THE CONSCIENCE
OF THE COURT

THE CONSCIENCE
OF THE COURT

❂ ❂ ❂

Selected Opinions

of

JUSTICE WILLIAM J. BRENNAN JR.

on Freedom and Equality

Edited by

Stephen L. Sepinuck and

Mary Pat Treuthart

Southern Illinois University Press

Carbondale and Edwardsville

02   01   00   99   4   3   2   1

Library of Congress Cataloging-in-Publication Data
The conscience of the court : selected opinions of
Justice William J. Brennan, Jr. on freedom and equality /
edited by Stephen L. Sepinuck and Mary Pat Treuthart.
    p.   cm.
Includes bibliographical references and index.
1. Brennan, William J. (William Joseph), 1906–   .
2. Civil rights—United States. 3. Equality before the law—
United States. I. Sepinuck, Stephen L., 1959–   .
II. Treuthart, Mary Pat, 1952–   .
KF213.B73S47   1999   98-33538
342.73′085—DC21   CIP
ISBN 0-8093-2234-x (cloth : alk. paper)

P4355

To Diane Handspicker, Jacob Landynski,
and all the other teachers who
inspire and enlighten.

Contents

Introduction ix

Note on Editorial Policy xiii

Table of Justices' Tenures xv

1. A Marketplace of Ideas 1

New York Times Co. v. Sullivan—Criticism of Public Officials 3

Lamont v. Postmaster General—Right to Receive Communications . . . 11

Paris Adult Theatre I v. Slaton—Obscenity 15

Elrod v. Burns—Political Patronage 27

FCC v. Pacifica Foundation—Control of the Airwaves 37

Hazelwood School District v. Kuhlmeier—Censorship of Student
   Newspapers 44

Texas v. Johnson—Flag Burning 53

2. One Nation under God 66

School District of Abington Township v. Schempp—Bible Reading
   in Public Schools 68

Marsh v. Chambers—Legislative Prayer 78

Lynch v. Donnelly—Public Religious Displays 85

Edwards v. Aguillard—Teaching Creationism 95

Sherbert v. Verner—Working on the Sabbath 103

Goldman v. Weinberger—Military Restrictions on Religious Attire .. 110

O'Lone v. Estate of Shabazz—Religious Practices in Prison 118

3. Alone Against the State 125

Schmerber v. California—Blood Testing Drivers 127

Goldberg v. Kelly—The Right to Be Heard 133

Furman v. Georgia—Capital Punishment 139

United States v. Ash—Assistance of Counsel 151

Parham v. J.R.—Commitment of Minors 160

United States v. Leon—The Exclusionary Rule 168

United States v. Verdugo-Urquidez—Search & Seizure Abroad 180

4. Different but Equal 188

Shapiro v. Thompson—The Right to Travel 191

Eisenstadt v. Baird—Marital Status & Privacy 197

Frontiero v. Richardson—Sex Discrimination 205

Regents of the University of California v. Bakke—Affirmative
Action 214

Plyler v. Doe—Education of Illegal Immigrants 226

Michael H. v. Gerald D.—Nontraditional Families 235

Selected Bibliography 245

Index of Cases Cited 249

General Index 253

INTRODUCTION

The words of modern political figures, even when available on audio or video tape, are remembered mostly in little snippets or sound bites. Think of the instruction in President Kennedy's inaugural address to "ask not what your country can do for you; ask what you can do for your country," or consider the familiar invocation from Martin Luther King's "I Have a Dream" speech.

The opinions of the Justices of the United States Supreme Court are far less well known. Nevertheless, they are well preserved. In addition to reciting their opinions from the bench, the Justices publish the entire text of each opinion in three different series of books—books that are readily available throughout the country, both in print and through computerized research services accessible to anyone with a computer, a telephone, and a modem.

Still, the public seldom reads the text of Supreme Court opinions. Instead, most nonlawyers assume that they lack the expertise necessary to understand the language of the law. Reading the opinions, then, becomes a task—and a delight—normally reserved to those with a formal legal education. The public's knowledge is generally limited to the results of selected—and usually controversial—cases, as reported by an often less than fully informed news media. Rarely is the public informed of the Justices' analyses, let alone their eloquence and persuasiveness. In short, the work and wit of the Justices is well preserved for posterity, but posterity shows little interest.

Yet judicial opinions need not be a proprietary enclave of the intellectual elite. Indeed, they are written *for* the public. Once stripped of their internal citations and cross-references, the judicial reasoning and rationale can readily be understood by anyone.

This book is designed to share with the public what we lawyers have known for almost forty years: that the words of the late Supreme Court Justice William J. Brennan Jr. are worth reading. Indeed, Justice Brennan may well be the best writer ever to have served on the Supreme Court of the United States. His judicial opinions have a remarkable clarity of analysis; his writing style was forceful yet persuasive. Even those readers who disagree with Brennan's arguments and conclusions find it difficult not to appreciate the manner in which he conveyed them.

What follows are extended excerpts from selected Brennan opinions involving issues of personal freedom, civil liberties, and equality. These excerpts were selected to bring the words and wisdom of Brennan to the public he served.

Their selection also serves another purpose: to highlight Brennan's approach to judicial decision making. For Brennan, the issues presented in the cases brought to the Supreme Court were not matters of mere academic interest or political philosophy. They were controversies that had real impact on identifiable people. Even when the litigants and the Court characterized a dispute as a narrow legal issue, Brennan chose to examine how people's lives were actually affected. Beyond that, Brennan had a rare ability to view issues from the perspective of people with whom he may never have had contact. Particularly for people and groups who lacked influence in society—Communists and flag burners, children and foreigners, criminal defendants and racial minorities—Brennan could be counted on to listen to their causes and judge them unmoved by the passions of the politically powerful. He was truly the conscience of the Court.

This book does not present a complete picture of Brennan's ideas and opinions on civil rights. By reproducing opinions authored only by Brennan, this book necessarily omits the opinions of other Justices that Brennan joined but did not write and the *per curiam* opinions, such as in *Brandenburg v. Ohio* and *Spence v. Washington,* which he may have drafted—in whole or in part— but which are not officially identified as his. This resulted in the omission of several substantive areas of law within the province of the Bill of Rights. For instance, even though Brennan participated in all of the landmark constitutional privacy cases of his time, his views on personal privacy are largely omitted from this book because he did not author opinions in most of the significant cases. We take comfort in the fact that Brennan was an extremely prolific member of the Court, particularly on civil rights issues, and thus there is, if anything, an overabundance of source material from which to choose. Moreover, only the opinions that Justice Brennan penned possess his unique and compelling style.

Choosing which of Brennan's opinions to excerpt here was both an arduous and wonderful project. It required review of hundreds of cases and thousands of pages of written material. Most of the reading was fascinating, however, and provided us with renewed respect both for almost every Justice to serve on the Court in the last fifty years and for the Solomon-like wisdom we tend to demand from them.

Still, selecting which opinions to include required consideration of numerous factors, such as their length, similarity to other opinions and issues, date (an attempt has been made to include cases from throughout Brennan's thirty-four-year tenure on the Court), persuasiveness and style, and, of course, the interest of the issue involved. This book contains a few more dissenting and concurring opinions than majority opinions. This was intentional. The author of a dissent or concurrence is free to say or not say whatever the author chooses, but those writing for a majority of the Court may be required to include or exclude certain statements in order to hold a fragile coalition together. Thus, Brennan's dissents and concurrences are presumed to be a slightly better reflection of his true sentiments than are his majority opinions.

Three prior books on Justices Holmes, Black, and Douglas excerpted many more opinions than are reproduced here but edited those opinions much more heavily. While there is much to be said for such an approach, we believe that heavy editing interferes with an accurate presentation of a judge's analysis. Accordingly, we decided to include fewer cases, but to leave them as intact as possible given page constraints and the need to focus on the issues. We hope readers find this approach effective.

We deeply appreciate the comments and editing assistance of Dan Webster.

Note on Editorial Policy

The excerpts included in this book were taken from the *United States Reports*, the official repository of Supreme Court decisions. Citations to the volume and pages in the United States Reports on which Justice Brennan's opinions may be found accompany each case. Deciphering these citations, along with others appearing at the end of the book, is easy once you know their pattern. For example, the citation *New York Times Co. v. Sullivan*, 376 U.S. 254 (1964), refers to a case by that name that can be found in volume 376 of the United States Reports, beginning on page 254. The year in parentheses is the year in which the Supreme Court rendered its decision. For more information on citations and their proper form, see *A Uniform System of Citation* (16th ed.).

All the opinions excerpted here retain the print style, including the use of italics, that appears in the *United States Reports*. The use of blocks for lengthy quotations has been changed to comport with the requirements of *A Uniform System of Citation*. Citations have been greatly shortened to minimize their distraction to the reader. Although this may provide some inconvenience to those who wish to know the precise origin of each quotation, the full citation to each cited case appears in an index at the end of this book. Moreover, the full text of the excerpted opinions, including the references to specific pages of cited material, are available in any law library.

Where textual material has been deleted, we have placed three asterisks; where the asterisks are centered on a line, one or more complete paragraphs have been omitted. The single exception is where the material removed consists solely of citations to cases or other supporting references. Such citations have been retained only when necessary to identify a quotation or when the source is discussed in the opinion or is excerpted or discussed elsewhere in this book.

We have chosen to include only those footnotes of Justice Brennan's that are useful to understanding the point Brennan was making or that are otherwise interesting. Footnote numbering is as in the original.

TABLE OF JUSTICES' TENURES

Justice Brennan took the oath of office on October 16, 1956, and retired on July 10, 1990. His almost 34-year term on the Supreme Court was longer than all but 6 other Justices. Of the 107 people who have served on the Court to date, Brennan served with 22. The following table shows the terms of Brennan's colleagues during his years of service.

Year						S. Reed		Harold H.
1956						S. Reed		Harold H.
1957						2/25/57		Burton
1958			Felix			3/25/57		10/13/58
1959			Frankfurter					10/14/58
1960						Charles E. Whittaker		
1961					Tom C. Clark			
1962	Earl		8/28/62		Clark	4/1/62		
1963	Warren		10/1/62			4/16/62		John M.
1964		Hugo L. Black	Arthur J. Goldberg					Harlan, II
1965			7/25/65	William O.				
1966			10/4/65	Douglas				
1967			Abe		6/12/67			
1968			Fortas		10/2/67			
1969	6/23/69		5/14/69					
1970	6/23/69							Potter
1971		9/17/71	6/9/70				9/23/71	Stewart
1972		1/7/72					1/7/72	
1973								
1974								
1975			11/12/75			Byron White		
1976			12/19/75					
1977	Warren E. Burger							
1978					Thurgood Marshall		William H. Rehnquist	
1979		Lewis F. Powell	Harry Blackmun					
1980								
1981								7/3/81
1982				John Paul Stevens				9/25/81
1983								
1984								
1985								Sandra Day
1986	9/26/86						9/26/86	O'Connor
1987	9/26/86	6/26/87					9/26/86	
1988	William H. Rehnquist	2/18/88					Antonin Scalia	
1989		Anthony Kennedy						
1990								

The Conscience
of the Court

❈ 1 ❈

A MARKETPLACE OF IDEAS

The First Amendment to the Constitution of the United States provides that "Congress shall make no law . . . abridging the freedom of speech or of the press, or of the right of the people peaceably to assemble, and to petition the government for a redress of grievances." This limitation on governmental power—like all of the restrictions in the Bill of Rights—was designed to restrain the power of the federal government, not the power of the individual states. However, the post–Civil War amendments to the Constitution drastically altered our system of federalism by directly limiting the activities of the states and by giving the federal government the authority to enforce those limitations.

In particular, the Fourteenth Amendment prohibits states from depriving "any person of life, liberty, or property without due process of law." Before Justice Brennan came to the federal bench, the Supreme Court had already begun to use this somewhat vague phrase to invalidate attempts by states to restrict traditional free speech rights. Although the Court has never adopted the position—championed by Justice Black—that the Fourteenth Amendment's Due Process Clause incorporates all the prohibitions on federal action in the Bill of Rights and makes them applicable to the states, it has concluded that the clause restricts states from interfering with "fundamental" rights. And, of course, most of the protections in the Bill of Rights could fairly be characterized as fundamental. Certainly freedom of expression is essential to any functional and legitimate democratic process, as the Court has long recognized.

When Brennan joined to the Supreme Court in 1956, the Justices were using the Fourteenth Amendment with increasing frequency, thereby constructing substantial safeguards for individual rights. This is not to say that all of the major decisions on freedom of expression made by the Warren Court or by Justice Brennan involved activities by individual states. Indeed, several of the opinions excerpted here involved actions by the federal government that infringed on expressive freedoms. What this background does show is that even though the First Amendment expressly restricts only "Congress," its principles, as applied through the Fourteenth Amendment, also restrict states and their subdivisions. Moreover, the application of First Amendment precepts to the States predates Brennan's arrival on the Court.

If the First Amendment, then, means more than its reference to Congress would indicate, it also means less than is implied by its phrase "no law." The Amendment does not say, after all, that Congress shall make no law "abridging speech"; it says that Congress shall make no law "abridging *the freedom of* speech." In other words, this freedom exists independently of the government and the Constitution, and is not granted by either. It is this *pre-existing* freedom of speech, this natural right to self-expression, that the Amendment protects, and no Justice ever to sit on the Court has believed that the right is absolute. As Justice Holmes said in his classic statement, "[t]he most stringent protection of free speech would not protect a man in falsely shouting fire in a theater and causing a panic."*

The precise extent of the right that the Amendment protects is something for the judiciary, in partnership with the other branches of government, to delineate. The cases excerpted here deal with criticism of public officials, the right to receive communications, obscenity, political patronage, governmental control of the airwaves, censorship of student newspapers, and flag burning. In each, Brennan advocated for a broad scope of the right to free expression, and his contribution to the nation's jurisprudence in this area has been substantial.

---

* *Schenk v. United States*, 249 U.S. 47, 52 (1919).

NEW YORK TIMES CO. V. SULLIVAN

March 9, 1964

Among legal circles, Justice Brennan is generally best known for his opinions for the Court in two cases: *Baker v. Carr* (1962), which held that courts could review legislatures' redistricting plans and which led to the Court's imposition of the "one person, one vote" standard; and this case. These decisions were Brennan's masterpieces, for "masterpieces" are what journeymen produce to become masters of their trade. Authored during Brennan's first decade on the Court, they demonstrated his ascendancy within it.

In this decision, the Court was confronted with whether and under what circumstances a state may require a person to pay civil damages for defaming a public official. The case arose out of the Civil Rights movement. On March 29, 1960, the New York Times printed a full-page advertisement paid for by the Committee to Defend Martin Luther King and the Struggle for Freedom in the South. The advertisement described "an unprecedented wave of terror" by those who would deny the benefits of the Constitution and the Bill of Rights to nonviolent student demonstrators in the South. The advertisement named no specific culprit. However, L. B. Sullivan, the City Commissioner for Montgomery, Alabama, who had oversight of the police, claimed that the advertisement impliedly referred to him. He brought a civil suit for libel against several Black clergymen and the New York Times. Sullivan pointed out some minor errors in two paragraphs of the advertisement but made no effort to prove that he suffered any actual loss because of them. Nevertheless, the Alabama jury awarded Sullivan $500,000 in damages, at that time the largest libel award in Alabama history.

The Court could have reversed the award on various narrow grounds. For example, it might have required proof of actual damages or an express reference to the plaintiff. Alternatively, it could have insulated advertisements from defamation awards. In a bold stroke, however, the Court invalidated a significant portion of state defamation law by holding that the First Amendment prohibits any award for libel or slander against a public official unless the injurious statement was both false and made maliciously—that is, made with knowledge of its falsity or with reckless disregard for its truth. Mere negligence would not suffice.

3

Over the next decade the Court struggled with how far to extend the malice requirement. First, the Court expanded the rule to cover criminal libel as well as civil libel. Then, in a series of cases over seven years, the Court broadened the rule to include candidates for public office and other public figures. Finally, in 1971, a plurality of the Court, led by Brennan, extended the malice requirement even further: to private persons embroiled in a public issue. He wrote that "[i]f a matter is of public or general interest, it cannot suddenly become less so because a private individual is involved." Three years later, however, the Court retreated; it ruled that people who are neither public officials nor public figures could recover damages for defamation on a showing of mere negligence. The more stringent *New York Times* standard did not apply to them in part because they, unlike public figures, may lack access to the channels of effective communication that would allow them to publicly challenge, if not effectively rebut, the false statements.

Despite this last ruling, *New York Times* remains the law for all defamation actions brought by public officials and public figures. While most decisions of the Supreme Court have little day-to-day effect on the great majority of us (after all, how often do we burn a flag or stand trial?) the decision in this case has a profound effect on what virtually all of us read and hear each day. Although all major news media have legal counsel review stories in advance for potential liability, the news and information we receive through print, television, radio, and the Internet would be filtered to a much greater extent if the press had to be more careful. While Brennan's opinion can be criticized as a license for negligence, it has undoubtedly made public debate a bit more "uninhibited, robust, and wide open."

Justice Brennan wrote the opinion for the Court, joined by Chief Justice Warren and Justices Clark, Harlan, Stewart, and White. Justices Black, Douglas, and Goldberg concurred in the result.

      ○   ○   ○

MR. JUSTICE BRENNAN delivered the opinion of the Court.

We are required in this case to determine for the first time the extent to which the constitutional protections for speech and press limit a State's power to award damages in a libel action brought by a public official against critics of his official conduct.

★ ★ ★

I

We may dispose at the outset of [one proposition] asserted to insulate the judgment of the Alabama courts from constitutional scrutiny[:] * * * that "The Fourteenth Amendment is directed against State action and not private action." That proposition has no application to this case. Although this is a civil lawsuit between private parties, the Alabama courts have applied a state rule of law which petitioners claim to impose invalid restrictions on their constitutional freedoms of speech and press. It matters not that that law has been applied in a civil action and that it is common law only, though supplemented by statute. The test is not the form in which state power has been applied but, whatever the form, whether such power has in fact been exercised.

* * *

II

Under Alabama law as applied in this case, a publication is "libelous per se" if the words "tend to injure a person . . . in his reputation" or to "bring [him] into public contempt"; the trial court stated that the standard was met if the words are such as to "injure him in his public office, or impute misconduct to him in his office, or want of official integrity, or want of fidelity to a public trust. . . . " The jury must find that the words were published "of and concerning" the plaintiff, but where the plaintiff is a public official his place in the governmental hierarchy is sufficient evidence to support a finding that his reputation has been affected by statements that reflect upon the agency of which he is in charge. Once "libel per se" has been established, the defendant has no defense as to stated facts unless he can persuade the jury that they were true in all their particulars. His privilege of "fair comment" for expressions of opinion depends on the truth of the facts upon which the comment is based. Unless he can discharge the burden of proving truth, general damages are presumed, and may be awarded without proof of pecuniary injury. * * *

The question before us is whether this rule of liability, as applied to an action brought by a public official against critics of his official conduct, abridges the freedom of speech and of the press that is guaranteed by the First and Fourteenth Amendments.

* * *

The general proposition that freedom of expression upon public questions is secured by the First Amendment has long been settled by our decisions. The constitutional safeguard, we have said, "was fashioned to assure unfettered interchange of ideas for the bringing about of political and social changes desired by the people." *Roth v. United States.* "The maintenance of the opportunity for free political discussion to the end that government may be responsive to the will of the people and that changes may be obtained by lawful means, an opportunity essential to the security of the Republic, is a fundamental principle of our constitutional system." *Stromberg v. California.* * * *

Thus we consider this case against the background of a profound national commitment to the principle that debate on public issues should be uninhibited, robust, and wide-open, and that it may well include vehement, caustic, and sometimes unpleasantly sharp attacks on government and public officials. The present advertisement, as an expression of grievance and protest on one of the major public issues of our time, would seem clearly to qualify for the constitutional protection. The question is whether it forfeits that protection by the falsity of some of its factual statements and by its alleged defamation of respondent.

Authoritative interpretations of the First Amendment guarantees have consistently refused to recognize an exception for any test of truth—whether administered by judges, juries, or administrative officials—and especially one that puts the burden of proving truth on the speaker. * * * As Madison said, "Some degree of abuse is inseparable from the proper use of every thing; and in no instance is this more true than in that of the press." * * * [E]rroneous statement is inevitable in free debate, and * * * it must be protected if the freedoms of expression are to have the "breathing space" that they "need . . . to survive," *NAACP v. Button.* * * *

Injury to official reputation affords no more warrant for repressing speech that would otherwise be free than does factual error. Where judicial officers are involved, this Court has held that concern for the dignity and reputation of the courts does not justify the punishment as criminal contempt of criticism of the judge or his decision. This is true even though the utterance contains "half-truths" and "misinformation." Such repression can be justified, if at all, only by a clear and present danger of the obstruction of justice. If judges are to be treated as "men of fortitude, able to thrive in a hardy climate," *Craig v. Harney,* surely the same must be true of other government officials, such as elected city commissioners. Criticism of their official conduct does not lose its constitutional protection merely because it is effective criticism and hence diminishes their official reputations.

If neither factual error nor defamatory content suffices to remove the constitutional shield from criticism of official conduct, the combination of the two elements is no less inadequate. This is the lesson to be drawn from the great controversy over the Sedition Act of 1798, which first crystallized a national awareness of the central meaning of the First Amendment. That statute made it a crime, punishable by a $5,000 fine and five years in prison,

> if any person shall write, print, utter or publish . . . any false, scandalous and malicious writing or writings against the government of the United States, or either house of the Congress . . . , or the President . . . , with intent to defame . . . or to bring them, or either of them, into contempt or disrepute; or to excite against them, or either or any of them, the hatred of the good people of the United States.

The Act allowed the defendant the defense of truth, and provided that the jury were to be judges both of the law and the facts. Despite these qualifications, the Act was vigorously condemned as unconstitutional in an attack joined in by Jefferson and Madison. * * *

Although the Sedition Act was never tested in this Court, the attack upon its validity has carried the day in the court of history. Fines levied in its prosecution were repaid by Act of Congress on the ground that it was unconstitutional. Calhoun, reporting to the Senate on February 4, 1836, assumed that its invalidity was a matter "which no one now doubts." Jefferson, as President, pardoned those who had been convicted and sentenced under the Act and remitted their fines, stating: "I discharged every person under punishment or prosecution under the sedition law, because I considered, and now consider, that law to be a nullity, as absolute and as palpable as if Congress had ordered us to fall down and worship a golden image." The invalidity of the Act has also been assumed by Justices of this Court. These views reflect a broad consensus that the Act, because of the restraint it imposed upon criticism of government and public officials, was inconsistent with the First Amendment.

* * *

What a State may not constitutionally bring about by means of a criminal statute is likewise beyond the reach of its civil law of libel. The fear of damage awards under a rule such as that invoked by the Alabama courts here may be markedly more inhibiting than the fear of prosecution under a criminal statute. Alabama, for example, has a criminal libel law which subjects to prosecution "any person who speaks, writes, or prints of and concerning another any accusation falsely and maliciously importing the commission by such person of a felony, or any other indictable offense involving moral turpitude," and which allows as punishment upon conviction a fine not exceeding $500 and a prison sentence of six months. Presumably a person charged with violation of this statute enjoys ordinary criminal-law safeguards such as the requirements of an indictment and of proof beyond a reasonable doubt. These safeguards are not available to the defendant in a civil action. The judgment awarded in this case—without the need for any proof of actual pecuniary loss—was one thousand times greater than the maximum fine provided by the Alabama criminal statute, and one hundred times greater than that provided by the Sedition Act. And since there is no double-jeopardy limitation applicable to civil lawsuits, this is not the only judgment that may be awarded against petitioners for the same publication. Whether or not a newspaper can survive a succession of such judgments, the pall of fear and timidity imposed upon those who would give voice to public criticism is an atmosphere in which the First Amendment freedoms cannot survive. Plainly the Alabama law of civil libel is "a form of regulation that creates hazards to protected freedoms markedly greater than those that attend reliance upon the criminal law." *Bantam Books, Inc. v. Sullivan.*

The state rule of law is not saved by its allowance of the defense of truth. * * * A rule compelling the critic of official conduct to guarantee the truth of all his factual assertions—and to do so on pain of libel judgments virtually unlimited in amount—leads to a comparable "self-censorship." Allowance of the defense of truth, with the burden of proving it on the defendant, does not mean that only false speech will be deterred.[19] Even courts accepting this defense as an adequate safeguard have recognized the difficulties of adducing legal proofs that the alleged libel was true in all its factual particulars. Under such a rule,

---

19. Even a false statement may be deemed to make a valuable contribution to public debate, since it brings about "the clearer perception and livelier impression of truth, produced by its collision with error." Mill, On Liberty 15 (Oxford, 1947).

would-be critics of official conduct may be deterred from voicing their criticism, even though it is believed to be true and even though it is in fact true, because of doubt whether it can be proved in court or fear of the expense of having to do so. They tend to make only statements which "steer far wider of the unlawful zone." *Speiser v. Randall.* The rule thus dampens the vigor and limits the variety of public debate. It is inconsistent with the First and Fourteenth Amendments.

The constitutional guarantees require, we think, a federal rule that prohibits a public official from recovering damages for a defamatory falsehood relating to his official conduct unless he proves that the statement was made with "actual malice"—that is, with knowledge that it was false or with reckless disregard of whether it was false or not. * * *

Such a privilege for criticism of official conduct is appropriately analogous to the protection accorded a public official when *he* is sued for libel by a private citizen. In *Barr v. Matteo*, this Court held the utterance of a federal official to be absolutely privileged if made "within the outer perimeter" of his duties. The States accord the same immunity to statements of their highest officers, although some differentiate their lesser officials and qualify the privilege they enjoy. But all hold that all officials are protected unless actual malice can be proved. The reason for the official privilege is said to be that the threat of damage suits would otherwise "inhibit the fearless, vigorous, and effective administration of policies of government" and "dampen the ardor of all but the most resolute, or the most irresponsible, in the unflinching discharge of their duties." *Id.* Analogous considerations support the privilege for the citizen-critic of government. It is as much his duty to criticize as it is the official's duty to administer. As Madison said, "the censorial power is in the people over the Government, and not in the Government over the people." It would give public servants an unjustified preference over the public they serve, if critics of official conduct did not have a fair equivalent of the immunity granted to the officials themselves.

We conclude that such a privilege is required by the First and Fourteenth Amendments.

III

We hold today that the Constitution delimits a State's power to award damages for libel in actions brought by public officials against critics of their official conduct. Since this is such an action, the rule requiring proof of actual malice is applicable. * * *

Applying these standards, we consider that the proof presented to show actual malice lacks the convincing clarity which the constitutional standard demands, and hence that it would not constitutionally sustain the judgment for respondent under the proper rule of law. * * * The statement by the Times' Secretary that * * * he thought the advertisement was "substantially correct," affords no constitutional warrant for the Alabama Supreme Court's conclusion that it was a "cavalier ignoring of the falsity of the advertisement [from which] the jury could not have but been impressed with the bad faith of The Times, and its maliciousness inferable therefrom." The statement does not indicate malice at the time of the publication; even if the advertisement was not "substantially correct"—although respondent's own proofs tend to show that it was—that opinion was at least a reasonable one, and there was no evidence to impeach the witness' good faith in holding it. * * *

Finally, there is evidence that the Times published the advertisement without checking its accuracy against the news stories in the Times' own files. The mere presence of the stories in the files does not, of course, establish that the Times "knew" the advertisement was false, since the state of mind required for actual malice would have to be brought home to the persons in the Times' organization having responsibility for the publication of the advertisement. With respect to the failure of those persons to make the check, the record shows that they relied upon their knowledge of the good reputation of many of those whose names were listed as sponsors of the advertisement, and upon the letter from [a person] known to them as a responsible individual, certifying that the use of the names was authorized. There was testimony that the persons handling the advertisement saw nothing in it that would render it unacceptable under the Times' policy of rejecting advertisements containing "attacks of a personal character"; their failure to reject it on this ground was not unreasonable. We think the evidence against the Times supports at most a finding of negligence in failing to discover the misstatements, and is constitutionally insufficient to show the recklessness that is required for a finding of actual malice.

* * *

The judgment of the Supreme Court of Alabama is reversed and the case is remanded to that court for further proceedings not inconsistent with this opinion.

Lamont v. Postmaster General

May 24, 1965

When Justice Brennan first joined the Court in 1956, the country was still in the midst of the Red Scare. Although the Senate had already censured Joseph McCarthy for his demagoguery and exploitation of the issue, the House Committee on Un-American Activities continued to investigate and expose what it suspected was Communist activity. In the process, the Committee destroyed the reputations and careers of numerous innocent people. The Committee's victims were not limited to celebrities, blacklisted authors, or selected State Department officials. Hundreds of people who were neither famous nor involved in making governmental policy—teachers, bus drivers, cafeteria workers, and the like—lost their jobs. Many were even imprisoned for refusing to answer questions about their political beliefs and associations.

It may be difficult for those who did not live through this time to fully understand or appreciate the climate that swept the country. It occurred before Watergate, before the age of cynicism, when most Americans trusted their elected officials. If congressmen and senators said there was a menace, then most people thought the threat was real.

Throughout Brennan's first decade on the Supreme Court, the Justices reviewed numerous constitutional challenges brought by persons imprisoned or discharged from their jobs for their alleged Communist beliefs or sympathies. In most of those cases, a sharply divided Court permitted the state and federal governments to do what they wished. Brennan generally refused to go along.

For example, in 1959 he dissented when the Court upheld the imprisonment for civil contempt of a man who refused to release the names of the guests at his summer retreat. Brennan argued that the constitutionally protected rights of speech and association could not be subordinated to the state's desire to expose such activities. Similarly, in 1961 Brennan voted to overturn the conviction of a man who refused to testify before the Un-American Activities Committee because the record indicated he was subpoenaed only because of his opposition to the Committee itself. Brennan regarded the state's action as exposure for exposure's sake, which was not a

11

legitimate legislative function and was antithetical to First Amendment free-doms.

This case involved a First Amendment challenge to a federal statute that authorized the U.S. Post Office to detain and potentially destroy correspondence characterized as "Communist political propaganda." Pursuant to this statute, the Post Office refrained from delivering such material while it notified the person to whom it was addressed. The intended recipient could then return a card specifically requesting delivery of the suspect material. Failure to do so resulted in non-delivery of the item and denied the intended recipient the opportunity to receive similar mailings in the future. The implications of this statute were clear: the Post Office would scrutinize the mails for subversive literature and maintain a list of those who wanted it.

The Court struck down the statute but skirted what was perhaps the most interesting issue: whether people had a right protected by the First Amendment to *receive* as well as send communications. In his concurring opinion, Brennan acknowledged there is no clear textual basis for such a right. Nevertheless, he concluded that it is a necessary corollary to the freedom of expression guaranteed in the First Amendment and thus constitutes a fundamental and protected right in and of itself. The Court ultimately embraced Brennan's view, effectively doubling the scope of the First Amendment.

Justice Douglas wrote the opinion of the Court, joined by Chief Justice Warren and Justices Black, Clark, and Stewart. Justices Harlan, Brennan, and Goldberg concurred.

❂　❂　❂

MR. JUSTICE BRENNAN, with whom MR. JUSTICE GOLDBERG joins, concurring.

These might be troublesome cases if the addressees predicated their claim for relief upon the First Amendment rights of the senders. To succeed, the addressees would then have to establish their standing to vindicate the senders' constitutional rights, as well as First Amendment protection for political propaganda prepared and printed abroad by or on behalf of a foreign government. However, those questions are not before us, since the addressees assert First Amendment claims in their own right: they contend that the Government is powerless to interfere with the delivery of the material because the First Amendment "necessarily protects the right to receive it." *Martin v. City of Struthers.* Since the decisions today uphold this contention, I join the Court's opinion.

It is true that the First Amendment contains no specific guarantee of access to publications. However, the protection of the Bill of Rights goes beyond the specific guarantees to protect from congressional abridgment those equally fundamental personal rights necessary to make the express guarantees fully meaningful. I think the right to receive publications is such a fundamental right. The dissemination of ideas can accomplish nothing if otherwise willing addressees are not free to receive and consider them. It would be a barren marketplace of ideas that had only sellers and no buyers.

Even if we were to accept the characterization of this statute as a regulation not intended to control the content of speech, but only incidentally limiting its unfettered exercise, we "have consistently held that only a compelling [governmental] interest in the regulation of a subject within [governmental] constitutional power to regulate can justify limiting First Amendment freedoms." *NAACP v. Button.* The Government's brief expressly disavows any support for this statute "in large public interests such as would be needed to justify a true restriction upon freedom of expression or inquiry." Rather the Government argues that, since an addressee taking the trouble to return the card can receive the publication named in it, only inconvenience and not an abridgment is involved. But inhibition as well as prohibition against the exercise of precious First Amendment rights is a power denied to government. * * * Moreover, the addressee's failure to return this form results in nondelivery not only of the particular publication but also of all similar publications or material. Thus, although the addressee may be content not to receive the particular publication, and hence does not return the card, the consequence is a denial of access to like publications which he may desire to receive. In any event, we cannot sustain an intrusion on First Amendment rights on the ground that the intrusion is only a minor one. * * *

The Government asserts that Congress enacted the statute in the awareness that Communist political propaganda mailed to addressees in the United States on behalf of foreign governments was often offensive to the recipients and constituted a subsidy to the very governments which bar the dissemination of publications from the United States. But the sensibilities of the unwilling recipient are fully safeguarded by [a regulation] under which the Post Office will honor his request to stop delivery; the statute under consideration, on the other hand, impedes delivery even to a willing addressee. In the area of First Amendment freedoms, government has the duty to confine itself to the least intrusive regulations which are adequate for the purpose. The argument that the statute is justified by the object of avoiding the subsidization of propaganda of foreign governments which bar American propaganda needs little comment. If the Government wishes to withdraw a subsidy or a privilege, it must do so by means and on terms which do not endanger First Amendment rights. That the governments which originate this propaganda themselves have no equivalent guarantees only highlights the cherished values of our constitutional framework; it can never justify emulating the practice of restrictive regimes in the name of expediency.

PARIS ADULT THEATRE I v. SLATON

June 21, 1973

Even the staunchest supporters of free speech acknowledge that the First Amendment is not absolute. Most agree, for example, that words designed to extort, incite a riot, or infringe upon a copyright can merit criminal or civil consequences. So, too, may words that disturb the peace, defame a person, reveal a confidence, or disclose a matter of national security. In each of these areas there is a fairly close connection between the type of speech and an identifiable harm. Also for each, the Court has settled on a standard for determining what is protected expression and what is not, although sometimes not before some difficult experimentation.

Another type of expression that the Court traditionally has regarded as outside the protection of the First Amendment is obscenity. For obscenity, however, the link between the words and their perceived harm—disruption to the social order and erosion of the community's moral fiber—is somewhat more attenuated. Some suggest that the true rationale for restricting obscene speech is morality based, and argue that moral considerations are not an adequate basis for restricting such a fundamental freedom. Others, often equating obscenity and pornography, contend that the sexually explicit material dehumanizes those it depicts, typically women, and thus contributes to their oppression.

For 15 years, Justice Brennan authored significant opinions for the Court on obscenity. His first opportunity to explore the issue arose shortly after he joined the Court, when he was assigned to write the majority opinion in the case of *Roth v. United States* (1957). That case involved two separate prosecutions: one of a New York publisher who mailed obscene materials in violation of federal law and another of a California bookstore owner who advertised and sold obscene works prohibited by a state statute. In both instances, the basic constitutional question was the same: whether the laws banning obscene materials violated the First Amendment. Brennan agreed with prior rulings of the Court that obscenity was not protected speech. He defined obscenity as "material which deals with sex in a manner appealing to the prurient interest," and he set forth a test for lower courts to use in determining if material is obscene: "whether to the average person, applying contemporary standards, the dominant theme of the material taken as a whole appeals to prurient interests." Using this standard, the Court upheld both convictions by a 6–3 vote.

Justice Harlan concurred but was troubled by the lack of specificity in the *Roth* test. Justices Black and Douglas dissented, taking an absolutist approach to the obscenity question. To them, it was constitutionally impermissible to prohibit obscene speech, however distasteful. Douglas warned his colleagues that the Court's review of possibly obscene material would be never ending, regardless of the test selected.

In subsequent cases, the Justices had trouble reaching consensus on how to apply the *Roth* test. Then, in a 1966 case involving John Cleland's *Memoirs*, Brennan, again writing for the Court, limited obscenity to material that was "utterly without redeeming social value." Despite the adjustment, it remained difficult for the Supreme Court, as well as for lower courts, to draw the line between acceptable erotica and objectionable obscenity.

The Court gradually recognized that judicial economy, if nothing else, necessitated a different approach to obscenity. Courts, including the Supreme Court, were too often called upon to scrutinize books and films to evaluate on which side of this vague standard they fell.

In 1973, the Court ruled on a group of five obscenity cases. In one of them, *Miller v. California*, the Court again tinkered with the definition of obscenity. The new standard, still applicable today, treats as obscene any material that appeals to prurient interests and "lacks serious literary, artistic, political or scientific value." In this case, decided the same day as *Miller*, Brennan broke with the mainstream of the Court. Joined by Justices Stewart and Marshall, he concluded that obscenity is simply not susceptible to a workable definition, and thus all speech appealing to prurient interests must be protected, at least where directed at consenting adults.

The subscription of Justice Stewart to this dissent is particularly noteworthy, since it was he who, perhaps unwittingly, had summed up the whole problem when he wrote in 1964 of "hard-core pornography:" "I shall not today attempt further to define the kinds of material I understand to be embraced within that shorthand description; and perhaps I could never succeed in doing so. But I know it when I see it."

Chief Justice Burger wrote the opinion of the Court, joined by Justices White, Blackmun, Powell, and Rehnquist. Justices Douglas, Brennan, Stewart, and Marshall dissented.

⦾   ⦾   ⦾

MR. JUSTICE BRENNAN, with whom MR. JUSTICE STEWART and MR. JUSTICE MARSHALL join, dissenting.

This case requires the Court to confront once again the vexing problem of reconciling state efforts to suppress sexually oriented expression with the protections of the First Amendment * * *. No other aspect of the First Amendment has, in recent years, demanded so substantial a commitment of our time, generated such disharmony of views, and remained so resistant to the formulation of stable and manageable standards. I am convinced that the approach initiated 16 years ago in *Roth v. United States*, and culminating in the Court's decision today, cannot bring stability to this area of the law without jeopardizing fundamental First Amendment values, and I have concluded that the time has come to make a significant departure from that approach.

* * *

III

Our experience with the *Roth* approach has certainly taught us that the outright suppression of obscenity cannot be reconciled with the fundamental principles of the First and Fourteenth Amendments. For we have failed to formulate a standard that sharply distinguishes protected from unprotected speech, and out of necessity, we have resorted to the approach, which resolves cases as between the parties, but offers only the most obscure guidance to legislation, adjudication by other courts, and primary conduct. * * * It comes as no surprise that judicial attempts to follow our lead conscientiously have often ended in hopeless confusion.

Of course, the vagueness problem would be largely of our own creation if it stemmed primarily from our failure to reach a consensus on any one standard. But after 16 years of experimentation and debate I am reluctantly forced to the conclusion that none of the available formulas, including the one announced today, can reduce the vagueness to a tolerable level while at the same time striking an acceptable balance between the protections of the First and Fourteenth Amendments, on the one hand, and on the other the asserted state interest in regulating the dissemination of certain sexually oriented materials. Any effort to draw a constitutionally acceptable boundary on state power must resort to such indefinite concepts as "prurient interest," "patent offensiveness," "serious literary value," and the like. The meaning of these concepts necessarily varies with the experience, outlook, and even idiosyncrasies of the person defining them. Although we have assumed that obscenity does exist and that we "know it when [we] see it," *Jacobellis v. Ohio* (Stewart, J., concurring), we are manifestly unable to describe it in advance except by reference to concepts so elusive that they fail to distinguish clearly between protected and unprotected speech.

We have more than once previously acknowledged that "constitutionally protected expression . . . is often separated from obscenity only by a dim and uncertain line." *Bantam Books, Inc. v. Sullivan.* Added to the "perhaps inherent residual vagueness" of each of the current multitude of standards, *Ginzburg v. United States,* is the further complication that the obscenity of any particular item may depend upon nuances of presentation and the context of its dissemination. * * * These considerations suggest that no one definition, no matter how precisely or narrowly drawn, can possibly suffice for all situations, or carve out fully suppressible expression from all media without also creating a substantial risk of encroachment upon the guarantees of the Due Process Clause and the First Amendment.

The vagueness of the standards in the obscenity area produces a number of separate problems, and any improvement must rest on an understanding that the problems are to some extent distinct. First, a vague statute fails to provide adequate notice to persons who are engaged in the type of conduct that the statute could be thought to proscribe. * * *

In addition to problems that arise when any criminal statute fails to afford fair notice of what it forbids, a vague statute in the areas of speech and press creates a second level of difficulty. We have indicated that "stricter standards of permissible statutory vagueness may be applied to a statute having a potentially inhibiting effect on speech; a man may the less be required to act at his peril here, because the free dissemination of ideas may be the loser." *Smith v. California.* * * *

The problems of fair notice and chilling protected speech are very grave standing alone. But it does not detract from their importance to recognize that a vague statute in this area creates a third, although admittedly more subtle, set of problems. These problems concern the institutional stress that inevitably results where the line separating protected from unprotected speech is excessively vague. In *Roth* we conceded that "there may be marginal cases in which it is difficult to determine the side of the line on which a particular fact situation falls. . . . " Our subsequent experience demonstrates that almost every case is "marginal." And since the "margin" marks the point of separation between protected and unprotected speech, we are left with a system in which almost every obscenity case presents a constitutional question of exceptional difficulty. * * *

As a result of our failure to define standards with predictable application to any given piece of material, there is no probability of regularity in obscenity decisions by state and lower federal courts. That is not to say that these courts have performed badly in this area or paid insufficient attention to the principles we have established. The problem is, rather, that one cannot say with certainty that material is obscene until at least five members of this Court, applying inevitably obscure standards, have pronounced it so. The number of obscenity cases on our docket gives ample testimony to the burden that has been placed upon this Court.

But the sheer number of the cases does not define the full extent of the institutional problem. For, quite apart from the number of cases involved and the need to make a fresh constitutional determination in each case, we are tied to the "absurd business of perusing and viewing the miserable stuff that pours into the Court. . . . " *Interstate Circuit, Inc. v. Dallas* (separate opinion of Harlan, J.). While the material may have varying degrees of social importance, it is hardly a source of edification to the members of this Court who are compelled to view it before passing on its obscenity.

* * *

The severe problems arising from the lack of fair notice, from the chill on protected expression, and from the stress imposed on the state and federal judicial machinery persuade me that a significant change in direction is urgently required. I turn, therefore, to the alternatives that are now open.

IV

1. The approach requiring the smallest deviation from our present course would be to draw a new line between protected and unprotected speech, still permitting the States to suppress all material on the unprotected side of the line. In my view, clarity cannot be obtained pursuant to this approach except by drawing a line that resolves all doubt in favor of state power and against the guarantees of the First Amendment. We could hold, for example, that any depiction or description of human sexual organs, irrespective of the manner or purpose of the portrayal,

is outside the protection of the First Amendment and therefore open to suppression by the States. That formula would, no doubt, offer much fairer notice of the reach of any state statute drawn at the boundary of the State's constitutional power. * * * But such a standard would be appallingly overbroad, permitting the suppression of a vast range of literary, scientific, and artistic masterpieces. Neither the First Amendment nor any free community could possibly tolerate such a standard. Yet short of that extreme it is hard to see how any choice of words could reduce the vagueness problem to tolerable proportions, so long as we remain committed to the view that some class of materials is subject to outright suppression by the State.

2. The alternative adopted by the Court today * * * [is] a restatement of the *Roth-Memoirs* definition of obscenity * * *.

The differences between this formulation and the three-pronged *Memoirs* test are, for the most part, academic. * * * The third component of the *Memoirs* test is that the material must be "utterly without redeeming social value." The Court's rephrasing requires that the work, taken as a whole, must be proved to lack "serious literary, artistic, political, or scientific value."

The Court evidently recognizes that difficulties with the *Roth* approach necessitate a significant change of direction. But the Court does not describe its understanding of those difficulties, nor does it indicate how the restatement of the *Memoirs* test is in any way responsive to the problems that have arisen. In my view, the restatement leaves unresolved the very difficulties that compel our rejection of the underlying *Roth* approach, while at the same time contributing substantial difficulties of its own. The modification of the *Memoirs* test may prove sufficient to jeopardize the analytic underpinnings of the entire scheme. And today's restatement will likely have the effect, whether or not intended, of permitting far more sweeping suppression of sexually oriented expression, including expression that would almost surely be held protected under our current formulation.

Although the Court's restatement substantially tracks the three-part test announced in *Memoirs v. Massachusetts*, it does purport to modify the "social value" component of the test. Instead of requiring, as did *Roth* and *Memoirs*, that state suppression be limited to materials utterly lacking in social value, the Court today permits suppression if the government can prove that the materials lack "*serious* literary, artistic, political or scientific value." But the definition of "obscenity" as expression utterly lacking in social importance is the key to the conceptual basis of *Roth* and our subsequent opinions. In *Roth* we held that certain expression is obscene, and thus outside the protection of the First Amendment, precisely *because* it lacks even the slightest redeeming social value.[14] The Court's approach necessarily assumes that some works will be deemed obscene—even though they clearly have *some* social value—because the State was able to prove that the value, measured by some unspecified standard, was not sufficiently "serious" to warrant constitutional protection. That result is not merely inconsistent with our holding in *Roth*; it is nothing less than a rejection of the fundamental First Amendment premises and rationale of the *Roth* opinion and an invitation to widespread suppression of sexually oriented speech. Before today, the protections of the First Amendment have never been thought limited to expressions of serious literary or political value.

* * *

In any case, even if the Court's approach left undamaged the conceptual framework of *Roth*, and even if it clearly barred the suppression of works with at least some social value, I would nevertheless be compelled to reject it. For it is beyond dispute that the approach can have no ameliorative impact on the cluster of problems that grow out of the vagueness of our current standards. Indeed, even the Court makes no argument that the reformulation will provide fairer notice to booksellers, theater owners, and the reading and viewing public. Nor does the Court contend that the approach will provide clearer guidance to law enforcement officials or reduce the chill on protected expression. Nor, finally, does the Court suggest that the approach will mitigate to the slightest degree the institutional problems that have plagued this Court and the state and federal judiciary as a direct result of the uncertainty inherent in any definition of obscenity.

* * *

3. I have also considered the possibility of reducing our own role, and the role of appellate courts generally, in determining whether particu-

---

14. "All ideas having even the slightest redeeming social importance—unorthodox ideas, controversial ideas, even ideas hateful to the prevailing climate of opinion—have the full protection of the guaranties, unless excludable because they encroach upon the limited area of more important interests. But implicit in the history of the First Amendment is the rejection of obscenity as utterly without redeeming social importance." *Roth.*

lar matter is obscene. Thus, we might conclude that juries are best suited to determine obscenity *vel non* and that jury verdicts in this area should not be set aside except in cases of extreme departure from prevailing standards. Or, more generally, we might adopt the position that where a lower federal or state court has conscientiously applied the constitutional standard, its finding of obscenity will be no more vulnerable to reversal by this Court than any finding of fact. * * * [However,] the First Amendment requires an independent review by appellate courts of the constitutional fact of obscenity. That result is required by principles applicable to the obscenity issue no less than to any other area involving free expression or other constitutional right. In any event, even if the Constitution would permit us to refrain from judging for ourselves the alleged obscenity of particular materials, that approach would solve at best only a small part of our problem. For while it would mitigate the institutional stress produced by the *Roth* approach, it would neither offer nor produce any cure for the other vices of vagueness. Far from providing a clearer guide to permissible primary conduct, the approach would inevitably lead to even greater uncertainty and the consequent due process problems of fair notice. And the approach would expose much protected, sexually oriented expression to the vagaries of jury determinations. Plainly, the institutional gain would be more than offset by the unprecedented infringement of First Amendment rights.

4. Finally, I have considered the view, urged so forcefully since 1957 by our Brothers Black and Douglas, that the First Amendment bars the suppression of any sexually oriented expression. That position would effect a sharp reduction, although perhaps not a total elimination, of the uncertainty that surrounds our current approach. Nevertheless, I am convinced that it would achieve that desirable goal only by stripping the States of power to an extent that cannot be justified by the commands of the Constitution, at least so long as there is available an alternative approach that strikes a better balance between the guarantee of free expression and the States' legitimate interests.

V

Our experience since *Roth* requires us not only to abandon the effort to pick out obscene materials on a case-by-case basis, but also to reconsider a fundamental postulate of *Roth*: that there exists a definable class of sexually oriented expression that may be totally suppressed by the

Federal and State Governments. Assuming that such a class of expression does in fact exist, I am forced to conclude that the concept of "obscenity" cannot be defined with sufficient specificity and clarity to provide fair notice to persons who create and distribute sexually oriented materials, to prevent substantial erosion of protected speech as a by-product of the attempt to suppress unprotected speech, and to avoid very costly institutional harms. Given these inevitable side effects of state efforts to suppress what is assumed to be *unprotected* speech, we must scrutinize with care the state interest that is asserted to justify the suppression. For in the absence of some very substantial interest in suppressing such speech, we can hardly condone the ill effects that seem to flow inevitably from the effort.

* * *

Because we assumed—incorrectly, as experience has proved—that obscenity could be separated from other sexually oriented expression without significant costs either to the First Amendment or to the judicial machinery charged with the task of safeguarding First Amendment freedoms, we had no occasion in *Roth* to probe the asserted state interest in curtailing unprotected, sexually oriented speech. Yet, as we have increasingly come to appreciate the vagueness of the concept of obscenity, we have begun to recognize and articulate the state interests at stake. Significantly, * * * [t]he opinions in [cases following *Roth*] reflected our emerging view that the state interests in protecting children and in protecting unconsenting adults may stand on a different footing from the other asserted state interests. It may well be, as one commentator has argued, that "exposure to [erotic material] is for some persons an intense emotional experience. A communication of this nature, imposed upon a person contrary to his wishes, has all the characteristics of a physical assault. . . . [And it] constitutes an invasion of his privacy. . . . " Similarly, if children are "not possessed of that full capacity for individual choice which is the presupposition of the First Amendment guarantees," *Ginsberg v. New York* (Stewart, J., concurring), then the State may have a substantial interest in precluding the flow of obscene materials even to consenting juveniles.

But, whatever the strength of the state interests in protecting juveniles and unconsenting adults from exposure to sexually oriented materials, those interests cannot be asserted in defense of the holding of the Georgia Supreme Court in this case. That court assumed for the purposes of its decision that the films in issue were exhibited only to persons over the age of 21 who viewed them willingly and with prior knowledge of the nature of their contents. And on that assumption the state court held that the films could still be suppressed. The justification for the suppression must be found, therefore, in some independent interest in regulating the reading and viewing habits of consenting adults.

At the outset it should be noted that virtually all of the interests that might be asserted in defense of suppression, laying aside the special interests associated with distribution to juveniles and unconsenting adults, were also posited in *Stanley v. Georgia,* where we held that the State could not make the "mere private possession of obscene material a crime." That decision presages the conclusions I reach here today.

In *Stanley* we pointed out that "[t]here appears to be little empirical basis for" the assertion that "exposure to obscene materials may lead to deviant sexual behavior or crimes of sexual violence."[26] In any event, we added that "if the State is only concerned about printed or filmed materials inducing antisocial conduct, we believe that in the context of private consumption of ideas and information we should adhere to the view that '[a]mong free men, the deterrents ordinarily to be applied to prevent crime are education and punishment for violations of the law. . . . '" *Id.,* quoting *Whitney v. California* (Brandeis, J., concurring).

Moreover, in *Stanley* we rejected as "wholly inconsistent with the philosophy of the First Amendment," the notion that there is a legitimate state concern in the "control [of] the moral content of a person's thoughts," and we held that a State "cannot constitutionally premise legislation on the desirability of controlling a person's private thoughts." That is not to say, of course, that a State must remain utterly indiffer-

---

26. Indeed, since *Stanley* was decided, the President's Commission on Obscenity and Pornography has concluded:

In sum, empirical research designed to clarify the question has found no evidence to date that exposure to explicit sexual materials plays a significant role in the causation of delinquent or criminal behavior among youth or adults. The Commission cannot conclude that exposure to erotic materials is a factor in the causation of sex crime or sex delinquency.

Report of the Commission on Obscenity and Pornography 27 (1970) (footnote omitted). To the contrary, the Commission found that "[o]n the positive side, explicit sexual materials are sought as a source of entertainment and information by substantial numbers of American adults. At times, these materials also appear to serve to increase and facilitate constructive communication about sexual matters within marriage." *Id.* at 53.

ent to—and take no action bearing on—the morality of the community. * * * But the State's interest in regulating morality by suppressing obscenity, while often asserted, remains essentially unfocused and ill defined. And, since the attempt to curtail unprotected speech necessarily spills over into the area of protected speech, the effort to serve this speculative interest through the suppression of obscene material must tread heavily on rights protected by the First Amendment.

* * *

If, as the Court today assumes, "a state legislature may . . . act on the . . . assumption that commerce in obscene books, or public exhibitions focused on obscene conduct, have a tendency to exert a corrupting and debasing impact leading to antisocial behavior," then it is hard to see how state-ordered regimentation of our minds can ever be forestalled. For if a State may, in an effort to maintain or create a particular moral tone, prescribe what its citizens cannot read or cannot see, then it would seem to follow that in pursuit of that same objective a State could decree that its citizens must read certain books or must view certain films. However laudable its goal—and that is obviously a question on which reasonable minds may differ—the State cannot proceed by means that violate the Constitution. * * *

In short, while I cannot say that the interests of the State—apart from the question of juveniles and unconsenting adults—are trivial or non-existent, I am compelled to conclude that these interests cannot justify the substantial damage to constitutional rights and to this Nation's judicial machinery that inevitably results from state efforts to bar the distribution even of unprotected material to consenting adults. I would hold, therefore, that at least in the absence of distribution to juveniles or obtrusive exposure to unconsenting adults, the First and Fourteenth Amendments prohibit the State and Federal Governments from attempting wholly to suppress sexually oriented materials on the basis of their allegedly "obscene" contents. Nothing in this approach precludes those governments from taking action to serve what may be strong and legitimate interests through regulation of the manner of distribution of sexually oriented material.

VI

* * * I do not pretend to have found a complete and infallible answer to what Mr. Justice Harlan called "the intractable obscenity problem."

Interstate Circuit, Inc. v. Dallas (separate opinion). Difficult questions must still be faced, notably in the areas of distribution to juveniles and offensive exposure to unconsenting adults. Whatever the extent of state power to regulate in those areas, it should be clear that the view I espouse today would introduce a large measure of clarity to this troubled area, would reduce the institutional pressure on this Court and the rest of the State and Federal Judiciary, and would guarantee fuller freedom of expression while leaving room for the protection of legitimate governmental interests. Since the Supreme Court of Georgia erroneously concluded that the State has power to suppress sexually oriented material even in the absence of distribution to juveniles or exposure to unconsenting adults, I would reverse that judgment and remand the case to that court for further proceedings not inconsistent with this opinion.

ELROD V. BURNS

June 28, 1976

"To the victor belongs the spoils" is a slogan long applicable to political as well as military campaigns. For two centuries, it had been an accepted practice in the United States to reward loyal partisans. Since the practice of patronage was so ingrained in our political culture, its constitutional implications were somewhat overlooked. The employees of the Sheriff of Cook County, Illinois, who brought this issue to the attention of the courts attacked not only this long-standing American tradition but another formidable institution as well: Chicago Mayor Richard J. Daley. His name, virtually synonymous with the best and worst of machine politics, appears among those listed as defendants in this action.

No clearly delineated constitutional guarantee is violated when workers are discharged from public employment after a member of the opposing party has won an election. Nevertheless, in announcing the Court's judgment, Justice Brennan spent little effort demonstrating that constitutional rights are indeed affected. Relying on earlier cases involving the practice of patronage for federal workers, Brennan concluded that conditioning employment on affiliation with a particular political party infringes upon the First Amendment rights of "belief and association."

Freedom of belief is not expressly guaranteed by the First Amendment, but it does logically follow from a right to free speech as well as from the First Amendment's protection of freedom of religion. Freedom of association has a less obvious connection to First Amendment principles and protections. Yet its constitutional foundation was confirmed in 1958 when the Court unanimously rejected Alabama's efforts to keep the NAACP from operating within its borders. In doing so, it noted that "[e]ffective advocacy of both public and private points of view, particularly controversial ones, is undeniably enhanced by group association."

Having concluded that the practice of political patronage infringes upon fundamental constitutional rights, Brennan examined the government's contention that effectiveness and efficiency justify this interference. He concluded, however, that both of these interests are often impaired, rather than enhanced, by staff turnover. Brennan was a bit more persuaded by the government's claim that political loyalty is essential to prevent holdover employees from thwarting the progress of a new administration. However, he differentiated between policymaking employees, typically those in higher level positions, and nonpolicymaking employees who are more likely to be support personnel. To Brennan, the government has a sufficient interest in discharging policymaking employees on the basis of political partisanship. In contrast, he believed that the interests of the nonpolicymaking group take precedence over those of the government, necessitating their retention.

Brennan then moved to the claim that the rewards and punishments doled out by patronage are essential to the preservation of the democratic process. Brennan scolded the government for confusing the political process with political parties. In footnote 22, he stated that "[p]artisan politics bears the imprimatur only of tradition, not the Constitution." Perhaps here is where Brennan alienated the concurring Justices. While agreeing with the result reached in this case, Justices Stewart and Blackmun could not sign onto Brennan's expansive pronouncements. They explicitly restricted their concurrence to the issue of firing nonpolicymaking employees, and left for another day whether political considerations could used in making hiring decisions. Justice Powell's dissenting opinion went further; it contradicted Brennan's characterization of the evils of patronage and instead lauded its benefits. Powell's discussion implicitly recognized that the Justices themselves may have benefitted at various points in their careers from a system of partisan rewards.

The demise of the political machines that dominated state and local government began decades before the Court's decision in this case. The ruling here all but ensured that they will not be resurrected. Despite a lack of consensus among the Justices, Brennan commanded a majority on the issue of firing nonpolicymaking employees for political reasons. In 1990, Brennan wrote the opinion for the Court in *Rutan v. Republican Party of Illinois*, which extended the point. Even in matters of hiring, transfer, and promotion, the political affiliation of nonpolicymaking public employees may not be considered. These two decisions continue to provide a substantial measure of job security for many civil servants, and are examples of how Brennan's jurisprudence was most sensitive to those who could least protect themselves.

Justice Brennan wrote an opinion announcing the judgment of the Court, joined by Justices White and Marshall. Justices Stewart and Blackmun concurred. Chief Justice Burger and Justices Powell and Rehnquist dissented.

o   o   o

MR. JUSTICE BRENNAN announced the judgment of the Court and delivered an opinion in which MR. JUSTICE WHITE and MR. JUSTICE MARSHALL joined.

This case presents the question whether public employees who allege that they were discharged or threatened with discharge solely because of their partisan political affiliation or nonaffiliation state a claim for deprivation of constitutional rights secured by the First and Fourteenth Amendments.

I

Respondents brought this suit in the United States District Court for the Northern District of Illinois against petitioners, Richard J. Elrod, Richard J. Daley, the Democratic Organization of Cook County, and the Democratic County Central Committee of Cook County. Their complaint alleged that they were discharged or threatened with discharge solely for the reason that they were not affiliated with or sponsored by the Democratic Party. * * *

II

In December 1970, the Sheriff of Cook County, a Republican, was replaced by Richard Elrod, a Democrat. At that time, respondents, all Republicans, were employees of the Cook County Sheriff's Office. They were non-civil-service employees and, therefore, not covered by any statute, ordinance, or regulation protecting them from arbitrary discharge. * * *

It has been the practice of the Sheriff of Cook County, when he assumes office from a Sheriff of a different political party, to replace non-civil-service employees of the Sheriff's Office with members of his own party when the existing employees lack or fail to obtain requisite support from, or fail to affiliate with, that party. Consequently, subsequent to Sheriff Elrod's assumption of office, respondents, with the exception of [one who is in imminent danger of being fired], were discharged from their employment solely because they did not support and were not members of the Democratic Party and had failed to obtain the sponsorship of one of its leaders. * * *

IV

The Cook County Sheriff's practice of dismissing employees on a partisan basis is but one form of the general practice of political patronage. The practice also includes placing loyal supporters in government jobs that may or may not have been made available by political discharges. Nonofficeholders may be the beneficiaries of lucrative government contracts for highway construction, buildings, and supplies. Favored wards may receive improved public services. Members of the judiciary may even engage in the practice through the appointment of receiverships, trusteeships, and refereeships. Although political patronage comprises a broad range of activities, we are here concerned only with the constitutionality of dismissing public employees for partisan reasons.

Patronage practice is not new to American politics. It has existed at the federal level at least since the Presidency of Thomas Jefferson, although its popularization and legitimation primarily occurred later, in the Presidency of Andrew Jackson. The practice is not unique to American politics. It has been used in many European countries, and in darker times, it played a significant role in the Nazi rise to power in Germany and other totalitarian states. More recent times have witnessed a strong decline in its use, particularly with respect to public employment. Indeed, only a few decades after Andrew Jackson's administration, strong discontent with the corruption and inefficiency of the patronage system of public employment eventuated in the Pendleton Act, the foundation of modern civil service. And on the state and local levels, merit systems have increasingly displaced the practice. This trend led the Court to observe in *CSC v. Letter Carriers* that "the judgment of Congress, the Executive, and the country appears to have been that partisan political activities by federal employees must be limited if the Government is to operate effectively and fairly, elections are to play their proper part in representative government, and employees themselves are to be sufficiently free from improper influences."

The decline of patronage employment is not, of course, relevant to the question of its constitutionality. It is the practice itself, not the magnitude of its occurrence, the constitutionality of which must be determined. Nor for that matter does any unacceptability of the practice signified by its decline indicate its unconstitutionality. Our inquiry does not begin with the judgment of history, though the actual operation of a practice viewed in retrospect may help to assess its workings with respect to constitutional limitations. Rather, inquiry must commence with identification of the constitutional limitations implicated by a challenged governmental practice.

V

The cost of the practice of patronage is the restraint it places on freedoms of belief and association. In order to maintain their jobs, respondents were required to pledge their political allegiance to the Democratic Party, work for the election of other candidates of the Democratic Party, contribute a portion of their wages to the Party, or obtain the sponsorship of a member of the Party, usually at the price of one of the first three alternatives. Regardless of the incumbent party's identity, Democratic or otherwise, the consequences for association and belief are the same. An individual who is a member of the out-party maintains affiliation with his own party at the risk of losing his job. He works for the election of his party's candidates and espouses its policies at the same risk. The financial and campaign assistance that he is induced to provide to another party furthers the advancement of that party's policies to the detriment of his party's views and ultimately his own beliefs, and any assessment of his salary is tantamount to coerced belief. Even a pledge of allegiance to another party, however ostensible, only serves to compromise the individual's true beliefs. Since the average public employee is hardly in the financial position to support his party and another, or to lend his time to two parties, the individual's ability to act according to his beliefs and to associate with others of his political persuasion is constrained, and support for his party is diminished.

It is not only belief and association which are restricted where political patronage is the practice. The free functioning of the electoral process also suffers. Conditioning public employment on partisan support prevents support of competing political interests. Existing employees are deterred from such support, as well as the multitude seeking jobs. As government employment, state or federal, becomes more pervasive, the greater the dependence on it becomes, and therefore the greater becomes the power to starve political opposition by commanding partisan support, financial and otherwise. Patronage thus tips the electoral process in favor of the incumbent party, and where the practice's scope is substantial relative to the size of the electorate, the impact on the process can be significant.

Our concern with the impact of patronage on political belief and association does not occur in the abstract, for political belief and association constitute the core of those activities protected by the First Amendment. * * *

There can no longer be any doubt that freedom to associate with others for the common advancement of political beliefs and ideas is a form of "orderly group activity" protected by the First and Fourteenth Amendments. The right to associate with the political party of one's choice is an integral part of this basic constitutional freedom.

Kusper v. Pontikes.

These protections reflect our "profound national commitment to the principle that debate on public issues should be uninhibited, robust, and wide-open," *New York Times Co. v. Sullivan,* a principle itself reflective of the fundamental understanding that "[c]ompetition in ideas and governmental policies is at the core of our electoral process." *Williams v. Rhodes.* Patronage, therefore, to the extent it compels or restrains belief and association, is inimical to the process which undergirds our system of government and is "at war with the deeper traditions of democracy embodied in the First Amendment." *Illinois State Employees Union v. Lewis.* As such, the practice unavoidably confronts decisions by this Court either invalidating or recognizing as invalid government action that inhibits belief and association through the conditioning of public employment on political faith.

* * *

VI

Although the practice of patronage dismissals clearly infringes First Amendment interests, our inquiry is not at an end, for the prohibition on encroachment of First Amendment protections is not an absolute. Restraints are permitted for appropriate reasons. * * * [The applicable standard, though, is an exacting one.] In short, if conditioning the retention of public employment on the employee's support of the in-party is to survive constitutional challenge, it must further some vital government end by a means that is least restrictive of freedom of belief and association in achieving that end, and the benefit gained must outweigh the loss of constitutionally protected rights.

One interest which has been offered in justification of patronage is the need to insure effective government and the efficiency of public employees. It is argued that employees of political persuasions not the same as that of the party in control of public office will not have the incentive to work effectively and may even be motivated to subvert the incumbent administration's efforts to govern effectively. We are not persuaded. The inefficiency resulting from the wholesale replacement of large numbers of public employees every time political office changes hands belies this justification. And the prospect of dismissal after an election in which the incumbent party has lost is only a disincentive to good work.[18] Further, it is not clear that dismissal in order to make room for a patronage appointment will result in replacement by a person more qualified to do the job, since appointment often occurs in exchange for the delivery of votes, or other party service, not job capability. More fundamentally, however, the argument does not succeed because it is doubtful that the mere difference of political persuasion motivates poor performance; nor do we think it legitimately may be used as a basis for imputing such behavior. The Court has consistently recognized that mere political association is an inadequate basis for imputing disposition to ill-willed conduct. * * * At all events, less drastic means for insuring government effectiveness and employee efficiency are available to the State. Specifically, employees may always be discharged for good cause, such as insubordination or poor job performance, when those bases in fact exist.

Even if the first argument that patronage serves effectiveness and efficiency be rejected, it still may be argued that patronage serves those interests by giving the employees of an incumbent party the incentive to perform well in order to insure their party's incumbency and thereby their jobs. Patronage, according to the argument, thus makes employees highly accountable to the public. But the ability of officials more directly accountable to the electorate to discharge employees for cause and the availability of merit systems, growth in the use of which has been quite significant, convince us that means less intrusive than patronage still exist for achieving accountability in the public work force and, thereby, effective and efficient government. The greater effectiveness of patronage over these less drastic means, if any, is at best marginal,

---

18. It does not appear that efficiency and effective government were the concerns of elected officials in this case. Employees originally dismissed were reinstated after obtaining sponsorship letters, a practice hardly promotive of efficiency if the employee's work had been less than par or if the employee had previously behaved in an insubordinate manner. Complaints by one supervisor that too many people were being discharged too fast, without adequately trained replacements, were met with the response that the number of dismissals was to be maintained because the job openings were needed for partisan appointments. * * *

a gain outweighed by the absence of intrusion on protected interests under the alternatives.

* * *

A second interest advanced in support of patronage is the need for political loyalty of employees, not to the end that effectiveness and efficiency be insured, but to the end that representative government not be undercut by tactics obstructing the implementation of policies of the new administration, policies presumably sanctioned by the electorate. The justification is not without force, but is nevertheless inadequate to validate patronage wholesale. Limiting patronage dismissals to policymaking positions is sufficient to achieve this governmental end. Nonpolicymaking individuals usually have only limited responsibility and are therefore not in a position to thwart the goals of the in-party.

No clear line can be drawn between policymaking and nonpolicymaking positions. While nonpolicymaking individuals usually have limited responsibility, that is not to say that one with a number of responsibilities is necessarily in a policymaking position. The nature of the responsibilities is critical. Employee supervisors, for example, may have many responsibilities, but those responsibilities may have only limited and well-defined objectives. An employee with responsibilities that are not well defined or are of broad scope more likely functions in a policymaking position. In determining whether an employee occupies a policymaking position, consideration should also be given to whether the employee acts as an adviser or formulates plans for the implementation of broad goals. Thus, the political loyalty "justification is a matter of proof, or at least argument, directed at particular kinds of jobs." *Lewis.* Since, as we have noted, it is the government's burden to demonstrate an overriding interest in order to validate an encroachment on protected interests, the burden of establishing this justification as to any particular respondent will rest on the petitioners on remand, cases of doubt being resolved in favor of the particular respondent.

It is argued that a third interest supporting patronage dismissals is the preservation of the democratic process. According to petitioners, "we have contrived no system for the support of party that does not place considerable reliance on patronage. The party organization makes a democratic government work and charges a price for its services." The argument is thus premised on the centrality of partisan politics to the democratic process.

Preservation of the democratic process is certainly an interest protection of which may in some instances justify limitations on First Amendment freedoms. But however important preservation of the two-party system or any system involving a fixed number of parties may or may not be,[22] we are not persuaded that the elimination of patronage practice or, as is specifically involved here, the interdiction of patronage dismissals, will bring about the demise of party politics. Political parties existed in the absence of active patronage practice prior to the administration of Andrew Jackson, and they have survived substantial reduction in their patronage power through the establishment of merit systems.

Patronage dismissals thus are not the least restrictive alternative to achieving the contribution they may make to the democratic process. The process functions as well without the practice, perhaps even better, for patronage dismissals clearly also retard that process. Patronage can result in the entrenchment of one or a few parties to the exclusion of others. And most indisputably, as we recognized at the outset, patronage is a very effective impediment to the associational and speech freedoms which are essential to a meaningful system of democratic government. Thus, if patronage contributes at all to the elective process, that contribution is diminished by the practice's impairment of the same. * * *

* * * The constitutional adjudication called for by this task is well within our province. The illuminating source to which we turn in performing the task is the system of government the First Amendment was intended to protect, a democratic system whose proper functioning is indispensably dependent on the unfettered judgment of each citizen on matters of political concern. Our decision in obedience to the guidance of that source does not outlaw political parties or political campaigning and management. Parties are free to exist and their concomitant activities are free to continue. We require only that the rights of every citizen to believe as he will and to act and associate according to his beliefs be free to continue as well.

In summary, patronage dismissals severely restrict political belief and association. Though there is a vital need for government efficiency and effectiveness, such dismissals are on balance not the least restrictive means for fostering that end. There is also a need to insure that policies

---

22. Partisan politics bears the imprimatur only of tradition, not the Constitution. * * *

which the electorate has sanctioned are effectively implemented. That interest can be fully satisfied by limiting patronage dismissals to policymaking positions. Finally, patronage dismissals cannot be justified by their contribution to the proper functioning of our democratic process through their assistance to partisan politics since political parties are nurtured by other, less intrusive and equally effective methods. More fundamentally, however, any contribution of patronage dismissals to the democratic process does not suffice to override their severe encroachment on First Amendment freedoms. We hold, therefore, that the practice of patronage dismissals is unconstitutional under the First and Fourteenth Amendments, and that respondents thus stated a valid claim for relief.

* * *

The judgment of the Court of Appeals is

Affirmed.

FCC v. Pacifica Foundation

July 3, 1978

This case arose when a New York radio station broadcast a recording of George Carlin's "Seven Dirty Words" monologue on a Tuesday afternoon. One man who claimed to have heard the broadcast while driving with his young son wrote a letter to the Federal Communications Commission, complaining that he could not understand why that recording would be broadcast over "the air that, supposedly, you control."

The FCC characterized Carlin's monologue as "patently offensive" but not "obscene." Nevertheless, based on this solitary complaint, it issued an order declaring that it could impose administrative sanctions on the broadcaster. Although the Commission chose not to impose such sanctions, it indicated that the matter would be added to the broadcaster's license file, and considered again if further complaints were received.

The broadcaster sued, arguing that the FCC lacked both statutory and constitutional authority to discipline a broadcaster for airing a program that was "indecent" but not obscene. By a 5–4 vote the Supreme Court upheld the FCC's statutory authority over indecent material. The majority also concluded that the government could, without transgressing the First Amendment, "channel" indecent material to times when children were not likely to be in the listening audience. It based this ruling in part on the intrusive ability of radio to enter the home and on the fact that it is accessible to children, even those too young to read. Apparently the Court did not regard Carlin's "indecent" monologue as overly offensive, however, because it attached the complete text—with interrupting laughter—as an appendix to its publicly announced decision.

Justice Brennan was one of four dissenters who believed the FCC lacked statutory authority to discipline broadcasters for airing nonobscene programs. Pursuant to a judicial tradition adopted during George Washington's administration, if a matter can be resolved on statutory grounds without reaching a constitutional question, courts should avoid deciding the constitutional issue. Brennan acknowledged this principle but was so outraged with the analysis offered by the majority that he was "unable to remain silent." He was not prepared to interpret the First Amendment to allow the government to restrict the adult population to hearing only what is fit for children. More than that, though, he saw and objected to a cultural bias in both the Court's and the FCC's action, a bias he deemed wholly incompatible with freedom of speech in a diverse culture.

Justice Stevens wrote the opinion of the Court, joined by Chief Justice Burger and Justices Blackmun, Powell, and Rehnquist. Justices Brennan, Stewart, White, and Marshall dissented.

o   o   o

MR. JUSTICE BRENNAN, with whom MR. JUSTICE MARSHALL joins, dissenting.

I agree with Mr. Justice Stewart that * * * [the FCC lacks statutory authority over non-obscene broadcasts]. I would, therefore, normally refrain from expressing my views on any constitutional issues implicated in this case. However, I find the Court's misapplication of fundamental First Amendment principles so patent, and its attempt to impose *its* notions of propriety on the whole of the American people so misguided, that I am unable to remain silent.

I

For the second time in two years, the Court refuses to embrace the notion, completely antithetical to basic First Amendment values, that the degree of protection the First Amendment affords protected speech varies with the social value ascribed to that speech by five Members of this Court. Moreover, as do all parties, all Members of the Court agree that the Carlin monologue aired by Station WBAI does not fall within one of the categories of speech, such as "fighting words," *Chaplinsky v. New Hampshire,* or obscenity, *Roth v. United States,* that is totally without First Amendment protection. * * * Yet despite the Court's refusal to create a sliding scale of First Amendment protection calibrated to this Court's perception of the worth of a communication's content, and despite our unanimous agreement that the Carlin monologue is protected speech, a majority of the Court nevertheless finds that, on the facts of this case, the FCC is not constitutionally barred from imposing sanctions on Pacifica for its airing of the Carlin monologue. This majority * * * rel[ies] principally on two factors in reaching this conclusion: (1) the capacity of a radio broadcast to intrude into the unwilling listener's home, and (2) the presence of children in the listening audience. Dispassionate analysis, removed from individual notions as to what is proper and what is not, starkly reveals that these justifications, whether individually or together, simply do not support even the professedly moderate degree of governmental homogenization of radio communications—if, indeed, such homogenization can ever be moderate given the pre-eminent status of the right of free speech in our constitutional scheme—that the Court today permits.

A

Without question, the privacy interests of an individual in his home are substantial and deserving of significant protection. In finding these interests sufficient to justify the content regulation of protected speech, however, the Court commits two errors. First, it misconceives the nature of the privacy interests involved where an individual voluntarily chooses to admit radio communications into his home. Second, it ignores the constitutionally protected interests of both those who wish to transmit and those who desire to receive broadcasts that many—including the FCC and this Court—might find offensive.

* * * I am in wholehearted agreement with my Brethren that an individual's right "to be let alone" when engaged in private activity within the confines of his own home is encompassed within the "substantial privacy interests" to which Mr. Justice Harlan referred in *Cohen v. California,* and is entitled to the greatest solicitude. However, I believe that an individual's actions in switching on and listening to communications transmitted over the public airways and directed to the public at large do not implicate fundamental privacy interests, even when engaged in within the home. Instead, because the radio is undeniably a public medium, these actions are more properly viewed as a decision to take part, if only as a listener, in an ongoing public discourse. Although an individual's decision to allow public radio communications into his home undoubtedly does not abrogate all of his privacy interests, the residual privacy interests he retains vis-à-vis the communication he voluntarily admits into his home are surely no greater than those of the people present in the corridor of the Los Angeles courthouse in *Cohen* who bore witness to the words "Fuck the Draft" emblazoned across Cohen's jacket. Their privacy interests were held insufficient to justify punishing Cohen for his offensive communication.

Even if an individual who voluntarily opens his home to radio communications retains privacy interests of sufficient moment to justify a ban on protected speech if those interests are "invaded in an essentially intolerable manner," *Cohen,* the very fact that those interests are threatened only by a radio broadcast precludes any intolerable invasion of privacy; for unlike other intrusive modes of communication, such as sound trucks, "[t]he radio can be turned off," *Lehman v. Shaker Heights*— and with a minimum of effort. ∗ ∗ ∗ Whatever the minimal discomfort suffered by a listener who inadvertently tunes into a program he finds offensive during the brief interval before he can simply extend his arm and switch stations or flick the "off" button, it is surely worth the candle to preserve the broadcaster's right to send, and the right of those interested to receive, a message entitled to full First Amendment protection. ∗ ∗ ∗

The Court's balance, of necessity, fails to accord proper weight to the interests of listeners who wish to hear broadcasts the FCC deems offensive. It permits majoritarian tastes completely to preclude a protected message from entering the homes of a receptive, unoffended minority. No decision of this Court supports such a result. Where the individuals constituting the offended majority may freely choose to reject the material being offered, we have never found their privacy interests of such moment to warrant the suppression of speech on privacy grounds. ∗ ∗ ∗

B

Most parents will undoubtedly find understandable as well as commendable the Court's sympathy with the FCC's desire to prevent offensive broadcasts from reaching the ears of unsupervised children. Unfortunately, the facial appeal of this justification for radio censorship masks its constitutional insufficiency. Although the government unquestionably has a special interest in the well-being of children and consequently "can adopt more stringent controls on communicative materials available to youths than on those available to adults," *Erznoznik v. Jacksonville,* the Court has accounted for this societal interest by adopting a "variable obscenity" standard that permits the prurient appeal of material available to children to be assessed in terms of the sexual interests of minors. ∗ ∗ ∗ Nevertheless, we have made it abundantly clear that "under any test of obscenity as to minors . . . to be obscene 'such expression must be, in some significant way, erotic.'" *Erznoznik,* quoting *Cohen.*

Because the Carlin monologue is obviously not an erotic appeal to the prurient interests of children, the Court, for the first time, allows the government to prevent minors from gaining access to materials that are not obscene, and are therefore protected, as to them. It thus ignores our recent admonition that "[speech] that is neither obscene as to youths nor subject to some other legitimate proscription cannot be suppressed solely to protect the young from ideas or images that a legislative body thinks unsuitable for them." *Id.* * * * The opinion of my Brother Powell acknowledges that there lurks in today's decision a potential for "[reducing] the adult population . . . to [hearing] only what is fit for children," but expresses faith that the FCC will vigilantly prevent this potential from ever becoming a reality. I am far less certain than my Brother Powell that such faith in the Commission is warranted; and even if I shared it, I could not so easily shirk the responsibility assumed by each Member of this Court jealously to guard against encroachments on First Amendment freedoms.

In concluding that the presence of children in the listening audience provides an adequate basis for the FCC to impose sanctions for Pacifica's broadcast of the Carlin monologue, the opinions of my Brother Powell and my Brother Stevens both stress the time-honored right of a parent to raise his child as he sees fit—a right this Court has consistently been vigilant to protect. Yet this principle supports a result directly contrary to that reached by the Court. [Our prior cases] hold that parents, *not* the government, have the right to make certain decisions regarding the upbringing of their children. As surprising as it may be to individual Members of this Court, some parents may actually find Mr. Carlin's unabashed attitude towards the seven "dirty words" healthy, and deem it desirable to expose their children to the manner in which Mr. Carlin defuses the taboo surrounding the words. Such parents may constitute a minority of the American public, but the absence of great numbers willing to exercise the right to raise their children in this fashion does not alter the right's nature or its existence. Only the Court's regrettable decision does that.

* * *

II

* * * Although the extent to which the Court stands ready to countenance FCC censorship of protected speech is unclear from today's decision, I find the reasoning by which my Brethren conclude that the

FCC censorship they approve will not significantly infringe on First Amendment values both disingenuous as to reality and wrong as a matter of law.

My Brother Stevens, in reaching a result apologetically described as narrow, takes comfort in his observation that "[a] requirement that indecent language be avoided will have its primary effect on the form, rather than the content, of serious communication," and finds solace in his conviction that "[t]here are few, if any, thoughts that cannot be expressed by the use of less offensive language." The idea that the content of a message and its potential impact on any who might receive it can be divorced from the words that are the vehicle for its expression is transparently fallacious. A given word may have a unique capacity to capsule an idea, evoke an emotion, or conjure up an image. Indeed, for those of us who place an appropriately high value on our cherished First Amendment rights, the word "censor" is such a word. Mr. Justice Harlan, speaking for the Court, recognized the truism that a speaker's choice of words cannot surgically be separated from the ideas he desires to express when he warned that "we cannot indulge the facile assumption that one can forbid particular words without also running a substantial risk of suppressing ideas in the process." *Cohen.* Moreover, even if an alternative phrasing may communicate a speaker's abstract ideas as effectively as those words he is forbidden to use, it is doubtful that the sterilized message will convey the emotion that is an essential part of so many communications. * * *

III

It is quite evident that I find the * * * result the Court reaches in this case dangerous as well as lamentable. Yet there runs throughout the opinions of my Brothers Powell and Stevens another vein I find equally disturbing: a depressing inability to appreciate that in our land of cultural pluralism, there are many who think, act, and talk differently from the Members of this Court, and who do not share their fragile sensibilities. It is only an acute ethnocentric myopia that enables the Court to approve the censorship of communications solely because of the words they contain.

"A word is not a crystal, transparent and unchanged, it is the skin of a living thought and may vary greatly in color and content according to the circumstances and the time in which it is used." *Towne v. Eisner.* The words that the Court and the Commission find so unpalatable may be the stuff of everyday conversations in some, if not many, of the innumerable subcultures that compose this Nation. Academic research indicates that this is indeed the case. As one researcher concluded, "[w]ords generally considered obscene like 'bullshit' and 'fuck' are considered neither obscene nor derogatory in the [black] vernacular except in particular contextual situations and when used with certain intonations."

Today's decision will thus have its greatest impact on broadcasters desiring to reach, and listening audiences composed of, persons who do not share the Court's view as to which words or expressions are acceptable and who, for a variety of reasons, including a conscious desire to flout majoritarian conventions, express themselves using words that may be regarded as offensive by those from different socio-economic backgrounds. In this context, the Court's decision may be seen for what, in the broader perspective, it really is: another of the dominant culture's inevitable efforts to force those groups who do not share its mores to conform to its way of thinking, acting, and speaking.

Pacifica, in response to an FCC inquiry about its broadcast of Carlin's satire on "the words you couldn't say on the public . . . airways," explained that "Carlin is not mouthing obscenities, he is merely using words to satirize as harmless and essentially silly our attitudes towards those words." In confirming Carlin's prescience as a social commentator by the result it reaches today, the Court evidences an attitude toward the "seven dirty words" that many others besides Mr. Carlin and Pacifica might describe as "silly." Whether today's decision will similarly prove "harmless" remains to be seen. One can only hope that it will.

HAZELWOOD SCHOOL DISTRICT V. KUHLMEIER

January 13, 1988

The Supreme Court has long recognized that "the constitutional rights of students in public schools are not automatically coextensive with the rights of adults in other settings." After all, when children exercise their individual rights in a manner that disrupts the classroom, their actions can frustrate the school's mission and interfere with the education of not only other students but of the disruptive students themselves.

In 1969, the Court established the basic parameters for student expression in public schools in *Tinker v. Des Moines School District*. School officials in *Tinker* had suspended junior high and high school students who wore black armbands to classes as a protest against the Vietnam war. The Court ruled that the symbolic act of wearing an armband for the purpose of expressing certain views is within the Free Speech Clause of the First Amendment. The opinion, authored by Justice Fortas, declared that neither students nor teachers "shed their constitutional rights to freedom of speech or expression at the schoolhouse gate." The Court then provided a standard that balanced the rights of children against the needs of public schools: school officials may ban expressive conduct if it "materially and substantially interferes with the requirements of appropriate discipline in the operation of the school." The school officials in *Tinker* were unable to make that showing.

Over the next two decades, however, the Court receded from the *Tinker* standard. For example, in 1986 the Court upheld the suspension of a high school student for making a speech filled with sexual innuendo at a student assembly. In doing so, the Court declined to independently assess the disruptive effect of the speech. Instead, a majority of Justices demonstrated a willingness to defer to the judgment of school officials about the level of disruption created by particular student conduct. In other cases, the Court created a distinction between a student's personal expression that occurred on school premises but not during instruction and student expression in school that took place under the auspices of a school-sponsored activity. Absent real interference with school discipline, the former is protected. The latter apparently may be prohibited if the *potential* for interference exists, a clear deviation from the showing required by *Tinker*.

This case arose in East Hazelwood, Missouri. When the high school principal objected to certain material in several articles planned for publication in the school newspaper, he ordered that the entire articles be excised prior to printing. His action thus presented a conflict between the Court's more deferential attitude toward public school officials and another time-honored First Amendment doctrine: intolerance for government censorship. The Court had traditionally held that it is one thing to punish people for abusing their right to free expression—such as by defaming someone or disturbing the peace—and quite another to restrain them from speaking or writing in the first place. Only the most extraordinary circumstances have prompted the Court to permit a prior restraint on expression.

The student reporters on the newspaper were involved in a school-sponsored activity, and thus arguably were subject to less protection. However, a prior restraint was involved. Moreover, the principal's reason for exercising editorial control was unrelated to concerns about interference with school discipline, whether actual or potential. Nevertheless, the Court upheld the principal's action. Although the majority continued to proclaim *Tinker's* vitality, it ruled that conduct of educators—including the blatant censorship exercised in this circumstance—was not offensive to the Constitution "so long as their actions are reasonably related to legitimate pedagogical concerns."

Justice Brennan's sharply worded dissenting opinion makes it obvious that he was disturbed by the Court's opinion. It is difficult to ascertain whether he was more troubled by the nearly complete dismantling of the *Tinker* framework or by the majority's disingenuous approach in doing so. In either case, to paraphrase the opening and closing lines of Brennan's dissent, there was a harsh civics lesson to be learned.

Justice White wrote the opinion of the Court, joined by Chief Justice Rehnquist and Justices Stevens, O'Connor, and Scalia. Justices Brennan, Marshall, and Blackmun dissented.

❂ ❂ ❂

JUSTICE BRENNAN, with whom JUSTICE MARSHALL and JUSTICE BLACKMUN join, dissenting.

When the young men and women of Hazelwood East High School registered for Journalism II, they expected a civics lesson. [As the court below noted,] Spectrum, the newspaper they were to publish, "was not just a class exercise in which students learned to prepare papers and hone writing skills, it was a . . . forum established to give students an opportunity to express their views while gaining an appreciation of their rights and responsibilities under the First Amendment to the United States Constitution." At the beginning of each school year, the student journalists published a Statement of Policy—tacitly approved each year by school authorities—announcing their expectation that "*Spectrum*, as a student-press publication, accepts all rights implied by the First Amendment. . . . Only speech that 'materially and substantially interferes with the requirements of appropriate discipline' can be found unacceptable and therefore prohibited." The school board itself affirmatively guaranteed the students of Journalism II an atmosphere conducive to fostering such an appreciation and exercising the full panoply of rights associated with a free student press. "School sponsored student publications," it vowed, "will not restrict free expression or diverse viewpoints within the rules of responsible journalism."

This case arose when the Hazelwood East administration breached its own promise, dashing its students' expectations. The school principal, without prior consultation or explanation, excised six articles—comprising two full pages—of the May 13, 1983, issue of Spectrum. He did so not because any of the articles would "materially and substantially interfere with the requirements of appropriate discipline," but simply because he considered two of the six "inappropriate, personal, sensitive, and unsuitable" for student consumption.

In my view the principal broke more than just a promise. He violated the First Amendment's prohibitions against censorship of any student expression that neither disrupts classwork nor invades the rights of others, and against any censorship that is not narrowly tailored to serve its purpose.

I

Public education serves vital national interests in preparing the Nation's youth for life in our increasingly complex society and for the duties of citizenship in our democratic Republic. The public school conveys to our young the information and tools required not merely to survive in, but to contribute to, civilized society. It also inculcates in tomorrow's leaders the "fundamental values necessary to the maintenance of a democratic political system." *Ambach v. Norwick.* All the while, the public educator nurtures students' social and moral development by transmitting to them an official dogma of "community values."

* * *

Free student expression undoubtedly sometimes interferes with the effectiveness of the school's pedagogical functions. Some brands of student expression do so by directly preventing the school from pursuing its pedagogical mission: The young polemic who stands on a soapbox during calculus class to deliver an eloquent political diatribe interferes with the legitimate teaching of calculus. And the student who delivers a lewd endorsement of a student-government candidate might so extremely distract an impressionable high school audience as to interfere with the orderly operation of the school. Other student speech, however, frustrates the school's legitimate pedagogical purposes merely by expressing a message that conflicts with the school's, without directly interfering with the school's expression of its message: A student who responds to a political science teacher's question with the retort, "socialism is good," subverts the school's inculcation of the message that capitalism is better. Even the maverick who sits in class passively sporting a symbol of protest against a government policy, cf. *Tinker v. Des Moines Independent Community School District*, or the gossip who sits in the student commons swapping stories of sexual escapade could readily muddle a clear official message condoning the government policy or condemning teenage sex. Likewise, the student newspaper that, like Spectrum, conveys a moral position at odds with the school's official stance might subvert the administration's legitimate inculcation of its own perception of community values.

If mere incompatibility with the school's pedagogical message were a constitutionally sufficient justification for the suppression of student speech, school officials could censor each of the students or student organizations in the foregoing hypotheticals, converting our public schools into "enclaves of totalitarianism," *id.*, that "strangle the free mind at its source," *West Virginia Board of Education v. Barnette*. The First Amendment permits no such blanket censorship authority. While the "constitutional rights of students in public school are not automatically coextensive with the rights of adults in other settings," *Bethel School Dist. No. 403 v. Fraser*, students in the public schools do not "shed their constitutional rights to freedom of speech or expression at the schoolhouse gate." *Tinker.* Just as the public on the street corner must, in the interest of fostering "enlightened opinion," tolerate speech that "tempt[s] [the listener] to throw [the speaker] off the street," *Cantwell v. Connecticut,* public educators must accommodate some student expression even if it offends them or offers views or values that contradict those the school wishes to inculcate.

In *Tinker,* this Court struck the balance. We held that official censorship of student expression—there the suspension of several students until they removed their armbands protesting the Vietnam war—is unconstitutional unless the speech "materially disrupts classwork or involves substantial disorder or invasion of the rights of others." School officials may not suppress "silent, passive expression of opinion, unaccompanied by any disorder or disturbance on the part of" the speaker. *Id.* The "mere desire to avoid the discomfort and unpleasantness that always accompany an unpopular viewpoint," *id.,* or an unsavory subject, does not justify official suppression of student speech in the high school.

* * *

II

Even if we were writing on a clean slate, I would reject the Court's rationale for abandoning *Tinker* in this case. The Court offers no more than an obscure tangle of three excuses to afford educators "greater control" over school-sponsored speech than the *Tinker* test would permit: the public educator's prerogative to control curriculum; the pedagogical interest in shielding the high school audience from objectionable viewpoints and sensitive topics; and the school's need to dissociate itself from student expression. None of the excuses, once disentangled, supports the distinction that the Court draws. *Tinker* fully addresses the first concern; the second is illegitimate; and the third is readily achievable through less oppressive means.

A

The Court is certainly correct that the First Amendment permits educators "to assure that participants learn whatever lessons the activity is designed to teach." That is, however, the essence of the *Tinker* test, not an excuse to abandon it. Under *Tinker,* school officials may censor only such student speech as would "materially disrup[t]" a legitimate curricular function. Manifestly, student speech is more likely to disrupt a curricular function when it arises in the context of a curricular activity—one that "is designed to teach" something—than when it arises in the context of a noncurricular activity. Thus, under *Tinker*, the school may constitutionally punish the budding political orator if he disrupts calculus class but not if he holds his tongue for the cafeteria. That is not because some more stringent standard applies in the curricular context. (After all, this Court applied the same standard whether the students in *Tinker* wore their armbands to the "classroom" or the "cafeteria.") It is because student speech in the noncurricular context is less likely to disrupt materially any legitimate pedagogical purpose.

I fully agree with the Court that the First Amendment should afford an educator the prerogative not to sponsor the publication of a newspaper article that is "ungrammatical, poorly written, inadequately researched, biased or prejudiced," or that falls short of the "high standards for . . . student speech that is disseminated under [the school's] auspices. . . . " But we need not abandon *Tinker* to reach that conclusion; we need only apply it. The enumerated criteria reflect the skills that the curricular newspaper "is designed to teach." The educator may, under *Tinker*, constitutionally "censor" poor grammar, writing, or research because to reward such expression would "materially disrup[t]" the newspaper's curricular purpose.

The same cannot be said of official censorship designed to shield the *audience* or dissociate the *sponsor* from the expression. Censorship so motivated might well serve (although, as I demonstrate *infra*, cannot legitimately serve) some other school purpose. But it in no way furthers the curricular purposes of a student *newspaper*, unless one believes that the purpose of the school newspaper is to teach students that the press ought never report bad news, express unpopular views, or print a thought that might upset its sponsors. Unsurprisingly, Hazelwood East claims no such pedagogical purpose.

* * *

B

The Court's second excuse for deviating from precedent is the school's interest in shielding an impressionable high school audience from material whose substance is "unsuitable for immature audiences." Specifically, the majority decrees that we must afford educators authority to shield high school students from exposure to "potentially sensitive topics" (like "the particulars of teenage sexual activity") or unacceptable social viewpoints (like the advocacy of "irresponsible se[x] or conduct otherwise inconsistent with 'the shared values of a civilized social order'") through school-sponsored student activities.

Tinker teaches us that the state educator's undeniable, and undeniably vital, mandate to inculcate moral and political values is not a general warrant to act as "thought police" stifling discussion of all but state- approved topics and advocacy of all but the official position. Otherwise educators could transform students into "closed-circuit recipients of only that which the State chooses to communicate," *Tinker,* and cast a perverse and impermissible "pall of orthodoxy over the classroom," *Keyishian v. Board of Regents.* Thus, the State cannot constitutionally prohibit its high school students from recounting in the locker room "the particulars of [their] teen-age sexual activity," nor even from advocating "irresponsible se[x]" or other presumed abominations of "the shared values of a civilized social order." Even in its capacity as educator the State may not assume an Orwellian "guardianship of the public mind," *Thomas v. Collins* (Jackson, J., concurring).

The mere fact of school sponsorship does not, as the Court suggests, license such thought control in the high school, whether through school suppression of disfavored viewpoints or through official assessment of topic sensitivity. The former would constitute unabashed and unconstitutional viewpoint discrimination, as well as an impermissible infringement of the students' "right to receive information and ideas," *Board of Education v. Pico.* Just as a school board may not purge its · state-funded library of all books that "offen[d] [its] social, political and moral tastes," *id.,* school officials may not, out of like motivation, discriminatorily excise objectionable ideas from a student publication. The State's prerogative to dissolve the student newspaper entirely (or to limit its subject matter) no more entitles it to dictate which viewpoints students may express on its pages, than the State's prerogative to close down the schoolhouse entitles it to prohibit the nondisruptive expression of antiwar sentiment within its gates.

Official censorship of student speech on the ground that it addresses "potentially sensitive topics" is, for related reasons, equally impermissible. I would not begrudge an educator the authority to limit the substantive scope of a school-sponsored publication to a certain, objectively definable topic, such as literary criticism, school sports, or an overview of the school year. Unlike those determinate limitations, "potential topic sensitivity" is a vaporous nonstandard * * * that invites manipulation to achieve ends that cannot permissibly be achieved through blatant viewpoint discrimination and chills student speech to which school officials might not object. In part because of those dangers, this Court has consistently condemned any scheme allowing a state official boundless discretion in licensing speech from a particular forum.

* * *

C

The sole concomitant of school sponsorship that might conceivably justify the distinction that the Court draws between sponsored and nonsponsored student expression is the risk "that the views of the individual speaker [might be] erroneously attributed to the school." Of course, the risk of erroneous attribution inheres in any student expression, including "personal expression" that, like the armbands in *Tinker*, "happens to occur on the school premises." Nevertheless, the majority is certainly correct that indicia of school sponsorship increase the likelihood of such attribution, and that state educators may therefore have a legitimate interest in dissociating themselves from student speech.

But "'[e]ven though the governmental purpose be legitimate and substantial, that purpose cannot be pursued by means that broadly stifle fundamental personal liberties when the end can be more narrowly achieved.'" *Keyishian v. Board of Regents* (quoting *Shelton v. Tucker*). Dissociative means short of censorship are available to the school. It could, for example, require the student activity to publish a disclaimer, such as the "Statement of Policy" that Spectrum published each school year announcing that "[a]ll . . . editorials appearing in this newspaper reflect the opinions of the Spectrum staff, which are not necessarily shared by the administrators or faculty of Hazelwood East," or it could simply issue its own response clarifying the official position on the matter and explaining why the student position is wrong. Yet, without so much as acknowledging the less oppressive alternatives, the Court approves of brutal censorship.

III

Since the censorship served no legitimate pedagogical purpose, it cannot by any stretch of the imagination have been designed to prevent "materia[l] disrup[tion of] classwork," *Tinker*. Nor did the censorship fall within the category that *Tinker* described as necessary to prevent student expression from "inva[ding] the rights of others." If that term is to have any content, it must be limited to rights that are protected by law. [As the Court of Appeals said below,] "[a]ny yardstick less exacting than [that] could result in school officials curtailing speech at the slightest fear of disturbance," a prospect that would be completely at odds with this Court's pronouncement that the "undifferentiated fear or apprehension of disturbance is not enough [even in the public school context] to overcome the right to freedom of expression." *Tinker*. And, as the Court of Appeals correctly reasoned, whatever journalistic impropriety these articles may have contained, they could not conceivably be tortious, much less criminal.

Finally, even if the majority were correct that the principal could constitutionally have censored the objectionable material, I would emphatically object to the brutal manner in which he did so. Where "[t]he separation of legitimate from illegitimate speech calls for more sensitive tools," *Speiser v. Randall*, the principal used a paper shredder. He objected to some material in two articles, but excised six entire articles. He did not so much as inquire into obvious alternatives, such as precise deletions or additions (one of which had already been made), rearranging the layout, or delaying publication. Such unthinking contempt for individual rights is intolerable from any state official. It is particularly insidious from one to whom the public entrusts the task of inculcating in its youth an appreciation for the cherished democratic liberties that our Constitution guarantees.

IV

The Court opens its analysis in this case by purporting to reaffirm *Tinker*'s time-tested proposition that public school students "do not shed their constitutional rights to freedom of speech or expression at the schoolhouse gate." That is an ironic introduction to an opinion that denudes high school students of much of the First Amendment protection that *Tinker* itself prescribed. Instead of "teach[ing] children to respect the diversity of ideas that is fundamental to the American system," *Pico* (Blackmun, J., concurring), and "that our Constitution is a living reality, not parchment preserved under glass," *Shanley v. Northeast Independent School District*, the Court today "teach[es] youth to discount important principles of our government as mere platitudes." *Barnette*. The young men and women of Hazelwood East expected a civics lesson, but not the one the Court teaches them today.

I dissent.

TEXAS V. JOHNSON

June 21, 1989

This decision, which invalidated a Texas flag desecration statute, received perhaps as much widespread public attention as any other case in the last quarter-century. In his dissent, Chief Justice Rehnquist made an emotional appeal to the flag's place in our hearts and in our history. In doing so, he cited such legal authorities as the Pledge of Allegiance, the Star-Spangled Banner, a Whittier poem, a Sousa march, and even the number of times the flag has appeared on U.S. postage stamps. Justice Brennan's opinion for the Court, on the other hand, presented a methodical and traditional First Amendment analysis that leads the reader to its inexorable conclusion.

Brennan's opinion relies heavily upon a series of Supreme Court decisions in flag cases dating back almost 60 years. In these decisions, the Court held that a person cannot be punished criminally for displaying a red flag, *Stromberg v. California* (1931), that people cannot be compelled to salute the flag, *West Virginia Board of Education v. Barnette* (1943), that no criminal sanctions may be imposed on those who speak critically of the flag, *Street v. New York* (1969), and that displaying a United States flag with a peace sign emblazoned on it is a form of protected political expression, *Spence v. Washington* (1974).

To some, the extension of the First Amendment's protection of speech to nonverbal conduct, such as that involving flags, might seem strange and beyond the textual mandate. However, the application of the Free Speech Clause to at least some forms of expressive conduct is well settled in First Amendment jurisprudence and is grounded in the rather obvious fact that many of the ways in which we express ourselves involve the use of symbols and symbolism. Indeed, if all expressive conduct were left wholly unprotected by the First Amendment, a person who is deaf and who communicates through sign language could be "silenced" at the whim of the government. Few scholars and judges would support such a miserly interpretation of our essential First Amendment freedoms.

Nevertheless, the Court has recognized that federal, state, and local governments may properly restrict conduct—even expressive conduct—more freely than it may restrict pure speech. Pursuant to the test announced in *United*

States v. O'Brien (1968), government regulation of expressive conduct will be constitutionally permissible "if it furthers an important or substantial governmental interest; if the governmental interest is unrelated to the suppression of free expression; and if the incidental restriction on alleged First Amendment freedoms is no greater than is essential to [further] that interest." However, when the governmental interest *is* related to suppressing expression, when its very purpose is to silence a particular view, the regulation will be confronted by the full force of the First Amendment and will be upheld only if it complies with the exacting standards applicable to government censorship of pure speech.

In 1982, Brennan broke a tradition of the Court by issuing a written dissent from the Court's refusal to review a lower court judgment. The defendants in that case, *Kime v. United States*, like the defendant in this one, raised First Amendment objections to a prosecution for flag burning. Brennan stated emphatically that the defendants' convictions violated their First Amendment rights because the government's interest in restricting flag burning was related to suppressing expression and could not be justified under traditional First Amendment analysis. In the *Johnson* decision, seven years later, Brennan persuaded a majority to join him.

The judgment in *Johnson* caused an uproar not only in political circles but throughout much of the nation. President Bush and other government and civic leaders called for a constitutional amendment to protect the flag. The controversy that raged that summer was almost surreal. Against the backdrop of Tiennamen Square, where Chinese students had struggled for their freedom only to be brutally suppressed, many in our country were trying to surrender some of our freedom for the sake of a symbolic piece of fabric.

After much debate, the Senate vote on a constitutional amendment—51 for, 48 against—fell far short of the required two-thirds majority, and Congress opted instead for a federal flag desecration statute. Mr. Johnson, among others, immediately protested against and challenged this statute by burning another flag on the steps of the Capitol. The Supreme Court took the cases on an expedited basis—directly from the federal trial courts rather than from one or more intermediate appellate courts—as the new federal act required, and it again held that flag desecration is protected expression. In another opinion authored by Brennan, *United States v. Eichman* (1990), the Court invalidated the federal statute, and the issue that had caused so much furor began to fade from public consciousness.

In the battle between emotionalism and the First Amendment, the country won.

Justice Brennan wrote the majority opinion, joined by Justices Marshall, Blackmun, Scalia, and Kennedy. Chief Justice Rehnquist dissented, as did Justices White, O'Connor, and Stevens.

⦿   ⦿   ⦿

JUSTICE BRENNAN delivered the opinion of the Court.

After publicly burning an American flag as a means of political protest, Gregory Lee Johnson was convicted of desecrating a flag in violation of Texas law. This case presents the question whether his conviction is consistent with the First Amendment. We hold that it is not.

I

While the Republican National Convention was taking place in Dallas in 1984, respondent Johnson participated in a political demonstration dubbed the "Republican War Chest Tour." As explained in literature distributed by the demonstrators and in speeches made by them, the purpose of this event was to protest the policies of the Reagan administration and of certain Dallas-based corporations. The demonstrators marched through the Dallas streets, chanting political slogans and stopping at several corporate locations to stage "die-ins" intended to dramatize the consequences of nuclear war. On several occasions they spray-painted the walls of buildings and overturned potted plants, but Johnson himself took no part in such activities. He did, however, accept an American flag handed to him by a fellow protestor who had taken it from a flag pole outside one of the targeted buildings.

The demonstration ended in front of Dallas City Hall, where Johnson unfurled the American flag, doused it with kerosene, and set it on fire. While the flag burned, the protestors chanted, "America, the red, white, and blue, we spit on you." After the demonstrators dispersed, a witness to the flag-burning collected the flag's remains and buried them in his backyard. No one was physically injured or threatened with injury, though several witnesses testified that they had been seriously offended by the flag-burning.

Of the approximately 100 demonstrators, Johnson alone was charged with a crime. The only criminal offense with which he was charged was the desecration of a venerated object in violation of Tex. Penal Code Ann. § 42.09(a)(3). After a trial, he was convicted, sentenced to one year in prison, and fined $2,000. The Court of Appeals for the Fifth

District of Texas at Dallas affirmed Johnson's conviction, but the Texas Court of Criminal Appeals reversed, holding that the State could not, consistent with the First Amendment, punish Johnson for burning the flag in these circumstances. * * * [We] now affirm.

II

* * * We must first determine whether Johnson's burning of the flag constituted expressive conduct, permitting him to invoke the First Amendment in challenging his conviction. If his conduct was expressive, we next decide whether the State's regulation is related to the suppression of free expression. If the State's regulation is not related to expression, then the less stringent standard we announced in *United States v. O'Brien* for regulations of noncommunicative conduct controls. If it is, then we are outside of *O'Brien's* test, and we must ask whether this interest justifies Johnson's conviction under a more demanding standard. * * *

The First Amendment literally forbids the abridgement only of "speech," but we have long recognized that its protection does not end at the spoken or written word. While we have rejected "the view that an apparently limitless variety of conduct can be labeled 'speech' whenever the person engaging in the conduct intends thereby to express an idea," *O'Brien*, we have acknowledged that conduct may be "sufficiently imbued with elements of communication to fall within the scope of the First and Fourteenth Amendments." *Spence v. Washington.*

In deciding whether particular conduct possesses sufficient communicative elements to bring the First Amendment into play, we have asked whether "[a]n intent to convey a particularized message was present, and [whether] the likelihood was great that the message would be understood by those who viewed it." *Id.* Hence, we have recognized the expressive nature of students' wearing of black armbands to protest American military involvement in Vietnam, *Tinker v. Des Moines Independent Community School District*; of a sit-in by blacks in a "whites only" area to protest segregation, *Brown v. Louisiana*; of the wearing of American military uniforms in a dramatic presentation criticizing American involvement in Vietnam, *Schacht v. United States*; and of picketing about a wide variety of causes, *see, e.g., Food Employees v. Logan Valley Plaza, Inc.*; *United States v. Grace.*

Especially pertinent to this case are our decisions recognizing the communicative nature of conduct relating to flags. Attaching a peace sign to the flag, *Spence*; saluting the flag, *West Virginia Board of Education v. Barnette*; and displaying a red flag, *Stromberg v. California*, we have held, all may find shelter under the First Amendment. That we have had little difficulty identifying an expressive element in conduct relating to flags should not be surprising. The very purpose of a national flag is to serve as a symbol of our country; it is, one might say, "the one visible manifestation of two hundred years of nationhood." *Smith v. Goguen* (Rehnquist, J., dissenting). Thus, we have observed:

> [T]he flag salute is a form of utterance. Symbolism is a primitive but effective way of communicating ideas. The use of an emblem or flag to symbolize some system, idea, institution, or personality, is a short cut from mind to mind. Causes and nations, political parties, lodges and ecclesiastical groups seek to knit the loyalty of their followings to a flag or banner, a color or design.

Barnette. Pregnant with expressive content, the flag as readily signifies this Nation as does the combination of letters found in "America."

We have not automatically concluded, however, that any action taken with respect to our flag is expressive. Instead, in characterizing such action for First Amendment purposes, we have considered the context in which it occurred. In *Spence*, for example, we emphasized that Spence's taping of a peace sign to his flag was "roughly simultaneous with and concededly triggered by the Cambodian incursion and the Kent State tragedy." The State of Washington had conceded, in fact, that Spence's conduct was a form of communication, and we stated that "the State's concession is inevitable on this record."

The State of Texas conceded for purposes of its oral argument in this case that Johnson's conduct was expressive conduct, and this concession seems to us as prudent as was Washington's in *Spence*. Johnson burned an American flag as part—indeed, as the culmination—of a political demonstration that coincided with the convening of the Republican Party and its renomination of Ronald Reagan for President. The expressive, overtly political nature of this conduct was both intentional and overwhelmingly apparent. At his trial, Johnson explained his reasons for burning the flag as follows: "The American Flag was burned as Ronald Reagan was being renominated as President. And a more powerful statement of symbolic speech, whether you agree with it or not, couldn't have been made at that time. It's quite a just position [juxtaposition]. We had new patriotism and no patriotism." In these circumstances, Johnson's burning of the flag was conduct "sufficiently imbued with elements of communication," *Spence,* to implicate the First Amendment.

III

The Government generally has a freer hand in restricting expressive conduct than it has in restricting the written or spoken word. It may not, however, proscribe particular conduct *because* it has expressive elements. "[W]hat might be termed the more generalized guarantee of freedom of expression makes the communicative nature of conduct an inadequate *basis* for singling out that conduct for proscription. A law *directed at* the communicative nature of conduct must, like a law directed at speech itself, be justified by the substantial showing of need that the First Amendment requires." *Community for Creative Non-Violence v. Watt,* (Scalia, J., dissenting) (emphasis in original). It is, in short, not simply the verbal or nonverbal nature of the expression, but the governmental interest at stake, that helps to determine whether a restriction on that expression is valid.

Thus, although we have recognized that where "'speech' and 'nonspeech' elements are combined in the same course of conduct, a sufficiently important governmental interest in regulating the nonspeech element can justify incidental limitations on First Amendment freedoms," *O'Brien,* we have limited the applicability of *O'Brien's* relatively lenient standard to those cases in which "the governmental interest is unrelated to the suppression of free expression." *Id.* * * *

In order to decide whether *O'Brien's* test applies here, therefore, we must decide whether Texas has asserted an interest in support of Johnson's conviction that is unrelated to the suppression of expression. If we find that an interest asserted by the State is simply not implicated on the facts before us, we need not ask whether *O'Brien's* test applies. The State offers two separate interests to justify this conviction: preventing breaches of the peace, and preserving the flag as a symbol of nationhood and national unity. We hold that the first interest is not implicated on this record and that the second is related to the suppression of expression.

A

Texas claims that its interest in preventing breaches of the peace justifies Johnson's conviction for flag desecration. However, no disturbance of the peace actually occurred or threatened to occur because of Johnson's burning of the flag. Although the State stresses the disruptive behavior of the protestors during their march toward City Hall, it admits that "no actual breach of the peace occurred at the time of the flagburning or in response to the flagburning." The State's emphasis on the protestors' disorderly actions prior to arriving at City Hall is not only somewhat surprising given that no charges were brought on the basis of this conduct, but it also fails to show that a disturbance of the peace was a likely reaction to Johnson's conduct. The only evidence offered by the State at trial to show the reaction to Johnson's actions was the testimony of several persons who had been seriously offended by the flag-burning.

The State's position, therefore, amounts to a claim that an audience that takes serious offense at particular expression is necessarily likely to disturb the peace and that the expression may be prohibited on this basis. Our precedents do not countenance such a presumption. On the contrary, they recognize that a principal "function of free speech under our system of government is to invite dispute. It may indeed best serve its high purpose when it induces a condition of unrest, creates dissatisfaction with conditions as they are, or even stirs people to anger." *Terminiello v. Chicago.* It would be odd indeed to conclude *both* that "if it is the speaker's opinion that gives offense, that consequence is a reason for according it constitutional protection," *FCC v. Pacifica Foundation* (opinion of Stevens, J.), *and* that the Government may ban the expression of certain disagreeable ideas on the unsupported presumption that their very disagreeableness will provoke violence.

Thus, we have not permitted the Government to assume that every expression of a provocative idea will incite a riot, but have instead required careful consideration of the actual circumstances surrounding such expression, asking whether the expression "is directed to inciting or producing imminent lawless action and is likely to incite or produce such action." *Brandenburg v. Ohio* (reviewing circumstances surrounding rally and speeches by Ku Klux Klan). To accept Texas' arguments that it need only demonstrate "the potential for a breach of the peace," and that every flag-burning necessarily possesses that potential, would be to eviscerate our holding in *Brandenburg.* This we decline to do.

* * *

We thus conclude that the State's interest in maintaining order is not implicated on these facts. The State need not worry that our holding will disable it from preserving the peace. We do not suggest that the First Amendment forbids a State to prevent "imminent lawless action." *Brandenburg.* And, in fact, Texas already has a statute specifically prohibiting breaches of the peace, which tends to confirm that Texas need not punish this flag desecration in order to keep the peace.

B

The State also asserts an interest in preserving the flag as a symbol of nationhood and national unity. In *Spence,* we acknowledged that the Government's interest in preserving the flag's special symbolic value "is directly related to expression in the context of activity" such as affixing a peace symbol to a flag. We are equally persuaded that this interest is related to expression in the case of Johnson's burning of the flag. The State, apparently, is concerned that such conduct will lead people to believe either that the flag does not stand for nationhood and national unity, but instead reflects other, less positive concepts, or that the concepts reflected in the flag do not in fact exist, that is, we do not enjoy unity as a Nation. These concerns blossom only when a person's treatment of the flag communicates some message, and thus are related "to the suppression of free expression" within the meaning of *O'Brien.* We are thus outside of *O'Brien's* test altogether.

IV

It remains to consider whether the State's interest in preserving the flag as a symbol of nationhood and national unity justifies Johnson's conviction.

As in *Spence,* "[w]e are confronted with a case of prosecution for the expression of an idea through activity," and "[a]ccordingly, we must examine with particular care the interests advanced by [petitioner] to support its prosecution." Johnson was not, we add, prosecuted for the expression of just any idea; he was prosecuted for his expression of dissatisfaction with the policies of this country, expression situated at the core of our First Amendment values.

Moreover, Johnson was prosecuted because he knew that his politically charged expression would cause "serious offense." If he had burned the flag as a means of disposing of it because it was dirty or torn, he would not have been convicted of flag desecration under this Texas law: federal law designates burning as the preferred means of disposing of a flag "when it is in such condition that it is no longer a fitting emblem for display," and Texas has no quarrel with this means of disposal. The Texas law is thus not aimed at protecting the physical integrity of the flag in all circumstances, but is designed instead to protect it only against impairments that would cause serious offense to others. Texas concedes as much: "Section 42.09(b) reaches only those severe acts of physical abuse of the flag carried out in a way likely to be offensive. The statute mandates intentional or knowing abuse, that is, the kind of mistreatment that is not innocent, but rather is intentionally designed to seriously offend other individuals." Brief for Petitioner.

* * * Johnson's political expression was restricted because of the content of the message he conveyed. We must therefore subject the State's asserted interest in preserving the special symbolic character of the flag to "the most exacting scrutiny." *Boos v. Barry.*

Texas argues that its interest in preserving the flag as a symbol of nationhood and national unity survives this close analysis. Quoting extensively from the writings of this Court chronicling the flag's historic and symbolic role in our society, the State emphasizes the "special place" reserved for the flag in our Nation. The State's argument is not that it has an interest simply in maintaining the flag as a symbol of something, no matter what it symbolizes; indeed, if that were the State's position, it would be difficult to see how that interest is endangered by highly symbolic conduct such as Johnson's. Rather, the State's claim is that it has an interest in preserving the flag as a symbol of *nationhood* and *national unity*, a symbol with a determinate range of meanings. According to Texas, if one physically treats the flag in a way that would tend to cast doubt on either the idea that nationhood and national unity are the flag's referents or that national unity actually exists, the message conveyed thereby is a harmful one and therefore may be prohibited.

If there is a bedrock principle underlying the First Amendment, it is that the Government may not prohibit the expression of an idea simply because society finds the idea itself offensive or disagreeable.

We have not recognized an exception to this principle even where our flag has been involved. In *Street v. New York*, we held that a State may not criminally punish a person for uttering words critical of the flag. Rejecting the argument that the conviction could be sustained on the ground that Street had "failed to show the respect for our national symbol which may properly be demanded of every citizen," we concluded that "the constitutionally guaranteed 'freedom to be intellectually . . .

diverse or even contrary,' and the 'right to differ as to things that touch the heart of the existing order,' encompass the freedom to express publicly one's opinion about our flag, including those opinions which are defiant or contemptuous." *Id.*, quoting *Barnette*. Nor may the Government, we have held, compel conduct that would evince respect for the flag. "To sustain the compulsory flag salute we are required to say that a Bill of Rights which guards the individual's right to speak his own mind, left it open to public authorities to compel him to utter what is not on his mind." *Id.*

In holding in *Barnette* that the Constitution did not leave this course open to the Government, Justice Jackson described one of our society's defining principles in words deserving of their frequent repetition: "If there is any fixed star in our constitutional constellation, it is that no official, high or petty, can prescribe what shall be orthodox in politics, nationalism, religion, or other matters of opinion of force citizens to confess by word or act their faith therein." In *Spence*, we held that the same interest asserted by Texas here was insufficient to support a criminal conviction under a flag-misuse statute for the taping of a peace sign to an American flag. "Given the protected character of [Spence's] expression and in light of the fact that no interest that State may have in preserving the physical integrity of a privately owned flag was significantly impaired on these facts," we held, "the conviction must be invalidated."

In short, nothing in our precedents suggests that a State may foster its own view of the flag by prohibiting expressive conduct relating to it. To bring its argument outside our precedents, Texas attempts to convince us that even if its interest in preserving the flag's symbolic role does not allow it to prohibit words or some expressive conduct critical of the flag, it does permit it to forbid the outright destruction of the flag. The State's argument cannot depend here on the distinction between written or spoken words and nonverbal conduct. That distinction, we have shown, is of no moment where the nonverbal conduct is expressive, as it is here, and where the regulation of that conduct is related to expression, as it is here. In addition, both *Barnette* and *Spence* involved expressive conduct, not only verbal communication, and both found that conduct protected.

Texas' focus on the precise nature of Johnson's expression, moreover, misses the point of our prior decisions: their enduring lesson, that the Government may not prohibit expression simply because it disagrees with its message, is not dependent on the particular mode in which one chooses to express an idea.[11] If we were to hold that a State may forbid flag-burning wherever it is likely to endanger the flag's symbolic role, but allow it wherever burning a flag promotes that role—as where, for example, a person ceremoniously burns a dirty flag—we would be saying that when it comes to impairing the flag's physical integrity, the flag itself may be used as a symbol—as a substitute for the written or spoken word or a "short cut from mind to mind"—only in one direction. We would be permitting a State to "prescribe what shall be orthodox" by saying that one may burn the flag to convey one's attitude toward it and its referents only if one does not endanger the flag's representation of nationhood and national unity.

We never before have held that the Government may ensure that a symbol be used to express only one view of that symbol or its referents. Indeed, in *Schacht v. United States*, we invalidated a federal statute permitting an actor portraying a member of one of our armed forces to "wear the uniform of that armed force if the portrayal does not intend to discredit that armed force." This proviso, we held, "which leaves Americans free to praise the war in Vietnam but can send persons like Schacht to prison for opposing it, cannot survive in a country which has the First Amendment."

We perceive no basis on which to hold that the principle underlying our decision in *Schacht* does not apply to this case. To conclude that the Government may permit designated symbols to be used to communicate only a limited set of messages would be to enter territory having no discernible or defensible boundaries. Could the Government, on this theory, prohibit the burning of state flags? Of copies of the Presidential seal? Of the Constitution? In evaluating these choices under the First Amendment, how would we decide which symbols were sufficiently special to warrant this unique status? To do so, we would be forced to consult our own political preferences, and impose them on the citizenry, in the very way that the First Amendment forbids us to do.

There is, moreover, no indication—either in the text of the Constitution or in our cases interpreting it—that a separate juridical category

---

11. The Chief Justice's dissent appears to believe that Johnson's conduct may be prohibited and, indeed, criminally sanctioned, because "his act . . . conveyed nothing that could not have been conveyed and was not conveyed just as forcefully in a dozen different ways." • • • [This assertion] ignores the fact that, in *Spence* we "rejected summarily" this very claim.

exists for the American flag alone. Indeed, we would not be surprised to learn that the persons who framed our Constitution and wrote the Amendment that we now construe were not known for their reverence for the Union Jack. The First Amendment does not guarantee that other concepts virtually sacred to our Nation as a whole—such as the principle that discrimination on the basis of race is odious and destructive—will go unquestioned in the marketplace of ideas. We decline, therefore, to create for the flag an exception to the joust of principles protected by the First Amendment.

* * *

We are fortified in today's conclusion by our conviction that forbidding criminal punishment for conduct such as Johnson's will not endanger the special role played by our flag or the feelings it inspires. To paraphrase Justice Holmes, we submit that nobody can suppose that this one gesture of an unknown man will change our Nation's attitude towards its flag. Indeed, Texas' argument that the burning of an American flag "is an act having a high likelihood to cause a breach of the peace," and its statute's implicit assumption that physical mistreatment of the flag will lead to "serious offense," tend to confirm that the flag's special role is not in danger; if it were, no one would riot or take offense because a flag had been burned.

We are tempted to say, in fact, that the flag's deservedly cherished place in our community will be strengthened, not weakened, by our holding today. Our decision is a reaffirmation of the principles of freedom and inclusiveness that the flag best reflects, and of the conviction that our toleration of criticism such as Johnson's is a sign and source of our strength. Indeed, one of the proudest images of our flag, the one immortalized in our own national anthem, is of the bombardment it survived at Fort McHenry. It is the Nation's resilience, not its rigidity, that Texas sees reflected in the flag—and it is that resilience that we reassert today.

The way to preserve the flag's special role is not to punish those who feel differently about these matters. It is to persuade them that they are wrong. * * * We can imagine no more appropriate response to burning a flag than waving one's own, no better way to counter a flag-burner's message than by saluting the flag that burns, no surer means of preserving the dignity even of the flag that burned than by—as one witness here did—according its remains a respectful burial. We do not consecrate the flag by punishing its desecration, for in doing so we dilute the freedom that this cherished emblem represents.

* * * The judgment of the Texas Court of Criminal Appeals is therefore

Affirmed.

◦ 2 ◦

ONE NATION UNDER GOD

This country has always struggled with the role religion should play in shaping public policy and in governing the populace. Many of the original colonies were settled by Europeans fleeing religious persecution. Yet it did not take long for some devout settlers to start imposing their convictions on others. Less than 15 years after the Mayflower landed at Plymouth, civil authorities banished Roger Williams for his views, prompting him to found Rhode Island as a haven for those oppressed by religious intolerance in Massachusetts.

In the more than three and a half centuries that have followed, the country has experienced the birth of new religions and occasional periods of zealous religious revivalism. Throughout most of that time, the nation has maintained a commitment to individual freedom of religious belief and worship while also valuing the religious training and heritage necessary to sustain a virtuous society capable of self-government.

The principal expression of this commitment to religious liberty is contained in the first two clauses of the First Amendment to the Constitution of the United States. They provide that "Congress shall make no law respecting an establishment of religion, or prohibiting the free exercise thereof." These two clauses, known respectively as the Establishment Clause and the Free Exercise Clause, set the framework for religious freedom in the country. The ongoing problems for the Supreme Court have been to define the scope of these clauses and to resolve the tensions between them.

The Establishment Clause, by prohibiting the creation of an official church, presumably also prohibits the government from setting one religion above, or preferring one religion over, all others. However, does this principle of neutrality also require that the government not prefer religion over nonreligion? May the government provide no public support for religious and moral values? Even if neutrality is the benchmark principle, how it is to be measured? For example, if the government provides generally available educational benefits, must those benefits be denied if used for religious training or if directed to a sectarian institution?

The Free Exercise Clause undoubtedly guarantees unfettered freedom for religious belief, but what about religious practices? Presumably followers of one faith may be restrained from slaying nonbelievers even though their religion commands them to do so, but what other governmental policies can justify suppression of religious freedom? For instance, does the societal interest in preventing drug and alcohol abuse permit the government to prevent Native Americans from using peyote? May the government prohibit minors from taking Communion if grape juice is not substituted for wine? Put more generally, when, if ever, does religious belief entitle the believer to an exemption from laws generally applicable to everyone else?

Perhaps most important, how are the two clauses to be reconciled when the principles underlying them are in conflict? Does it violate the Free Exercise Clause to tax church property? Does it violate the Establishment Clause to provide churches an exemption from such a tax?

The opinions excerpted in this chapter deal with four Establishment Clause issues and three Free Exercise issues: Bible reading in public schools, invocations and prayer at legislative sessions, religious displays supported by public funds, mandatory instruction in creationism, working on the sabbath, military restrictions on religious attire, and religious practices in prison. In each, Justice Brennan manifested a profound respect for people of different faiths and traditions as he helped shape the nation's jurisprudence on some of the most controversial issues ever presented to a panel of judges.

SCHOOL DISTRICT OF ABINGTON TOWNSHIP V. SCHEMPP

June 17, 1963

In 1962, the Supreme Court issued its controversial ruling in *Engel v. Vitale*, striking down the use of a nondenominational morning prayer in New York public schools. Despite common belief, the case did *not* ban prayer in public schools. Rather, it banned only *compulsory* school prayer. Nothing in the Court's language or reasoning in any way suggested that students, teachers, or administrators were forbidden to offer private prayer in a nondisruptive manner. Instead, it was the state's role in composing and imposing the prayer that was critical. As the Court noted, "[i]t is no part of the business of government to compose official prayers."

The case excerpted here consolidated two disputes involving a related issue: whether mandatory readings from the Bible in primary and elementary public schools violate the First Amendment's mandate that government "make no law respecting an establishment of religion." The lower federal court in one of the cases, arising out of Abington, Pennsylvania, held that the practice does violate the Constitution. A divided state court in the other case, originating in Baltimore, ruled to the contrary.

By a vote of 8–1, the Supreme Court sided with the lower federal court and held that mandatory Bible reading in public schools is constitutionally impermissible under the Establishment Clause. Justice Clark's opinion for the Court occupied slightly more than 22 pages in the official reporter and analyzed the issue through a "purpose and effect" test. Under this test, government action is permissible only if there be "a secular purpose and a primary effect that neither advances nor inhibits religion." According to the Court, compulsory Bible reading in public schools fails both parts of this test. In reaching this conclusion, the Court indicated that state neutrality toward religion is the touchstone of the Establishment Clause.

Justice Brennan's concurring opinion, which by necessity is heavily edited here, extended for 74 pages. He examined in detail the history behind the Establishment Clause and explored the intent of the Framers. Brennan concluded that there were differences of opinion among the Framers about the extent of separation between Church and State required by the First Amendment. In any event, the intent of the Framers was, in Brennan's view,

68

not dispositive. He believed the Court needed to consider the issue in the context of current realities, such as greater religious diversity in twentieth-century American society and the enactment of compulsory education laws.

Brennan did not advocate complete separation of church and state. He emphasized at the end of his concurrence that the Court's ruling does not prohibit public schools from teaching about the Holy Scriptures or about the differences between religions in literature or history classes. "Indeed," he went on, "whether or not the Bible is involved, it would be impossible to teach meaningfully many subjects in the social sciences or the humanities without some mention of religion." However, he noted, the compulsory nature of the type of religious training at issue here presents a problem under the Free Exercise Clause as well as with the Establishment Clause.

The care with which Brennan crafted his opinion and his appreciation for people's deeply held convictions are evident. His analysis, particularly his description of the various factors to be considered, helped shape the Court's approach to Establishment Clause issues in many subsequent cases.

Justice Clark wrote the opinion of the Court, joined by Chief Justice Warren and Justices Black, Douglas, and White. Justices Harlan, Brennan, and Goldberg concurred. Justice Stewart dissented.

❂   ❂   ❂

MR. JUSTICE BRENNAN, concurring.

* * * [T]he line which separates the secular from the sectarian in American life is elusive. The difficulty of defining the boundary with precision inheres in a paradox central to our scheme of liberty. While our institutions reflect a firm conviction that we are a religious people, those institutions by solemn constitutional injunction may not officially involve religion in such a way as to prefer, discriminate against, or oppress, a particular sect or religion. * * *

I join fully in the opinion and the judgment of the Court. I see no escape from the conclusion that the exercises called in question in these two cases violate the constitutional mandate. The reasons we gave only last Term in *Engel v. Vitale* for finding in the New York Regents' prayer an impermissible establishment of religion, compel the same judgment of the practices at bar. The involvement of the secular with the religious is no less intimate here; and it is constitutionally irrelevant that the State has not composed the material for the inspirational exercises

presently involved. It should be unnecessary to observe that our holding does not declare that the First Amendment manifests hostility to
the practice or teaching of religion, but only applies prohibitions incor-
porated in the Bill of Rights in recognition of historic needs shared by
Church and State alike. While it is my view that not every involvement
of religion in public life is unconstitutional, I consider the exercises
at bar a form of involvement which clearly violates the Establishment
Clause.

The importance of the issue and the deep conviction with which
views on both sides are held seem to me to justify detailing at some
length my reasons for joining the Court's judgment and opinion.

I

The First Amendment forbids both the abridgment of the free exercise of religion and the enactment of laws "respecting an establishment
of religion." The two clauses, although distinct in their objectives and
their applicability, emerged together from a common panorama of history. The inclusion of both restraints upon the power of Congress to
legislate concerning religious matters shows unmistakably that the Framers of the First Amendment were not content to rest the protection of
religious liberty exclusively upon either clause. * * *

It is true that the Framers' immediate concern was to prevent the setting up of an official federal church of the kind which England and
some of the Colonies had long supported. But nothing in the text of the
Establishment Clause supports the view that the prevention of the setting up of an official church was meant to be the full extent of the prohibitions against official involvements in religion. * * *

The specific question before us has * * * aroused vigorous dispute
whether the architects of the First Amendment—James Madison and
Thomas Jefferson particularly—understood the prohibition against any
"law respecting an establishment of religion" to reach devotional exercises in the public schools. * * * A more fruitful inquiry, it seems to me,
is whether the practices here challenged threaten those consequences
which the Framers deeply feared; whether, in short, they tend to promote that type of interdependence between religion and state which
the First Amendment was designed to prevent. Our task is to translate
"the majestic generalities of the Bill of Rights, conceived as part of the
pattern of liberal government in the eighteenth century, into concrete
restraints on officials dealing with the problems of the twentieth century." *West Virginia Board of Education v. Barnette.*

A too literal quest for the advice of the Founding Fathers upon the issues of these cases seems to me futile and misdirected for several reasons: First, on our precise problem the historical record is at best ambiguous, and statements can readily be found to support either side of the proposition. The ambiguity of history is understandable if we recall the nature of the problems uppermost in the thinking of the statesmen who fashioned the religious guarantees; they were concerned with far more flagrant intrusions of government into the realm of religion than any that our century has witnessed. While it is clear to me that the Framers meant the Establishment Clause to prohibit more than the creation of an established federal church such as existed in England, I have no doubt that, in their preoccupation with the imminent question of established churches, they gave no distinct consideration to the particular question whether the clause also forbade devotional exercises in public institutions.

Second, the structure of American education has greatly changed since the First Amendment was adopted. In the context of our modern emphasis upon public education available to all citizens, any views of the eighteenth century as to whether the exercises at bar are an "establishment" offer little aid to decision. Education, as the Framers knew it, was in the main confined to private schools more often than not under strictly sectarian supervision. Only gradually did control of education pass largely to public officials. It would, therefore, hardly be significant if the fact was that the nearly universal devotional exercises in the schools of the young Republic did not provoke criticism; even today religious ceremonies in church-supported private schools are constitutionally unobjectionable.

Third, our religious composition makes us a vastly more diverse people than were our forefathers. They knew differences chiefly among Protestant sects. Today the Nation is far more heterogeneous religiously, including as it does substantial minorities not only of Catholics and Jews but as well of those who worship according to no version of the Bible and those who worship no God at all. In the face of such profound changes, practices which may have been objectionable to no one in the time of Jefferson and Madison may today be highly offensive to many persons, the deeply devout and the nonbelievers alike.

* * *

Fourth, * * * the history and character of American public education that the public schools serve a uniquely public function: the training of

American citizens in an atmosphere free of parochial, divisive, or sepa-
ratist influences of any sort—an atmosphere in which children may as-
similate a heritage common to all American groups and religions. This
is a heritage neither theistic nor atheistic, but simply civic and patriotic.

* * *

IV

I turn now to the cases before us. The religious nature of the exercises
here challenged seems plain. Unless *Engel v. Vitale* is to be overruled, or
we are to engage in wholly disingenuous distinction, we cannot sustain
these practices. Daily recital of the Lord's Prayer and the reading of
passages of Scripture are quite as clearly breaches of the command of
the Establishment Clause as was the daily use of the rather bland Regents' Prayer in the New York public schools. Indeed, I would suppose
that, if anything, the Lord's Prayer and the Holy Bible are more clearly
sectarian, and the present violations of the First Amendment consequently more serious. * * *

A

First, it is argued that however clearly religious may have been the
origins and early nature of daily prayer and Bible reading, these practices today serve so clearly secular educational purposes that their religious attributes may be overlooked. I do not doubt, for example, that
morning devotional exercises may foster better discipline in the classroom, and elevate the spiritual level on which the school day opens. The
Pennsylvania Superintendent of Public Instruction, testifying by depo-
sition in the *Schempp* case, offered his view that daily Bible reading
"places upon the children or those hearing the reading of this, and the
atmosphere which goes on in the reading . . . one of the last vestiges of
moral value that we have left in our school system." The exercise thus
affords, the Superintendent concluded, "a strong contradiction to the
materialistic trends of our time." Baltimore's Superintendent of Schools
expressed a similar view of the practices challenged in the *Murray* case,
to the effect that "[t]he acknowledgment of the existence of God as
symbolized in the opening exercises establishes a discipline tone which
tends to cause each individual pupil to constrain his overt acts and to
consequently conform to accepted standards of behavior during his attendance at school." These views are by no means novel.

It is not the business of this Court to gainsay the judgments of experts on matters of pedagogy. Such decisions must be left to the discretion of those administrators charged with the supervision of the Nation's public schools. The limited province of the courts is to determine whether the means which the educators have chosen to achieve legitimate pedagogical ends infringe the constitutional freedoms of the First Amendment. The secular purposes which devotional exercises are said to serve fall into two categories—those which depend upon an immediately religious experience shared by the participating children; and those which appear sufficiently divorced from the religious content of the devotional material that they can be served equally by nonreligious materials. With respect to the first objective, much has been written about the moral and spiritual values of infusing some religious influence or instruction into the public school classroom. To the extent that only *religious* materials will serve this purpose, it seems to me that the purpose as well as the means is so plainly religious that the exercise is necessarily forbidden by the Establishment Clause. The fact that purely secular benefits may eventually result does not seem to me to justify the exercises * * *.

The second justification assumes that religious exercises at the start of the school day may directly serve solely secular ends—for example, by fostering harmony and tolerance among the pupils, enhancing the authority of the teacher, and inspiring better discipline. To the extent that such benefits result not from the content of the readings and recitation, but simply from the holding of such a solemn exercise at the opening assembly or the first class of the day, it would seem that less sensitive materials might equally well serve the same purpose. * * * It has not been shown that readings from the speeches and messages of great Americans, for example, or from the documents of our heritage of liberty, daily recitation of the Pledge of Allegiance, or even the observance of a moment of reverent silence at the opening of class, may not adequately serve the solely secular purposes of the devotional activities without jeopardizing either the religious liberties of any members of the community or the proper degree of separation between the spheres of religion and government. Such substitutes would, I think, be unsatisfactory or inadequate only to the extent that the present activities do in fact serve religious goals. While I do not question the judgment of experienced educators that the challenged practices may well achieve valuable secular ends, it seems to me that the State acts unconstitutionally if it either sets about to attain even indirectly religious ends by religious means, or if it uses religious means to serve secular ends where secular means would suffice.

B

Second, it is argued that the particular practices involved in the two cases before us are unobjectionable because they prefer no particular sect or sects at the expense of others. Both the Baltimore and Abington procedures permit, for example, the reading of any of several versions of the Bible, and this flexibility is said to ensure neutrality sufficiently to avoid the constitutional prohibition. One answer, which might be dispositive, is that any version of the Bible is inherently sectarian, else there would be no need to offer a system of rotation or alternation of versions in the first place, that is, to allow different sectarian versions to be used on different days. The sectarian character of the Holy Bible has been at the core of the whole controversy over religious practices in the public schools throughout its long and often bitter history. To vary the version as the Abington and Baltimore schools have done may well be less offensive than to read from the King James version every day, as once was the practice. But the result even of this relatively benign procedure is that majority sects are preferred in approximate proportion to their representation in the community and in the student body, while the smaller sects suffer commensurate discrimination. So long as the subject matter of the exercise is sectarian in character, these consequences cannot be avoided.

The argument contains, however, a more basic flaw. There are persons in every community—often deeply devout—to whom any version of the Judaeo-Christian Bible is offensive. There are others whose reverence for the Holy Scriptures demands private study or reflection and to whom public reading or recitation is sacrilegious, as one of the expert witnesses at the trial of the *Schempp* case explained. To such persons it is not the fact of using the Bible in the public schools, nor the content of any particular version, that is offensive, but only the *manner* in which it is used.[60] For such persons, the anathema of public communion is even more pronounced when prayer is involved. Many deeply devout persons have always regarded prayer as a necessarily private expe-

---

60. Rabbi Solomon Grayzel testified before the District Court, "In Judaism the Bible is not read, it is studied. There is no special virtue attached to a mere reading of the Bible; there is a great deal of virtue attached to a study of the Bible." ⋅ ⋅ ⋅

rience. One Protestant group recently commented, for example: "When one thinks of prayer as sincere outreach of a human soul to the Creator, 'required prayer' becomes an absurdity." There is a similar problem with respect to comment upon the passages of Scripture which are to be read. Most present statutes forbid comment, and this practice accords with the views of many religious groups as to the manner in which the Bible should be read. However, as a recent survey discloses, scriptural passages read without comment frequently convey no message to the younger children in the school. Thus there has developed a practice in some schools of bridging the gap between faith and understanding by means of "definitions," even where "comment" is forbidden by statute. The present practice therefore poses a difficult dilemma: While Bible reading is almost universally required to be without comment, since only by such a prohibition can sectarian interpretation be excluded from the classroom, the rule breaks down at the point at which rudimentary definitions of Biblical terms are necessary for comprehension if the exercise is to be meaningful at all.

* * *

C

A third element which is said to absolve the practices involved in these cases from the ban of the religious guarantees of the Constitution is the provision to excuse or exempt students who wish not to participate. Insofar as these practices are claimed to violate the Establishment Clause, I find the answer which the District Court gave after our remand of *Schempp* to be altogether dispositive:

> The fact that some pupils, or theoretically all pupils, might be excused from attendance at the exercises does not mitigate the obligatory nature of the ceremony . . . . The exercises are held in the school buildings and perforce are conducted by and under the authority of the local school authorities and during school sessions. Since the statute requires the reading of the "Holy Bible," a Christian document, the practice, as we said in our first opinion, prefers the Christian religion. The record demonstrates that it was the intention of the General Assembly of the Commonwealth of Pennsylvania to introduce a religious ceremony into the public schools of the Commonwealth.

Thus the short, and to me sufficient, answer is that the availability of excusal or exemption simply has no relevance to the establishment question, if it is once found that these practices are essentially religious exercises designed at least in part to achieve religious aims through the use of public school facilities during the school day.

* * * [Moreover,] the excusal procedure itself necessarily operates in such a way as to infringe the rights of free exercise of those children who wish to be excused. We have held in *Barnette* and *Torcaso v. Watkins*, respectively, that a State may require neither public school students nor candidates for an office of public trust to profess beliefs offensive to religious principles. By the same token the State could not constitutionally require a student to profess publicly his disbelief as the prerequisite to the exercise of his constitutional right of abstention. * * * [B]y requiring what is tantamount in the eyes of teachers and schoolmates to a profession of disbelief, or at least of nonconformity, the procedure may well deter those children who do not wish to participate for any reason based upon the dictates of conscience from exercising an indisputably constitutional right to be excused.[68] Thus the excusal provision in its operation subjects them to a cruel dilemma. In consequence, even devout children may well avoid claiming their right and simply continue to participate in exercises distasteful to them because of an understandable reluctance to be stigmatized as atheists or nonconformists simply on the basis of their request.

Such reluctance to seek exemption seems all the more likely in view of the fact that children are disinclined at this age to step out of line or to flout "peer-group norms." Such is the widely held view of experts who have studied the behaviors and attitudes of children. * * *

V

These considerations bring me to a final contention of the school officials in these cases: that the invalidation of the exercises at bar permits this Court no alternative but to declare unconstitutional every vestige, however slight, of cooperation or accommodation between religion and government. I cannot accept that contention. While it is not, of course, appropriate for this Court to decide questions not presently

---

68. See the testimony of Edward L. Schempp, the father of the children in the Abington schools concerning his reasons for not asking that his children be excused from the morning exercises after excusal was made available through amendment of the statute:

We originally objected to our children being exposed to the reading of the King James version of the Bible ... and under those conditions we would have theoretically liked to have had the children excused. But we felt that the penalty of having our children labelled as "odd balls" before their teachers and classmates every day in the year was even less satisfactory than the other problem. ...

before it, I venture to suggest that religious exercises in the public schools present a unique problem. For not every involvement of religion in public life violates the Establishment Clause. Our decision in these cases does not clearly forecast anything about the constitutionality of other types of interdependence between religious and other public institutions.

Specifically, I believe that the line we must draw between the permissible and the impermissible is one which accords with history and faithfully reflects the understanding of the Founding Fathers. It is a line which the Court has consistently sought to mark in its decisions expounding the religious guarantees of the First Amendment. What the Framers meant to foreclose, and what our decisions under the Establishment Clause have forbidden, are those involvements of religious with secular institutions which (a) serve the essentially religious activities of religious institutions; (b) employ the organs of government for essentially religious purposes; or (c) use essentially religious means to serve governmental ends, where secular means would suffice. When the secular and religious institutions become involved in such a manner, there inhere in the relationship precisely those dangers—as much to church as to state—which the Framers feared would subvert religious liberty and the strength of a system of secular government. On the other hand, there may be myriad forms of involvements of government with religion which do not import such dangers and therefore should not, in my judgment, be deemed to violate the Establishment Clause. Nothing in the Constitution compels the organs of government to be blind to what everyone else perceives—that religious differences among Americans have important and pervasive implications for our society. Likewise nothing in the Establishment Clause forbids the application of legislation having purely secular ends in such a way as to alleviate burdens upon the free exercise of an individual's religious beliefs. Surely the Framers would never have understood that such a construction sanctions that involvement which violates the Establishment Clause. Such a conclusion can be reached, I would suggest, only by using the words of the First Amendment to defeat its very purpose.

* * *

The principles which we reaffirm and apply today can hardly be thought novel or radical. They are, in truth, as old as the Republic itself, and have always been as integral a part of the First Amendment as the very words of that charter of religious liberty. * * *

MARSH V. CHAMBERS

July 5, 1983

In the 1960s, the *Engel v. Vitale* and *Schempp* (p. 68) cases outlawed, respectively, compulsory prayer and Bible reading in public schools. Both cases concerned situations where the Establishment Clause and the Free Exercise Clause pulled the Court in the same direction: in each case, the government sponsorship of the religious activity raised Establishment Clause concerns and the compulsory involvement of students raised problems under the Free Exercise Clause. After *Engel* and *Schempp*, a different type of Establishment Clause case concerning schools reached the Court. In 1971, the Court decided *Lemon v. Kurtzman*, a case involving financial support to church-related schools. In that case, whatever issues of free exercise existed were secondary and largely unaddressed. The primary issue was whether and to what extent public financial support for sectarian institutions violated the Establishment Clause.

The Court used that opportunity to revise the "purpose and effect" test it had previously developed. In its place the Court adopted a new three-prong standard to evaluate Establishment Clause problems. Under this *Lemon* test, government action will survive constitutional scrutiny only if: (1) its purpose is secular; (2) its principal effect neither advances nor inhibits religion; and (3) it does not foster "an excessive government entanglement with religion."

The *Lemon* test may have added some specificity to the jurisprudence in this area but it provided little clarity. Nevertheless, the Court attempted to apply this test in cases where government action allegedly conflicted with the Establishment Clause. Public schools remained a particularly fertile ground for such issues. Using the *Lemon* test, the Court analyzed such things as classroom display of the Ten Commandments, a moment of silence for prayer and reflection, and clergy participation in graduation ceremonies. In each instance, the Court ruled that these religiously connected activities in the public schools violated the Establishment Clause.

Outside the school context, however, the results in Establishment Clause cases were mixed and difficult to predict, and the *Lemon* test itself came under increasing criticism from some members of the Court. Nowhere was the dissatisfaction with *Lemon* more evident than in the majority's decision in the case excerpted here. The Court upheld legislative prayer: the long-standing practice of having clergy lead a religious invocation at the opening of legislative sessions. In making its ruling, the Court relied on historical practice and conspicuously refrained from directly applying or even citing to the *Lemon* standard.

Justice Brennan dissented, and criticized the majority for failing to use the *Lemon* test, which he strongly supported. He also acknowledged his own fallibility. As in *Slaton* (p. 15), where Brennan announced he could no longer continue to support the Court's efforts to craft a workable definition of obscenity, Brennan here publicly confessed to a change of heart about the scope of the Establishment Clause. Referring to his 20-year-old concurring opinion in *Schempp*, in which he suggested that legislative prayer was constitutionally permissible, he wrote, "I have come to the conclusion that I was wrong." Such a willingness to reevaluate and change his views was exactly what Brennan feared public officials would lose if political debate became polarized by religious ideology.

Chief Justice Burger wrote the opinion of the Court, joined by Justices White, Blackmun, Powell, Rehnquist, and O'Connor. Justices Brennan, Stewart, and Marshall dissented.

o   o   o

JUSTICE BRENNAN, with whom JUSTICE MARSHALL joins, dissenting.

The Court today has written a narrow and, on the whole, careful opinion. In effect, the Court holds that officially sponsored legislative prayer, primarily on account of its "unique history," is generally exempted from the First Amendment's prohibition against "an establishment of religion." The Court's opinion is consistent with dictum in at least one of our prior decisions, and its limited rationale should pose little threat to the overall fate of the Establishment Clause. Moreover, disagreement with the Court requires that I confront the fact that some 20 years ago, in a concurring opinion in one of the cases striking down official prayer and ceremonial Bible reading in the public schools, I came very close to endorsing essentially the result reached by the Court today. Nevertheless, after much reflection, I have come to the conclusion that I was wrong then and that the Court is wrong today. I now believe that the practice of official invocational prayer, as it exists in

Nebraska and most other state legislatures, is unconstitutional. It is contrary to the doctrine as well the underlying purposes of the Establishment Clause, and it is not saved either by its history or by any of the other considerations suggested in the Court's opinion.

I respectfully dissent.

I

The Court makes no pretense of subjecting Nebraska's practice of legislative prayer to any of the formal "tests" that have traditionally structured our inquiry under the Establishment Clause. That it fails to do so is, in a sense, a good thing, for it simply confirms that the Court is carving out an exception to the Establishment Clause rather than reshaping Establishment Clause doctrine to accommodate legislative prayer. For my purposes, however, I must begin by demonstrating what should be obvious: that, if the Court were to judge legislative prayer through the unsentimental eye of our settled doctrine, it would have to strike it down as a clear violation of the Establishment Clause.

The most commonly cited formulation of prevailing Establishment Clause doctrine is found in *Lemon v. Kurtzman*:

> Every analysis in this area must begin with consideration of the cumulative criteria developed by the Court over many years. Three such tests may be gleaned from our cases. First, the statute [at issue] must have a secular legislative purpose; second, its principal or primary effect must be one that neither advances nor inhibits religion; finally, the statute must not foster "an excessive government entanglement with religion."

That the "purpose" of legislative prayer is pre-eminently religious rather than secular seems to me to be self-evident. "To invoke Divine guidance on a public body entrusted with making the laws," [as the majority describes the practice,] is nothing but a religious act. Moreover, whatever secular functions legislative prayer might play—formally opening the legislative session, getting the members of the body to quiet down, and imbuing them with a sense of seriousness and high purpose—could so plainly be performed in a purely nonreligious fashion that to claim a secular purpose for the prayer is an insult to the perfectly honorable individuals who instituted and continue the practice.

The "primary effect" of legislative prayer is also clearly religious. As we said in the context of officially sponsored prayers in the public schools, "prescribing a particular form of religious worship," even if the individuals involved have the choice not to participate, places "indirect coercive pressure upon religious minorities to conform to the prevailing officially approved religion." *Engel v. Vitale.* More importantly, invocations in Nebraska's legislative halls explicitly link religious belief and observance to the power and prestige of the State. "[T]he mere appearance of a joint exercise of legislative authority by Church and State provides a significant symbolic benefit to religion in the minds of some by reason of the power conferred." *Larkin v. Grendel's Den, Inc.*

Finally, there can be no doubt that the practice of legislative prayer leads to excessive "entanglement" between the State and religion. *Lemon* pointed out that "entanglement" can take two forms: First, a state statute or program might involve the state impermissibly in monitoring and overseeing religious affairs. In the case of legislative prayer, the process of choosing a "suitable" chaplain, whether on a permanent or rotating basis, and insuring that the chaplain limits himself of herself to "suitable" prayers, involves precisely the sort of supervision that agencies of government should if at all possible avoid.

Second, excessive "entanglement" might arise out of "the divisive political potential" of a state statute or program.

> Ordinarily political debate and division, however vigorous or even partisan, are normal and healthy manifestations of our democratic system of government, but political division along religious lines was one of the principal evils against which the First Amendment was intended to protect. The potential divisiveness of such conflict is a threat to the normal political process.

Lemon. In this case, this second aspect of entanglement is also clear. The controversy between Senator Chambers and his colleagues, which had reached the stage of difficulty and rancor long before this lawsuit was brought, has split the Nebraska Legislature precisely on issues of religion and religious conformity. The record in this case also reports a series of instances, involving legislators other than Senator Chambers, in which invocations by Reverend Palmer and others led to controversy along religious lines. And in general, the history of legislative prayer has been far more eventful—and divisive—than a hasty reading of the Court's opinion might indicate.

In sum, I have no doubt that, if any group of law students were asked to apply the principles of *Lemon* to the question of legislative prayer, they would nearly unanimously find the practice to be unconstitutional.

* * *

III

* * *

A

The Court's main argument for carving out an exception sustaining legislative prayer is historical. The Court cannot—and does not—purport to find a pattern of "undeviating acceptance" of legislative prayer. It also disclaims exclusive reliance on the mere longevity of legislative prayer. The Court does, however, point out that, only three days before the First Congress reached agreement on the final wording of the Bill of Rights, it authorized the appointment of paid chaplains for its own proceedings, and the Court argues that in light of this "unique history," the actions of Congress reveal its intent as to the meaning of the Establishment Clause. I agree that historical practice is "of considerable import in the interpretation of abstract constitutional language," *Walz v. Tax Commission*, (Brennan, J., concurring). This is a case, however, in which—absent the Court's invocation of history—there would be no question that the practice at issue was unconstitutional. And despite the surface appeal of the Court's argument, there are at least three reasons why specific historical practice should not in this case override that clear constitutional imperative.

First, it is significant that the Court's historical argument does not rely on the legislative history of the Establishment Clause itself. Indeed, that formal history is profoundly unilluminating on this and most other subjects. * * *

Second, the Court's analysis treats the First Amendment simply as an Act of Congress, as to whose meaning the intent of Congress is the single touchstone. Both the Constitution and its Amendments, however, became supreme law only by virtue of their ratification by the States, and the understanding of the States should be as relevant to our analysis as the understanding of Congress.[32] * * *

---

32. As a practical matter, "we know practically nothing about what went on in the state legislatures" during the process of ratifying the Bill of Rights. 2 B. Schwartz, The Bill of Rights: A Documentary History 1171 (1971). Moreover, looking to state practices is, as the Court admits, of dubious relevance because the Establishment Clause did not originally apply to the States. Nevertheless, these difficulties give us no warrant to give controlling weight on the constitutionality of a specific practice to the collateral acts of the Members of Congress who proposed the Bill of Rights to the States.

Finally, and most importantly, the argument tendered by the Court is misguided because the Constitution is not a static document whose meaning on every detail is fixed for all time by the life experience of the Framers. We have recognized in a wide variety of constitutional contexts that the practices that were in place at the time any particular guarantee was enacted into the Constitution do not necessarily fix forever the meaning of that guarantee. To be truly faithful to the Framers, "our use of the history of their time must limit itself to broad purposes, not specific practices." *School District of Abington Township v. Schempp* (Brennan, J., concurring). Our primary task must be to translate "the majestic generalities of the Bill of Rights, conceived as part of the pattern of liberal government in the eighteenth century, into concrete restraints on officials dealing with the problems of the twentieth century." *West Virginia Board of Education v. Barnette.*

* * *

B

Of course, the Court does not rely entirely on the practice of the First Congress in order to validate legislative prayer. There is another theme which, although implicit, also pervades the Court's opinion. It is exemplified by the Court's comparison of legislative prayer with the formulaic recitation of "God save the United States and this Honorable Court." It is also exemplified by the Court's apparent conclusion that legislative prayer is, at worst, a "mere shadow" on the Establishment Clause rather than a "real threat" to it. Simply put, the Court seems to regard legislative prayer as at most a *de minimis* violation, somehow unworthy of our attention. I frankly do not know what should be the proper disposition of features of our public life such as "God save the United States and this Honorable Court," "In God We Trust," "One Nation Under God," and the like. I might well adhere to the view expressed in *Schempp* that such mottos are consistent with the Establishment Clause, not because their import is *de minimis*, but because they have lost any true religious significance. Legislative invocations, however, are very different.

* * * Prayer is serious business—serious theological business—and it is not a mere "acknowledgment of beliefs widely held among the people of this country" for the State to immerse itself in that business. Some religious individuals or groups find it theologically problematic to engage in joint religious exercises predominantly influenced by faiths not

their own. Some might object even to the attempt to fashion a "nonsec-tarian" prayer. Some would find it impossible to participate in any "prayer opportunity," marked by Trinitarian references. Some would find a prayer *not* invoking the name of Christ to represent a flawed view of the relationship between human beings and God. Some might find any petitionary prayer to be improper. Some might find any prayer that lacked a petitionary element to be deficient. Some might be troubled by what they consider shallow public prayer, or nonspontaneous prayer, or prayer without adequate spiritual preparation or concentration. Some might, of course, have *theological* objections to any prayer sponsored by an organ of government. Some might object on theological grounds to the level of political neutrality generally expected of government-sponsored invocational prayer. And some might object on theological grounds to the Court's requirement that prayer, even though religious, not be proselytizing. * * * [W]e are faced with potential religious objections to an activity at the very center of religious life, and it is simply beyond the competence of government, and inconsistent with our conceptions of liberty, for the State to take upon itself the role of ecclesiastical arbiter.

IV

The argument is made occasionally that a strict separation of religion and state robs the Nation of its spiritual identity. I believe quite the contrary. It may be true that individuals cannot be "neutral" on the question of religion. But the judgment of the Establishment Clause is that neutrality by the organs of *government* on questions of religion is both possible and imperative. * * * If the Court had struck down legislative prayer today, it would likely have stimulated a furious reaction. But it would also, I am convinced, have invigorated both the "spirit of religion" and the "spirit of freedom."

I respectfully dissent.

LYNCH V. DONNELLY

March 5, 1984

Some holidays, such as Memorial Day, are intended to be solemn occasions when we commemorate and honor those who have sacrificed their lives for their country. Others are intended to be jubilant affairs, such as Independence Day, when we celebrate our heritage and liberty. Religious holidays, even the festive type, present a difficult problem. If the government sponsors or participates in the celebration, its action often offends those of different faiths and appears to deviate from the Establishment Clause's mandate of neutrality. If the government chooses not to be involved, observers of the holiday often brand it as hostile to their religion, or to religion generally. Joyous occasions thus become the source of conflict and anger. This case is one example.

For many years, the City of Pawtucket, Rhode Island, erected a Christmas display in a downtown park. The display was paid for and installed with public funds, and included a life-size nativity scene that re-created the biblically described birth of Christ. Some residents challenged the practice as an impermissible establishment of religion.

The City defended this method of celebrating the national holiday as a means of attracting people to the downtown area "in order to promote pre-Christmas retail sales and to help engender the spirit of goodwill commonly associated with the season." To justify the inclusion of the nativity scene in the display, the City downplayed the significance of the crèche as a religious symbol.

By a 5–4 vote, the Court accepted this explanation and upheld the City's practice. The Court acknowledged that the crèche was not completely secular but determined that it was primarily "a reminder of the origins of Christmas," and thus no different from other things or activities the Court had previously permitted. Justice O'Connor joined the Court's opinion, but also wrote a separate concurrence in which she suggested that the critical inquiry is whether the City could be perceived as purposefully endorsing a religious message. She concluded that on these facts there was no such endorsement and that the display should be allowed.

Justice Brennan, in dissent, admonished the Court for effectively equating a crèche with Santa's house or reindeer, a proposition that could easily offend both supporters and detractors of Pawtucket's display. He characterized the Court's reference to a shared religious history as contradictory to the diversity and religious pluralism in the United States. For Brennan, though, the Court's methodology was more significant than its conclusion. Whereas eight months earlier in *Marsh* the Court had avoided the *Lemon* test, and relied primarily on history and tradition, here it purported to apply *Lemon*. Thus, while *Marsh* could be viewed as an aberration or exception to the usual analytical framework for Establishment Clause problems, the Court's seemingly conciliatory attitude toward state-sponsored religious activity now looked more like a trend than a deviation. Brennan criticized the Court for applying the *Lemon* test in a "less-than-vigorous" manner. If *Lemon* were applied as intended, he argued, it was inescapable that the Pawtucket display violated the Establishment Clause.

After the decision in this case, it was inevitable that other cases with slightly different factual twists would follow. In 1989, the Court determined that an elaborately displayed nativity scene with a written religious message in a county courthouse violated the Establishment Clause but that a city's display of a menorah and Christmas tree with a secular written message did not. In doing so, the Court seemed to embrace the "no endorsement" test advocated by O'Connor. Thoroughly frustrated, Brennan again dissented.

Chief Justice Burger wrote the opinion of the Court, joined by Justices White, Powell, Rehnquist, and O'Connor. Justices Brennan, Marshall, Blackmun, and Stevens dissented.

❂   ❂   ❂

JUSTICE BRENNAN, with whom JUSTICE MARSHALL, JUSTICE BLACKMUN, and JUSTICE STEVENS join, dissenting.

The principles announced in the compact phrases of the Religion Clauses have, as the Court today reminds us, proved difficult to apply. Faced with that uncertainty, the Court properly looks for guidance to the settled test announced in *Lemon v. Kurtzman*, for assessing whether a challenged governmental practice involves an impermissible step toward the establishment of religion. Applying that test to this case, the Court reaches an essentially narrow result which turns largely upon the particular holiday context in which the city of Pawtucket's nativity scene appeared. The Court's decision implicitly leaves open questions concerning the constitutionality of the public display on public property of a crèche standing alone, or the public display of other distinctively religious symbols such as a cross. Despite the narrow contours of the Court's opinion, our precedents in my view compel the holding that Pawtucket's inclusion of a life-sized display depicting the biblical description of the birth of Christ as part of its annual Christmas celebration is unconstitutional. Nothing in the history of such practices or the setting in which the city's crèche is presented obscures or diminishes the plain fact that Pawtucket's action amounts to an impermissible governmental endorsement of a particular faith.

I

Last Term, I expressed the hope that the Court's decision in *Marsh v. Chambers* would prove to be only a single, aberrant departure from our settled method of analyzing Establishment Clause cases. That the Court today returns to the settled analysis of our prior cases gratifies that hope. At the same time, the Court's less-than-vigorous application of the *Lemon* test suggests that its commitment to those standards may only be superficial. After reviewing the Court's opinion, I am convinced that this case appears hard not because the principles of decision are obscure, but because the Christmas holiday seems so familiar and agreeable. Although the Court's reluctance to disturb a community's chosen method of celebrating such an agreeable holiday is understandable, that cannot justify the Court's departure from controlling precedent. In my view, Pawtucket's maintenance and display at public expense of a symbol as distinctively sectarian as a crèche simply cannot be squared with our prior cases. And it is plainly contrary to the purposes and values of the Establishment Clause to pretend, as the Court does, that the otherwise secular setting of Pawtucket's nativity scene dilutes in some fashion the crèche's singular religiosity, or that the city's annual display reflects nothing more than an "acknowledgment" of our shared national heritage. Neither the character of the Christmas holiday itself, nor our heritage of religious expression supports this result. Indeed, our remarkable and precious religious diversity as a Nation, which the Establishment Clause seeks to protect, runs directly counter to today's decision.

A

As we have sought to meet new problems arising under the Establishment Clause, our decisions, with few exceptions, have demanded that a challenged governmental practice satisfy the following criteria:

> First, the [practice] must have a secular legislative purpose; second, its principal or primary effect must be one that neither advances nor inhibits religion; finally, [it] must not foster "an excessive government entanglement with religion."

Lemon v. Kurtzman

This well-defined three-part test expresses the essential concerns animating the Establishment Clause. Thus, the test is designed to ensure that the organs of government remain strictly separate and apart from religious affairs, for "a union of government and religion tends to destroy government and degrade religion." *Engel v. Vitale.* And it seeks to guarantee that government maintains a position of neutrality with respect to religion and neither advances nor inhibits the promulgation and practice of religious beliefs. In this regard, we must be alert in our examination of any challenged practice not only for an official establishment of religion, but also for those other evils at which the Clause was aimed—"sponsorship, financial support, and active involvement of the sovereign in religious activity." *Committee for Public Education & Religious Liberty v. Nyquist.*

Applying the three-part test to Pawtucket's crèche, I am persuaded that the city's inclusion of the crèche in its Christmas display simply does not reflect a "clearly secular . . . purpose." *Nyquist.* * * *

[In addition, t]he "primary effect" of including a nativity scene in the city's display is, as the District Court found, to place the government's imprimatur of approval on the particular religious beliefs exemplified by the crèche. * * * The effect on minority religious groups, as well as on those who may reject all religion, is to convey the message that their views are not similarly worthy of public recognition nor entitled to public support. It was precisely this sort of religious chauvinism that the Establishment Clause was intended forever to prohibit. * * *

In sum, considering the District Court's careful findings of fact under the three-part analysis called for by our prior cases, I have no difficulty concluding that Pawtucket's display of the crèche is unconstitutional.

B

The Court advances two principal arguments to support its conclusion that the Pawtucket crèche satisfies the *Lemon* test. Neither is persuasive.

First—The Court, by focusing on the holiday "context" in which the nativity scene appeared, seeks to explain away the clear religious import of the crèche and the findings of the District Court that most observers understood the crèche as both a symbol of Christian beliefs and a symbol of the city's support for those beliefs. Thus, although the Court concedes that the city's inclusion of the nativity scene plainly serves "to depict the origins" of Christmas as a "significant historical religious event," and that the crèche "is identified with one religious faith," we are nevertheless expected to believe that Pawtucket's use of the crèche does not signal the city's support for the sectarian symbolism that the nativity scene evokes. The effect of the crèche, of course, must be gauged not only by its inherent religious significance but also by the overall setting in which it appears. But it blinks reality to claim, as the Court does, that by including such a distinctively religious object as the crèche in its Christmas display, Pawtucket has done no more than make use of a "traditional" symbol of the holiday, and has thereby purged the crèche of its religious content and conferred only an "incidental and indirect" benefit on religion.

The Court's struggle to ignore the clear religious effect of the crèche seems to me misguided for several reasons. In the first place, the city has positioned the crèche in a central and highly visible location within the Hodgson Park display. * * *

Moreover, the city has done nothing to disclaim government approval of the religious significance of the crèche, to suggest that the crèche represents only one religious symbol among many others that might be included in a seasonal display truly aimed at providing a wide catalog of ethnic and religious celebrations, or to disassociate itself from the religious content of the crèche. In *School District of Abington Township v. Schempp*, we noted that reading aloud from the Bible would be a permissible schoolroom exercise only if it was "presented objectively as part of a secular program of education" that would remove any message of governmental endorsement of religion. Similarly, when the Court of Appeals for the District of Columbia Circuit approved the inclusion of a crèche as part of a national "Pageant of Peace" on federal parkland adjacent to the White House, it did so on the express condition that the Government would erect "explanatory plaques" disclaiming any sponsorship of religious beliefs associated with the crèche. In this case, by contrast, Pawtucket has made no effort whatever to provide a similar cautionary message.

* * *

Finally, and most importantly, even in the context of Pawtucket's seasonal celebration, the crèche retains a specifically Christian religious meaning. I refuse to accept the notion implicit in today's decision that non-Christians would find that the religious content of the crèche is eliminated by the fact that it appears as part of the city's otherwise secular celebration of the Christmas holiday. The nativity scene is clearly distinct in its purpose and effect from the rest of the Hodgson Park display for the simple reason that it is the only one rooted in a biblical account of Christ's birth. It is the chief symbol of the characteristically Christian belief that a divine Savior was brought into the world and that the purpose of this miraculous birth was to illuminate a path toward salvation and redemption. For Christians, that path is exclusive, precious, and holy. But for those who do not share these beliefs, the symbolic reenactment of the birth of a divine being who has been miraculously incarnated as a man stands as a dramatic reminder of their differences with Christian faith. * * * To be so excluded on religious grounds by one's elected government is an insult and an injury that, until today, could not by countenanced by the Establishment Clause.

Second—The Court also attempts to justify the crèche by entertaining a beguilingly simple, yet faulty syllogism. The Court begins by noting that government may recognize Christmas Day as a public holiday; the Court then asserts that the crèche is nothing more than a traditional element of Christmas celebrations; and it concludes that the inclusion of a crèche as part of a government's annual Christmas celebration is constitutionally permissible. The Court apparently believes that once it finds that the designation of Christmas as a public holiday is constitutionally acceptable, it is then free to conclude that virtually every form of governmental association with the celebration of the holiday is also constitutional. The vice of this dangerously superficial argument is that it overlooks the fact that the Christmas holiday in our national culture contains both secular and sectarian elements. To say that government may recognize the holiday's traditional, secular elements of gift-giving, public festivities, and community spirit, does not mean that government may indiscriminately embrace the distinctively sectarian aspects of the holiday. Indeed, in its eagerness to approve the crèche, the Court has advanced a rationale so simplistic that it would appear to allow the Mayor of Pawtucket to participate in the celebration of a Christmas Mass, since this would be just another unobjectionable way for the city to "celebrate the holiday." As is demonstrated below, the Court's logic is fundamentally flawed both because it obscures the reason why public designation of Christmas Day as a holiday is constitutionally acceptable, and blurs the distinction between the secular aspects of Christmas and its distinctively religious character, as exemplified by the crèche.

When government decides to recognize Christmas Day as a public holiday, it does no more than accommodate the calendar of public activities to the plain fact that many Americans will expect on that day to spend time visiting with their families, attending religious services, and perhaps enjoying some respite from preholiday activities. The Free Exercise Clause, of course, does not necessarily compel the government to provide this accommodation, but neither is the Establishment Clause offended by such a step. Because it is clear that the celebration of Christmas has both secular and sectarian elements, it may well be that by taking note of the holiday, the government is simply seeking to serve the same kinds of wholly secular goals—for instance, promoting goodwill and a common day of rest—that were found to justify Sunday Closing Laws. If public officials go further and participate in the *secular* celebration of Christmas—by, for example, decorating public places with such secular images as wreaths, garlands, or Santa Claus figures—they move closer to the limits of their constitutional power but nevertheless remain within the boundaries set by the Establishment Clause. But when those officials participate in or appear to endorse the distinctively religious elements of this otherwise secular event, they encroach upon First Amendment freedoms. For it is at that point that the government brings to the forefront the theological content of the holiday, and places the prestige, power, and financial support of a civil authority in the service of a particular faith.

The inclusion of a crèche in Pawtucket's otherwise secular celebration on Christmas clearly violates these principles. * * * To suggest, as the Court does, that such a symbol is merely "traditional" and therefore no different from Santa's house or reindeer is not only offensive to those for whom the crèche has profound significance, but insulting to those who insist for religious or personal reasons that the story of Christ is in no sense a part of "history" nor an unavoidable element of our national "heritage."

For these reasons, the crèche in this context simply cannot be viewed as playing the same role that an ordinary museum display does. The Court seems to assume that prohibiting Pawtucket from displaying a crèche would be tantamount to prohibiting a state college from including the Bible or Milton's Paradise Lost in a course on English literature. But in those cases the religiously inspired materials are being considered solely as literature. The purpose is plainly not to single out the particular religious beliefs that may have inspired the authors, but to see in these writings the outlines of a larger imaginative universe shared with other forms of literary expression. The same may be said of a course devoted to the study of art; when the course turns to Gothic architecture, the emphasis is not on the religious beliefs which the cathedrals exalt, but rather upon the "aesthetic consequences of [such religious] thought."

In this case, by contrast, the crèche plays no comparable secular role. Unlike the poetry of Paradise Lost which students in a literature course will seek to appreciate primarily for aesthetic or historical reasons, the angels, shepherds, Magi, and infant of Pawtucket's nativity scene can only be viewed as symbols of a particular set of religious beliefs. It would be another matter if the crèche were displayed in a museum setting, in the company of other religiously inspired artifacts, as an example, among many, of the symbolic representation of religious myths. In that setting, we would have objective guarantees that the crèche could not suggest that a particular faith has been singled out for public favor and recognition. The effect of Pawtucket's crèche, however, is not confined by any of these limiting attributes. In the absence of any other religious symbols or of any neutral disclaimer, the inescapable effect of the crèche will be to remind the average observer of the religious roots of the celebration he is witnessing and to call to mind the scriptural message that the nativity symbolizes. * * *

III

The American historical experience concerning the public celebration of Christmas, if carefully examined, provides no support for the

Court's decision. The opening sections of the Court's opinion, while seeking to rely on historical evidence, do no more than recognize the obvious: because of the strong religious currents that run through our history, an inflexible or absolutistic enforcement of the Establishment Clause would be both imprudent and impossible. This observation is at once uncontroversial and unilluminating. Simply enumerating the various ways in which the Federal Government has recognized the vital role religion plays in our society does nothing to help decide the question presented in this case.

Indeed, the Court's approach suggests a fundamental misapprehension of the proper uses of history in constitutional interpretation. Certainly, our decisions reflect the fact that an awareness of historical practice often can provide a useful guide in interpreting the abstract language of the Establishment Clause. But historical acceptance of a particular practice alone is never sufficient to justify a challenged governmental action, since, as the Court has rightly observed, "no one acquires a vested or protected right in violation of the Constitution by long use, even when that span of time covers our entire national existence and indeed predates it." *Walz v. Tax Commission.* * * *

The intent of the Framers with respect to the public display of nativity scenes is virtually impossible to discern primarily because the widespread celebration of Christmas did not emerge in its present form until well into the nineteenth century. * * *

The historical evidence with respect to public financing and support for governmental displays of nativity scenes is even more difficult to gauge. * * *

In sum, there is no evidence whatsoever that the Framers would have expressly approved a federal celebration of the Christmas holiday including public displays of a nativity scene; accordingly, the Court's repeated invocation of the decision in *Marsh* is not only baffling, it is utterly irrelevant. Nor is there any suggestion that publicly financed and supported displays of Christmas crèches are supported by a record of widespread, undeviating acceptance that extends throughout our history. Therefore, our prior decisions which relied upon concrete, specific historical evidence to support a particular practice simply have no bearing on the question presented in this case. Contrary to today's careless decision, those prior cases have all recognized that the "illumination" provided by history must always be focused on the particular practice at issue in a given case. Without that guiding principle and the intellectual discipline it imposes, the Court is at sea, free to select random elements of America's varied history solely to suit the views of five members of this Court.

IV

Under our constitutional scheme, the role of safeguarding our "religious heritage" and of promoting religious beliefs is reserved as the exclusive prerogative of our Nation's churches, religious institutions, and spiritual leaders. Because the Framers of the Establishment Clause understood that "religion is too personal, too sacred, too holy to permit its 'unhallowed perversion' by civil [authorities]," *Engel v. Vitale*, the Clause demands that government play no role in this effort. The Court today brushes aside these concerns by insisting that Pawtucket has done nothing more than include a "traditional" symbol of Christmas in its celebration of this national holiday, thereby muting the religious content of the crèche. But the city's action should be recognized for what it is: a coercive, though perhaps small, step toward establishing the sectarian preferences of the majority at the expense of the minority, accomplished by placing public facilities and funds in support of the religious symbolism and theological tidings that the crèche conveys. * * * That the Constitution sets [the] realm of [religious] thought and feeling apart from the pressures and antagonisms of government is one of its supreme achievements. Regrettably, the Court today tarnishes that achievement.

I dissent.

EDWARDS V. AGUILLARD

June 19, 1987

He that troubleth his own house shall inherit the wind." This line from Proverbs 11:29 provided the title and the moral for the play and film about the 1925 Scopes "Monkey Trial." John T. Scopes was a Tennessee teacher whose instruction on evolution in public school violated a state statute. His ensuing criminal prosecution truly was the trial of the century, featuring two of the country's most famous attorneys: Clarence Darrow for the defense and Williams Jennings Bryan as special prosecutor. The jury convicted Scopes and the court fined him $100. On appeal, the State Supreme Court upheld the constitutionality of the statute but overturned the fine as excessive.

The United States Supreme Court never reviewed the *Scopes* case, but in 1968, a year after Tennessee repealed its anti-evolution statute, the Court struck down a similar Arkansas law. In that case, *Epperson v. Arkansas*, the Court unanimously concluded that the Arkansas law violated the Establishment Clause of the First Amendment.

Some years later, Louisiana attempted to circumvent the Court's ruling in *Epperson* by requiring instruction in "creation science" whenever the theory of evolution was taught. "Creation science" is somewhat of a misnomer. Whereas modern scientific method is premised on a search for truth with an open mind, creationism involves a search for evidence to justify a religious belief. Despite the clear religious foundation of creationism, the State defended its law as a legitimate protection for academic freedom and a means of ensuring comprehensive instruction in science.

Justice Brennan, writing for the Court, applied the *Lemon* test and had little difficulty determining that the statute had no valid secular purpose. He concluded that the State's explanation was a mere pretext and that the legislature's true purpose was to undermine the teaching of evolution theory. Because there was a religious rather than a secular purpose behind the law, the first prong of the *Lemon* test was not met and the legislation was constitutionally defective. It was one of Brennan's last major pronouncements on the separation of church and state.

Justice Brennan wrote the opinion of the Court, joined by Justices Marshall, Blackmun, Powell, and Stevens. Justices White and O'Connor concurred. Chief Justice Rehnquist and Justice Scalia dissented.

⬦ ⬦ ⬦

JUSTICE BRENNAN delivered the opinion of the Court.

The question for decision is whether Louisiana's "Balanced Treatment for Creation-Science and Evolution-Science in Public School Instruction" Act (Creationism Act) is facially invalid as violative of the Establishment Clause of the First Amendment.

I

The Creationism Act forbids the teaching of the theory of evolution in public schools unless accompanied by instruction in "creation science." No school is required to teach evolution or creation science. If either is taught, however, the other must also be taught. The theories of evolution and creation science are statutorily defined as "the scientific evidences for [creation or evolution] and inferences from those scientific evidences."

Appellees, who include parents of children attending Louisiana public schools, Louisiana teachers, and religious leaders, challenged the constitutionality of the Act in District Court, seeking an injunction and declaratory relief. Appellants, Louisiana officials charged with implementing the Act, defended on the ground that the purpose of the Act is to protect a legitimate secular interest, namely, academic freedom. * * * [T]he Court of Appeals held that the Act violated the Establishment Clause. * * * [We] now affirm.

II

The Establishment Clause forbids the enactment of any law "respecting an establishment of religion." The Court has applied a three-pronged test to determine whether legislation comports with the Establishment Clause. First, the legislature must have adopted the law with a secular purpose. Second, the statute's principal or primary effect must be one that neither advances nor inhibits religion. Third, the statute must not result in an excessive entanglement of government with religion. *Lemon v. Kurtzman.* State action violates the Establishment Clause if it fails to satisfy any of these prongs.

In this case, the Court must determine whether the Establishment Clause was violated in the special context of the public elementary and secondary school system. States and local school boards are generally afforded considerable discretion in operating public schools. "At the same time . . . we have necessarily recognized that the discretion of the States and local school boards in matters of education must be exercised in a manner that comports with the transcendent imperatives of the First Amendment." *Board of Education v. Pico.*

The Court has been particularly vigilant in monitoring compliance with the Establishment Clause in elementary and secondary schools. Families entrust public schools with the education of their children, but condition their trust on the understanding that the classroom will not purposely be used to advance religious views that may conflict with the private beliefs of the student and his or her family. Students in such institutions are impressionable and their attendance is involuntary. *See, e.g., School District of Abington Township v. Schempp* (Brennan, J., concurring). The State exerts great authority and coercive power through mandatory attendance requirements, and because of the students' emulation of teachers as role models and the children's susceptibility to peer pressure.[5] Furthermore, "[t]he public school is at once the symbol of our democracy and the most pervasive means for promoting our common destiny. In no activity of the State is it more vital to keep out divisive forces than in its schools." *Illinois ex rel. McCollum v. Board of Education* (opinion of Frankfurter, J.).

Consequently, the Court has been required often to invalidate statutes which advance religion in public elementary and secondary schools. *See, e.g., Grand Rapids School District v. Ball* (school district's use of religious school teachers in public schools); *Wallace v. Jaffree* (Alabama statute authorizing moment of silence for school prayer); *Stone v. Graham* (posting copy of Ten Commandments on public classroom wall); *Epperson v. Arkansas* (statute forbidding teaching of evolution); *School District of Abington Township v. Schempp* (daily reading of Bible); *Engel v. Vitale* (recitation of "denominationally neutral" prayer).

Therefore, in employing the three-pronged *Lemon* test, we must do so

---

5. The potential for undue influence is far less significant with regard to college students who voluntarily enroll in courses. "This distinction warrants a difference in constitutional results." *Schempp* (Brennan, J., concurring). Thus, for instance, the Court has not questioned the authority of state colleges and universities to offer courses on religion or theology.

mindful of the particular concerns that arise in the context of public elementary and secondary schools. We now turn to the evaluation of the Act under the *Lemon* test.

III

Lemon's first prong focuses on the purpose that animated adoption of the Act. "The purpose prong of the *Lemon* test asks whether government's actual purpose is to endorse or disapprove of religion." *Lynch v. Donnelly* (O'Connor, J., concurring). A governmental intention to promote religion is clear when the State enacts a law to serve a religious purpose. This intention may be evidenced by promotion of religion in general, or by advancement of a particular religious belief, *e.g., Stone v. Graham* (invalidating requirement to post Ten Commandments, which are "undeniably a sacred text in the Jewish and Christian faiths"); *Epperson v. Arkansas* (holding that banning the teaching of evolution in public schools violates the First Amendment since "teaching and learning" must not "be tailored to the principles or prohibitions of any religious sect or dogma"). If the law was enacted for the purpose of endorsing religion, "no consideration of the second or third criteria [of *Lemon*] is necessary." *Wallace v. Jaffree.* In this case, appellants have identified no clear secular purpose for the Louisiana Act.

True, the Act's stated purpose is to protect academic freedom. This phrase might, in common parlance, be understood as referring to enhancing the freedom of teachers to teach what they will. The Court of Appeals, however, correctly concluded that the Act was not designed to further that goal. * * * Even if "academic freedom" is read to mean "teaching all of the evidence" with respect to the origin of human beings, the Act does not further this purpose. The goal of providing a more comprehensive science curriculum is not furthered either by outlawing the teaching of evolution or by requiring the teaching of creation science.

A

While the Court is normally deferential to a State's articulation of a secular purpose, it is required that the statement of such purpose be sincere and not a sham. * * *

It is clear from the legislative history that the purpose of the legislative sponsor, Senator Bill Keith, was to narrow the science curriculum. During the legislative hearings, Senator Keith stated: "My preference would be that neither [creationism nor evolution] be taught." Such a ban on teaching does not promote—indeed, it undermines—the provision of a comprehensive scientific education.

It is equally clear that requiring schools to teach creation science with evolution does not advance academic freedom. The Act does not grant teachers a flexibility that they did not already possess to supplant the present science curriculum with the presentation of theories, besides evolution, about the origin of life. Indeed, the Court of Appeals found that no law prohibited Louisiana public school teachers from teaching any scientific theory. As the president of the Louisiana Science Teachers Association testified, "[a]ny scientific concept that's based on established fact can be included in our curriculum already, and no legislation allowing this is necessary." The Act provides Louisiana schoolteachers with no new authority. Thus the stated purpose is not furthered by it.

* * *

If the Louisiana Legislature's purpose was solely to maximize the comprehensiveness and effectiveness of science instruction, it would have encouraged the teaching of all scientific theories about the origins of humankind. But under the Act's requirements, teachers who were once free to teach any and all facets of this subject are now unable to do so. Moreover, the Act fails even to ensure that creation science will be taught, but instead requires the teaching of this theory only when the theory of evolution is taught. Thus we agree with the Court of Appeals' conclusion that the Act does not serve to protect academic freedom, but has the distinctly different purpose of discrediting "evolution by counterbalancing its teaching at every turn with the teaching of creationism."

B

Stone v. Graham invalidated the State's requirement that the Ten Commandments be posted in public classrooms. "The Ten Commandments are undeniably a sacred text in the Jewish and Christian faiths, and no legislative recitation of a supposed secular purpose can blind us to that fact." As a result, the contention that the law was designed to provide instruction on a "fundamental legal code" was "not sufficient to avoid conflict with the First Amendment." Similarly [*Schempp*] held unconstitutional a statute "requiring the selection and reading at the opening of the school day of verses from the Holy Bible and the recitation of the Lord's Prayer by the students in unison," despite the proffer of such secular purposes as the "promotion of moral values, the contradiction to the materialistic trends of our times, the perpetuation of our institutions and the teaching of literature."

As in *Stone* and [*Schempp*], we need not be blind in this case to the legislature's preeminent religious purpose in enacting this statute. There is a historic and contemporaneous link between the teachings of certain religious denominations and the teaching of evolution. It was this link that concerned the Court in *Epperson v. Arkansas*, which also involved a facial challenge to a statute regulating the teaching of evolution. In that case, the Court reviewed an Arkansas statute that made it unlawful for an instructor to teach evolution or to use a textbook that referred to this scientific theory. Although the Arkansas antievolution law did not explicitly state its predominate religious purpose, the Court could not ignore that "[t]he statute was a product of the upsurge of 'fundamentalist' religious fervor" that has long viewed this particular scientific theory as contradicting the literal interpretation of the Bible. After reviewing the history of antievolution statutes, the Court determined that "there can be no doubt that the motivation for the [Arkansas] law was the same [as other anti-evolution statutes]: to suppress the teaching of a theory which, it was thought, 'denied' the divine creation of man." The Court found that there can be no legitimate state interest in protecting particular religions from scientific views "distasteful to them," and concluded "that the First Amendment does not permit the State to require that teaching and learning must be tailored to the principles or prohibitions of any religious sect or dogma."

These same historic and contemporaneous antagonisms between the teachings of certain religious denominations and the teaching of evolution are present in this case. The preeminent purpose of the Louisiana Legislature was clearly to advance the religious viewpoint that a supernatural being created humankind. * * * The legislative history documents that the Act's primary purpose was to change the science curriculum of public schools in order to provide persuasive advantage to a particular religious doctrine that rejects the factual basis of evolution in its entirety. The sponsor of the Creationism Act, Senator Keith, explained during the legislative hearings that his disdain for the theory of evolution resulted from the support that evolution supplied to views contrary to his own religious beliefs. According to Senator Keith, the theory of evolution was consonant with the "cardinal principle[s] of religious humanism, secular humanism, theological liberalism, aetheistism [sic]." The state senator repeatedly stated that scientific evidence supporting his religious views should be included in the public school curriculum to redress the fact that the theory of evolution incidentally coincided with what he characterized as religious beliefs antithetical to his own. The legislation therefore sought to alter the science curriculum to reflect endorsement of a religious view that is antagonistic to the theory of evolution.

In this case, the purpose of the Creationism Act was to restructure the science curriculum to conform with a particular religious viewpoint. Out of many possible science subjects taught in the public schools, the legislature chose to affect the teaching of the one scientific theory that historically has been opposed by certain religious sects. As in *Epperson*, the legislature passed the Act to give preference to those religious groups which have as one of their tenets the creation of humankind by a divine creator. The "overriding fact" that confronted the Court in *Epperson* was "that Arkansas' law selects from the body of knowledge a particular segment which it proscribes for the sole reason that it is deemed to conflict with . . . a particular interpretation of the Book of Genesis by a particular religious group." Similarly, the Creationism Act is designed either to promote the theory of creation science which embodies a particular religious tenet by requiring that creation science be taught whenever evolution is taught or to prohibit the teaching of a scientific theory disfavored by certain religious sects by forbidding the teaching of evolution when creation science is not also taught. The Establishment Clause, however, "forbids *alike* the preference of a religious doctrine *or* the prohibition of theory which is deemed antagonistic to a particular dogma." *Id.* (emphasis added). Because the primary purpose of the Creationism Act is to advance a particular religious belief, the Act endorses religion in violation of the First Amendment.

We do not imply that a legislature could never require that scientific critiques of prevailing scientific theories be taught. Indeed, the Court acknowledged in *Stone* that its decision forbidding the posting of the Ten Commandments did not mean that no use could ever be made of the Ten Commandments, or that the Ten Commandments played an exclusively religious role in the history of Western Civilization. In a similar way, teaching a variety of scientific theories about the origins of humankind to schoolchildren might be validly done with the clear secular intent of enhancing the effectiveness of science instruction. But because the primary purpose of the Creationism Act is to endorse a particular religious doctrine, the Act furthers religion in violation of the Establishment Clause.

* * *

V

    The Louisiana Creationism Act advances a religious doctrine by requiring either the banishment of the theory of evolution from public school classrooms or the presentation of a religious viewpoint that rejects evolution in its entirety. The Act violates the Establishment Clause of the First Amendment because it seeks to employ the symbolic and financial support of government to achieve a religious purpose. The judgment of the Court of Appeals therefore is

Affirmed.

SHERBERT V. VERNER

June 17, 1963

This case, decided on the same day as *Schempp* (p. 68), involved the other issue of religious freedom under the First Amendment: the Free Exercise Clause. As in many free exercise cases, the question presented was whether a person should be exempt from laws of general applicability that impose a burden on the individual's religious beliefs or practices. Specifically, the case involved a Seventh-day Adventist who lost her job when she refused to work on Saturday, the designated Sabbath of her faith. The state then denied her unemployment benefits because her unavailability for Saturday labor contravened the state's unemployment regulation that she be available for suitable work.

In prior cases, the Court had concluded that there was a constitutionally relevant distinction between religious beliefs and religious practices. Under the Free Exercise Clause, the former could not be regulated by the government, but the latter could be restricted if a threat to public safety, peace, or order existed. Justice Brennan, writing for the majority in this case, decided that the claimant's challenge was not based on conduct that constituted any sort of threat.

Brennan created a two-part inquiry to be applied in free exercise cases. First, the Court determines if the law infringed upon free exercise of religion. If so, the Court then inquires whether the infringement is justified by a compelling state interest. Brennan concluded that this claimant's free exercise was infringed by the unemployment regulation because she was forced to choose between violating a basic tenet of her faith or receiving benefits. This same type of choice, Brennan pointed out, was not foisted upon Sunday worshippers. Having concluded that the first part of the test was satisfied, Brennan examined the state's interest. The state contended that its primary interest was to prevent fraudulent claims by those feigning religious objections to Saturday labor. Brennan responded by declaring that, under the compelling interest test, the state would have to show that there were no alternative ways to prevent such abuses, something the state had failed to do.

The compelling interest test is a difficult standard for a state to satisfy. Nine years after *Sherbert*, in *Wisconsin v. Yoder* (1972), the Court used that standard to provide an exemption for Amish schoolchildren from compulsory education beyond the eighth grade. The Court based its ruling on a combination of factors, including the unusual features of the Amish religion and way of life, the free exercise rights of the children, and the right of parents to direct their children's education. The Court was unusually careful in distinguishing between the religious beliefs and practices involved in the case, and implied that other groups might not receive similar treatment. Thereafter, the Court began to retreat from the *Sherbert-Yoder* compelling interest test. With the exception of those cases arising in the unemployment context, an increasing number of free exercise challenges were denied. The Court limited *Sherbert*'s holding to the unemployment situation and distinguished *Yoder* due to its unique factual circumstances.

In 1990, the Court was presented with another unemployment case when two Native Americans drug counselors were dismissed from their jobs for ingesting peyote in a tribal religious ceremony. The state's criminal drug laws provided no exemption for religious use of peyote, a banned substance. The state denied unemployment benefits to the workers because it determined that their discharge was the result of "work-related misconduct." Over Brennan's dissent, the Court upheld the denial of benefits ostensibly because of the violation of criminal law. In doing so, however, the Court expressed great reluctance to continue to use the *Sherbert-Yoder* compelling interest test.

Three years later, Congress responded by enacting the Religious Freedom Restoration Act, which attempted to reinstate the compelling interest test in free exercise cases, the approach Brennan championed in *Sherbert* and throughout his tenure on the Court. However, in 1997, the Court struck down the Act, concluding that it was beyond the power of Congress. Brennan's opinion in *Sherbert* remains, therefore, one of the Court's broadest interpretations of the Free Exercise Clause. It also evidences Brennan's unwavering commitment to the principle that the government must reasonably accommodate an individual's free exercise of religion.

Justice Brennan wrote the opinion of the Court, joined by Chief Justice Warren and Justices Black, Douglas, Clark, and Goldberg. Justice Stewart concurred. Justices Harlan and White dissented.

⋄ ⋄ ⋄

MR. JUSTICE BRENNAN delivered the opinion of the Court.

Appellant, a member of the Seventh-day Adventist Church, was discharged by her South Carolina employer because she would not work on Saturday, the Sabbath Day of her faith.[1] When she was unable to obtain other employment because from conscientious scruples she would not take Saturday work,[2] she filed a claim for unemployment compensation benefits under the South Carolina Unemployment Compensation Act. That law provides that, to be eligible for benefits, a claimant must be "able to work and . . . available for work"; and, further, that a claimant is ineligible for benefits "[i]f . . . he has failed, without good cause . . . to accept available suitable work when offered him by the employment office or the employer. . . . " The appellee Employment Security Commission, in administrative proceedings under the statute, found that appellant's restriction upon her availability for Saturday work brought her within the provision disqualifying for benefits insured workers who fail, without good cause, to accept "suitable work when offered . . . by the employment office or the employer. . . . " The Commission's finding was sustained by the Court of Common Pleas for Spartanburg County. That court's judgment was in turn affirmed by the South Carolina Supreme Court, which rejected appellant's contention that, as applied to her, the disqualifying provisions of the South Carolina statute abridged her right to the free exercise of her religion secured under the Free Exercise Clause of the First Amendment through the Fourteenth Amendment. * * * We reverse the judgment of the South Carolina Supreme Court and remand for further proceedings not inconsistent with this opinion.

I

The door of the Free Exercise Clause stands tightly closed against any governmental regulation of religious *beliefs* as such. Government may neither compel affirmation of a repugnant belief; nor penalize or discriminate against individuals or groups because they hold religious views abhorrent to the authorities; nor employ the taxing power to inhibit the dissemination of particular religious views. On the other

---

1. Appellant became a member of the Seventh-day Adventist Church in 1957, at a time when her employer, a textile-mill operator, permitted her to work a five-day week. It was not until 1959 that the work week was changed to six days, including Saturday, for all three shifts in the employer's mill. No question has been raised in this case concerning the sincerity of appellant's religious beliefs. Nor is there any doubt that the prohibition against Saturday labor is a basic tenet of the Seventh-day Adventist creed, based upon that religion's interpretation of the Holy Bible.

2. After her discharge, appellant sought employment with three other mills in the Spartanburg area, but found no suitable five-day work available at any of the mills. In filing her claim with the Commission, she expressed a willingness to accept employment at other mills, or even in another industry, so long as Saturday work was not required. * * *

hand, the Court has rejected challenges under the Free Exercise Clause to governmental regulation of certain overt acts prompted by religious beliefs or principles, for "even when the action is in accord with one's religious convictions, [it] is not totally free from legislative restrictions." *Braunfeld v. Brown.* The conduct or actions so regulated have invariably posed some substantial threat to public safety, peace or order.

Plainly enough, appellant's conscientious objection to Saturday work constitutes no conduct prompted by religious principles of a kind within the reach of state legislation. If, therefore, the decision of the South Carolina Supreme Court is to withstand appellant's constitutional challenge, it must be either because her disqualification as a beneficiary represents no infringement by the State of her constitutional rights of free exercise, or because any incidental burden on the free exercise of appellant's religion may be justified by a "compelling state interest in the regulation of a subject within the State's constitutional power to regulate." *NAACP v. Button.*

II

We turn first to the question whether the disqualification for benefits imposes any burden on the free exercise of appellant's religion. We think it is clear that it does. In a sense the consequences of such a disqualification to religious principles and practices may be only an indirect result of welfare legislation within the State's general competence to enact; it is true that no criminal sanctions directly compel appellant to work a six-day week. But this is only the beginning, not the end, of our inquiry. For "[i]f the purpose or effect of a law is to impede the observance of one or all religions or is to discriminate invidiously between religions, that law is constitutionally invalid even though the burden may be characterized as being only indirect." *Braunfeld.* Here not only is it apparent that appellant's declared ineligibility for benefits derives solely from the practice of her religion, but the pressure upon her to forego that practice is unmistakable. The ruling forces her to choose between following the precepts of her religion and forfeiting benefits, on the one hand, and abandoning one of the precepts of her religion in order to accept work, on the other hand. Governmental imposition of such a choice puts the same kind of burden upon the free exercise of religion as would a fine imposed against appellant for her Saturday worship.

Nor may the South Carolina court's construction of the statute be saved from constitutional infirmity on the ground that unemployment compensation benefits are not appellant's "right" but merely a "privilege." It is too late in the day to doubt that the liberties of religion and expression may be infringed by the denial of or placing of conditions upon a benefit or privilege. For example, in *Flemming v. Nestor* the Court recognized with respect to Federal Social Security benefits that "[t]he interest of a covered employee under the Act is of sufficient substance to fall within the protection from arbitrary governmental action afforded by the Due Process Clause." In *Speiser v. Randall,* we emphasized that conditions upon public benefits cannot be sustained if they so operate, whatever their purpose, as to inhibit or deter the exercise of First Amendment freedoms. We there struck down a condition which limited the availability of a tax exemption to those members of the exempted class who affirmed their loyalty to the state government granting the exemption. While the State was surely under no obligation to afford such an exemption, we held that the imposition of such a condition upon even a gratuitous benefit inevitably deterred or discouraged the exercise of First Amendment rights of expression and thereby threatened to "produce a result which the State could not command directly." "To deny an exemption to claimants who engage in certain forms of speech is in effect to penalize them for such speech." *Id.* Likewise, to condition the availability of benefits upon this appellant's willingness to violate a cardinal principle of her religious faith effectively penalizes the free exercise of her constitutional liberties.

Significantly South Carolina expressly saves the Sunday worshipper from having to make the kind of choice which we here hold infringes the Sabbatarian's religious liberty. When in times of "national emergency" the textile plants are authorized by the State Commissioner of Labor to operate on Sunday, "no employee shall be required to work on Sunday . . . who is conscientiously opposed to Sunday work; and if any employee should refuse to work on Sunday on account of conscientious . . . objections he or she shall not jeopardize his or her seniority by such refusal or be discriminated against in any other manner." S. C. Code, § 64-4. No question of the disqualification of a Sunday worshipper for benefits is likely to arise, since we cannot suppose that an employer will discharge him in violation of this statute. The unconstitutionality of the disqualification of the Sabbatarian is thus compounded by the religious discrimination which South Carolina's general statutory scheme necessarily effects.

III

We must next consider whether some compelling state interest enforced in the eligibility provisions of the South Carolina statute justifies the substantial infringement of appellant's First Amendment right. It is basic that no showing merely of a rational relationship to some colorable state interest would suffice; in this highly sensitive constitutional area, "[only] the gravest abuses, endangering paramount interests, give occasion for permissible limitation," *Thomas v. Collins.* No such abuse or danger has been advanced in the present case. The appellees suggest no more than a possibility that the filing of fraudulent claims by unscrupulous claimants feigning religious objections to Saturday work might not only dilute the unemployment compensation fund but also hinder the scheduling by employers of necessary Saturday work. But that possibility is not apposite here because no such objection appears to have been made before the South Carolina Supreme Court, and we are unwilling to assess the importance of an asserted state interest without the views of the state court. Nor, if the contention had been made below, would the record appear to sustain it; there is no proof whatever to warrant such fears of malingering or deceit as those which the respondents now advance. Even if consideration of such evidence is not foreclosed by the prohibition against judicial inquiry into the truth or falsity of religious beliefs—a question as to which we intimate no view since it is not before us—it is highly doubtful whether such evidence would be sufficient to warrant a substantial infringement of religious liberties. For even if the possibility of spurious claims did threaten to dilute the fund and disrupt the scheduling of work, it would plainly be incumbent upon the appellees to demonstrate that no alternative forms of regulation would combat such abuses without infringing First Amendment rights.

In these respects, then, the state interest asserted in the present case is wholly dissimilar to the interests which were found to justify the less direct burden upon religious practices in *Braunfeld v. Brown.* The Court recognized that the Sunday closing law which that decision sustained undoubtedly served "to make the practice of [the Orthodox Jewish merchants'] . . . religious beliefs more expensive." But the statute was nevertheless saved by a countervailing factor which finds no equivalent in the instant case—a strong state interest in providing one uniform day of rest for all workers. That secular objective could be achieved, the Court found, only by declaring Sunday to be that day of rest. Requiring exemptions for Sabbatarians, while theoretically possible, appeared to present an administrative problem of such magnitude, or to afford the exempted class so great a competitive advantage, that such a requirement would have rendered the entire statutory scheme unworkable. In the present case no such justifications underlie the determination of the state court that appellant's religion makes her ineligible to receive benefits.

IV

In holding as we do, plainly we are not fostering the "establishment" of the Seventh-day Adventist religion in South Carolina, for the extension of unemployment benefits to Sabbatarians in common with Sunday worshippers reflects nothing more than the governmental obligation of neutrality in the face of religious differences, and does not represent that involvement of religious with secular institutions which it is the object of the Establishment Clause to forestall. Nor does the recognition of the appellant's right to unemployment benefits under the state statute serve to abridge any other person's religious liberties. Nor do we, by our decision today, declare the existence of a constitutional right to unemployment benefits on the part of all persons whose religious convictions are the cause of their unemployment. This is not a case in which an employee's religious convictions serve to make him a nonproductive member of society. Finally, nothing we say today constrains the States to adopt any particular form or scheme of unemployment compensation. Our holding today is only that South Carolina may not constitutionally apply the eligibility provisions so as to constrain a worker to abandon his religious convictions respecting the day of rest. This holding but reaffirms a principle that we announced a decade and a half ago, namely that no State may "exclude individual Catholics, Lutherans, Mohammedans, Baptists, Jews, Methodists, Nonbelievers, Presbyterians, or the members of any other faith, *because of their faith, or lack of it,* from receiving the benefits of public welfare legislation." *Everson v. Board of Education.*

* * *

The judgment of the South Carolina Supreme Court is reversed and the case is remanded for further proceedings not inconsistent with this opinion.

It is so ordered.

GOLDMAN V. WEINBERGER

March 25, 1986

Captain S. Simcha Goldman was an Orthodox Jew and ordained rabbi who served as a clinical psychologist in the Air Force. In 1981, he testified as a defense witness in a court martial while wearing a yarmulke, the head covering worn by many Jews as a show of devotion to God. Opposing counsel complained to Goldman's commanding officer that the yarmulke violated Air Force regulations that prohibited wearing headgear indoors. The commander responded by ordering Goldman not to wear the yarmulke while on duty, except in the base hospital. After Goldman protested to the Air Force General Counsel, the commander revised his instructions to prohibit Goldman from wearing the yarmulke anywhere on the base. The commander also threatened Goldman with court martial and withdrew a recommendation to extend Goldman's term of active service. Goldman sued, arguing that the Air Force regulation violated his right to freely exercise his religion.

Oversight of military rules and regulations puts the judiciary in a precarious position. No judge wants to undermine the readiness or effectiveness of the nation's military forces, and no judge is insensitive to the need for rigorous military training and discipline. However, military personnel do not lose their constitutional rights by virtue of their military service. While those who are drafted into the military may have a stronger basis for asserting their rights, even those who enlist are entitled to express themselves and practice their faiths without undue interference.

The question for the Supreme Court becomes how much deference to give to military claims of necessity. In the case of *Brown v. Glines* (1980), for example, the Court upheld Navy, Air Force, and Marine Corps regulations that restrict circulation of petitions. The services argued that these restrictions are essential to good military discipline, and the Court unhesitatingly accepted this argument. Justice Brennan, though, dissented, characterizing the justifications as "a series of platitudes about the special nature and overwhelming importance of military necessity."

When Goldman's case reached the Supreme Court, a majority of five again deferred to the military's claim of necessity. It freely admitted that its "review of military regulations challenged on First Amendment grounds is far more deferential than constitutional review of similar laws or regulations designed for civilian authority." In reality, however, its review was not merely deferential, it was nonexistent. In its six-page opinion, half of which described the facts, the majority made no effort to evaluate the reasonableness of the regulation. It summed up both the facts and the extent of its review by noting that "[t]he desirability of dress regulations in the military is decided by the appropriate military officials."

Brennan sharply disagreed, and in characteristic style stressed the importance of the issue to someone in Goldman's position. At the end of his dissent, he made a plea for Congress to intervene. That plea was heard. Twenty-one months after this decision, in December 1987, Congress enacted a statute drafted by Goldman's attorney. That law authorizes military personnel to wear "neat and conservative" religious apparel while in uniform, except when such clothing interferes with the wearer's military duties. The legislative history makes it clear that religious apparel does not interfere with the wearer's military duties merely because it is "nonuniform."

This statute did not, however, save Goldman's military career. Following this litigation, the Air Force declined to renew his commission.

Justice Rehnquist wrote the opinion of the Court, joined by Chief Justice Burger and Justices White, Powell, and Stevens. Justices Brennan, Marshall, Blackmun, and O'Connor dissented.

◈ ◈ ◈

JUSTICE BRENNAN, with whom JUSTICE MARSHALL joins, dissenting.

Simcha Goldman invokes this Court's protection of his First Amendment right to fulfill one of the traditional religious obligations of a male Orthodox Jew—to cover his head before an omnipresent God. The Court's response to Goldman's request is to abdicate its role as principal expositor of the Constitution and protector of individual liberties in favor of credulous deference to unsupported assertions of military necessity. I dissent.

I

In ruling that the paramount interests of the Air Force override Dr. Goldman's free exercise claim, the Court overlooks the sincere and serious nature of his constitutional claim. It suggests that the desirability of certain dress regulations, rather than a First Amendment right, is at issue. The Court declares that in selecting dress regulations, "military officials . . . are under no constitutional mandate to abandon their considered professional judgment." If Dr. Goldman wanted to wear a hat to keep his head warm or to cover a bald spot I would join the majority. Mere personal preferences in dress are not constitutionally protected. The First Amendment, however, restrains the Government's ability to prevent an Orthodox Jewish serviceman from, or punish him for, wearing a yarmulke.[1]

The Court also attempts, unsuccessfully, to minimize the burden that was placed on Dr. Goldman's rights. The fact that "the regulations do not permit the wearing of . . . a yarmulke," does not simply render military life for observant Orthodox Jews "objectionable." It sets up an almost absolute bar to the fulfillment of a religious duty. Dr. Goldman spent most of his time in uniform indoors, where the dress code forbade him even to cover his head with his service cap. Consequently, he was asked to violate the tenets of his faith virtually every minute of every workday.

II

A

Dr. Goldman has asserted a substantial First Amendment claim, which is entitled to meaningful review by this Court. The Court, however, evades its responsibility by eliminating, in all but name only, judicial review of military regulations that interfere with the fundamental constitutional rights of service personnel.

Our cases have acknowledged that in order to protect our treasured liberties, the military must be able to command service members to sacrifice a great many of the individual freedoms they enjoyed in the civilian community and to endure certain limitations on the freedoms they retain. *See, e.g., Brown v. Glines.* Notwithstanding this acknowledgment, we have steadfastly maintained that "our citizens in uniform may not be stripped of basic rights simply because they have doffed their civilian clothes." *Chappell v. Wallace.* And, while we have hesitated, due to our lack of expertise concerning military affairs and our

---

1. The yarmulke worn by Dr. Goldman was a dark-colored skullcap measuring approximately 5 1/2 inches in diameter.

respect for the delegated authority of a coordinate branch, to strike down restrictions on individual liberties which could reasonably be justified as necessary to the military's vital function, we have never abdicated our obligation of judicial review.

Today the Court eschews its constitutionally mandated role. It adopts for review of military decisions affecting First Amendment rights a subrational-basis standard—absolute, uncritical "deference to the professional judgment of military authorities." If a branch of the military declares one of its rules sufficiently important to outweigh a service person's constitutional rights, it seems that the Court will accept that conclusion, no matter how absurd or unsupported it may be.

A deferential standard of review, however, need not, and should not, mean that the Court must credit arguments that defy common sense. When a military service burdens the free exercise rights of its members in the name of necessity, it must provide, as an initial matter and at a minimum, a *credible* explanation of how the contested practice is likely to interfere with the proffered military interest.[2] Unabashed *ipse dixit* cannot outweigh a constitutional right.

In the present case, the Air Force asserts that its interests in discipline and uniformity would be undermined by an exception to the dress code permitting observant male Orthodox Jews to wear yarmulkes. The Court simply restates these assertions without offering any explanation how the exception Dr. Goldman requests reasonably could interfere with the Air Force's interests. Had the Court given actual consideration to Goldman's claim, it would have been compelled to decide in his favor.

B

1

The Government maintains in its brief that discipline is jeopardized whenever exceptions to military regulations are granted. Service personnel must be trained to obey even the most arbitrary command

---

2. I continue to believe that Government restraints on First Amendment rights, including limitations placed on military personnel, may be justified only upon showing a compelling state interest which is precisely furthered by a narrowly tailored regulation. *See, e.g.,* Brown v. Glines (Brennan, J., dissenting). I think that any special needs of the military can be accommodated in the compelling-interest prong of the test. My point here is simply that even under a more deferential test Dr. Goldman should prevail.

reflexively. Non-Jewish personnel will perceive the wearing of a yarmulke by an Orthodox Jew as an unauthorized departure from the rules and will begin to question the principle of unswerving obedience. Thus shall our fighting forces slip down the treacherous slope toward unkempt appearance, anarchy, and, ultimately, defeat at the hands of our enemies.

The contention that the discipline of the Armed Forces will be subverted if Orthodox Jews are allowed to wear yarmulkes with their uniforms surpasses belief. It lacks support in the record of this case, and the Air Force offers no basis for it as a general proposition. While the perilous slope permits the services arbitrarily to refuse exceptions requested to satisfy mere personal preferences, before the Air Force may burden free exercise rights it must advance, at the *very least*, a rational reason for doing so.

Furthermore, the Air Force cannot logically defend the content of its rule by insisting that discipline depends upon absolute adherence to whatever rule is established. If, as General Usher admitted at trial, the dress code codified religious exemptions from the "no-headgear-indoors" regulation, then the wearing of a yarmulke would be sanctioned by the code and could not be considered an unauthorized deviation from the rules.

2

The Government also argues that the services have an important interest in uniform dress, because such dress establishes the preeminence of group identity, thus fostering esprit de corps and loyalty to the service that transcends individual bonds. In its brief, the Government characterizes the yarmulke as an assertion of individuality and as a badge of religious and ethnic identity, strongly suggesting that, as such, it could drive a wedge of divisiveness between members of the services.

First, the purported interests of the Air Force in complete uniformity of dress and in elimination of individuality or visible identification with any group other than itself are belied by the service's own regulations. The dress code expressly abjures the need for total uniformity:

(1) The American public and its elected representatives draw certain conclusions on military effectiveness based on what they see; that is, the image the Air Force presents. The image must instill public confidence

and leave no doubt that the service member lives by a common standard and responds to military order and discipline.

(2) Appearance in uniform is an important part of this image. . . . Neither the Air Force nor the public expects absolute uniformity of appearance. Each member has the right, within limits, to express individuality through his or her appearance. However, the image of a disciplined service member who can be relied on to do his or her job excludes the extreme, the unusual, and the fad.

It cannot be seriously contended that a serviceman in a yarmulke presents so extreme, so unusual, or so faddish an image that public confidence in his ability to perform his duties will be destroyed. Under the Air Force's own standards, then, Dr. Goldman should have and could have been granted an exception to wear his yarmulke.

The dress code also allows men to wear up to three rings and one identification bracelet of "neat and conservative," but nonuniform, design. This jewelry is apparently permitted even if, as is often the case with rings, it associates the wearer with a denominational school or a religious or secular fraternal organization. If these emblems of religious, social, and ethnic identity are not deemed to be unacceptably divisive, the Air Force cannot rationally justify its bar against yarmulkes on that basis.

Moreover, the services allow, and rightly so, other manifestations of religious diversity. It is clear to all service personnel that some members attend Jewish services, some Christian, some Islamic, and some yet other religious services. Barracks mates see Mormons wearing temple garments, Orthodox Jews wearing tzitzit, and Catholics wearing crosses and scapulars. That they come from different faiths and ethnic backgrounds is not a secret that can or should be kept from them.

I find totally implausible the suggestion that the overarching group identity of the Air Force would be threatened if Orthodox Jews were allowed to wear yarmulkes with their uniforms. To the contrary, a yarmulke worn with a United States military uniform is an eloquent reminder that the shared and proud identity of United States serviceman embraces and unites religious and ethnic pluralism.

Finally, the Air Force argues that while Dr. Goldman describes his yarmulke as an "unobtrusive" addition to his uniform, obtrusiveness is a purely relative, standardless judgment. The Government notes that

while a yarmulke might not seem obtrusive to a Jew, neither does a tur-
ban to a Sikh, a saffron robe to a Satchidananda Ashram-Integral Yogi,
nor dreadlocks to a Rastafarian. If the Court were to require the Air
Force to permit yarmulkes, the service must also allow all of these other
forms of dress and grooming.

The Government dangles before the Court a classic parade of hor-
ribles, the specter of a brightly-colored, "rag-tag band of soldiers." Although turbans, saffron robes, and dreadlocks are not before us in this
case and must each be evaluated against the reasons a service branch
offers for prohibiting personnel from wearing them while in uniform,
a reviewing court could legitimately give deference to dress and grooming rules that have a *reasoned* basis in, for example, functional utility,
health and safety considerations, and the goal of a polished, professional appearance.[4] It is the lack of any reasoned basis for prohibiting
yarmulkes that is so striking here.

Furthermore, contrary to its intimations, the Air Force has available
to it a familiar standard for determining whether a particular style of
yarmulke is consistent with a polished, professional military appearance—the "neat and conservative" standard by which the service judges
jewelry. No rational reason exists why yarmulkes cannot be judged by
the same criterion. Indeed, at argument Dr. Goldman declared himself
willing to wear whatever style and color yarmulke the Air Force believes
best comports with its uniform.

* * *

III

Through our Bill of Rights, we pledged ourselves to attain a level of
human freedom and dignity that had no parallel in history. Our constitutional commitment to religious freedom and to acceptance of religious pluralism is one of our greatest achievements in that noble en-
deavor. Almost 200 years after the First Amendment was drafted,
tolerance and respect for all religions still set us apart from most other
countries and draws to our shores refugees from religious persecution
from around the world.

---

4. For example, the Air Force could no doubt justify regulations ordering troops to wear uniforms, prohibiting garments that could become entangled in machinery, and requiring hair to be
worn short so that it may not be grabbed in combat and may be kept louse-free in field conditions.

Guardianship of this precious liberty is not the exclusive domain of federal courts. It is the responsibility as well of the States and of the other branches of the Federal Government. Our military services have a distinguished record of providing for many of the religious needs of their personnel. But that they have satisfied much of their constitutional obligation does not remove their actions from judicial scrutiny. Our Nation has preserved freedom of religion, not through trusting to the good faith of individual agencies of government alone, but through the constitutionally mandated vigilant oversight and checking authority of the judiciary.

It is not the province of the federal courts to second-guess the professional judgments of the military services, but we are bound by the Constitution to assure ourselves that there exists a rational foundation for assertions of military necessity when they interfere with the free exercise of religion. "The concept of military necessity is seductively broad," *Glines* (Brennan, J., dissenting), and military decisionmakers themselves are as likely to succumb to its allure as are the courts and the general public. Definitions of necessity are influenced by decisionmakers' experiences and values. As a consequence, in pluralistic societies such as ours, institutions dominated by a majority are inevitably, if inadvertently, insensitive to the needs and values of minorities when these needs and values differ from those of the majority. The military, with its strong ethic of conformity and unquestioning obedience, may be particularly impervious to minority needs and values. A critical function of the Religion Clauses of the First Amendment is to protect the rights of members of minority religions against quiet erosion by majoritarian social institutions that dismiss minority beliefs and practices as unimportant, because unfamiliar. It is the constitutional role of this Court to ensure that this purpose of the First Amendment be realized.

The Court and the military services have presented patriotic Orthodox Jews with a painful dilemma—the choice between fulfilling a religious obligation and serving their country. Should the draft be reinstated, compulsion will replace choice. Although the pain the services inflict on Orthodox Jewish servicemen is clearly the result of insensitivity rather than design, it is unworthy of our military because it is unnecessary. The Court and the military have refused these servicemen their constitutional rights; we must hope that Congress will correct this wrong.

O'LONE V. ESTATE OF SHABAZZ

June 9, 1987

Few opinions demonstrate Justice Brennan's compassion for and under-standing of the difficulties faced by minorities as ably as this one does. The case arose when officials at New Jersey's Leesburg State Prison initiated a re-quirement that all nondangerous inmates work outside the prison facility for the entire day. This new rule prevented Muslim inmates from participating in Jumu'ah, a prayer service that the Koran commands Muslims to observe every Friday afternoon.

Muslims are a very small percentage of our society, their faith is not widely understood, and they are often wrongly perceived as connected to the fanati-cism of fundamentalists in the Middle East. Convicted felons are an even greater focus of suspicion. They evoke little sympathy and they are thought by many to have waived their rights by violating the rights of others. Yet in the second and third paragraphs of this opinion, Brennan persuasively ar-gued that the Muslim prisoners who petitioned the Court deserve to have their claims closely scrutinized and their rights zealously guarded not *in spite of* their status, but in part *because of* it.

The majority of the Court ruled that as long as prison officials are acting reasonably, any deprivation of inmates' constitutional rights is permissible. In making this determination, the Court was unwilling to examine whether prison officials had alternatives that would achieve their objectives while not infringing on inmates' rights. Instead, it placed great emphasis on the fact that the inmates had alternative ways to exercise their religious obligations.

Brennan took issue with this approach. In *Goldman v. Weinberger* (p. 110), he questioned the military's claimed justifications for prohibiting Captain Goldman and other Jewish personnel from wearing yarmulkes. Simi-larly, Brennan here refused to accept at face value prison officials' contentions that permitting Muslim inmates to participate in the peaceful weekly prayer service would undermine prison administration.

Critics of Brennan argue that he was not sufficiently deferential to execu-tive officials whose judgments are often based on experience and expertise. Yet in this case, Brennan neither replaced prison officials' judgment with his own nor rejected their judgment as incorrect. He insisted that such officials merely provide the Court with evidence supporting their actions, something they had not done in this case. Furthermore, he suggested that by failing to require such a showing, the Court empowered executive officials to trample on people's fundamental rights merely by asserting that such action is necessary to promote some governmental objective. In essence, Brennan asserted that if the Court is to be the guardian of individual liberties, it must guard them from the other branches of the government, not blindly defer to the unsupported and perhaps insupportable actions of executive agencies.

Chief Justice Rehnquist wrote the opinion of the Court, joined by Justices White, Powell, O'Connor, and Scalia. Justices Brennan, Marshall, Blackmun, and Stevens dissented.

◦　◦　◦

JUSTICE BRENNAN, with whom JUSTICE MARSHALL, JUSTICE BLACKMUN, and JUSTICE STEVENS join, dissenting.

The religious ceremony that these respondents seek to attend is not presumptively dangerous, and the prison has completely foreclosed respondents' participation in it. I therefore would require prison officials to demonstrate that the restrictions they have imposed are necessary to further an important government interest, and that these restrictions are no greater than necessary to achieve prison objectives. As a result, I would affirm the Court of Appeals' order to remand the case to the District Court, and would require prison officials to make this showing.
* * *

I

Prisoners are persons whom most of us would rather not think about. Banished from everyday sight, they exist in a shadow world that only dimly enters our awareness. They are members of a "total institution" that controls their daily existence in a way that few of us can imagine. * * *

It is thus easy to think of prisoners as members of a separate netherworld, driven by its own demands, ordered by its own customs, ruled by those whose claim to power rests on raw necessity. Nothing can change the fact, however, that the society that these prisoners inhabit is our own. Prisons may exist on the margins of that society, but no act of will can sever them from the body politic. When prisoners emerge from the shadows to press a constitutional claim, they invoke no alien set of principles drawn from a distant culture. Rather, they speak the language of the charter upon which all of us rely to hold official power accountable. They ask us to acknowledge that power exercised in the shadows must be restrained at least as diligently as power that acts in the sunlight.

In reviewing a prisoner's claim of the infringement of a constitutional right, we must therefore begin from the premise that, as members of this society, prisoners retain constitutional rights that limit the exercise of official authority against them. At the same time, we must acknowledge that incarceration by its nature changes an individual's status in society. Prison officials have the difficult and often thankless job of preserving security in a potentially explosive setting, as well as of attempting to provide rehabilitation that prepares some inmates for re-entry into the social mainstream. Both these demands require the curtailment and elimination of certain rights.

The challenge for this Court is to determine how best to protect those prisoners' rights that remain. Our objective in selecting a standard of review is therefore not, as the Court declares, "[t]o ensure that courts afford appropriate deference to prison officials." The Constitution was not adopted as a means of enhancing the efficiency with which government officials conduct their affairs, nor as a blueprint for ensuring sufficient reliance on administrative expertise. Rather, it was meant to provide a bulwark against infringements that might otherwise be justified as necessary expedients of governing. The practice of Europe, wrote James Madison, was "charters of liberty . . . granted by power"; of America, "charters of power granted by liberty." While we must give due consideration to the needs of those in power, this Court's role is to ensure that fundamental *restraints* on that power are enforced.

In my view, adoption of "reasonableness" as a standard of review for *all* constitutional challenges by inmates is inadequate to this task. Such a standard is categorically deferential, and does not discriminate among degrees of deprivation. From this perspective, restricting use of the prison library to certain hours warrants the same level of scrutiny as preventing inmates from reading at all. Various "factors" may be weighed differently in each situation, but the message to prison officials is clear: merely act "reasonably" and your actions will be upheld. If a directive that officials act "reasonably" were deemed sufficient to check all exercises of power, the Constitution would hardly be necessary. Yet the

Court deems this single standard adequate to restrain *any* type of conduct in which prison officials might engage.

It is true that the degree of deprivation is one of the factors in the Court's reasonableness determination. This by itself does not make the standard of review appropriate, however. If it did, we would need but a single standard for evaluating all constitutional claims, as long as every relevant factor were considered under its rubric. Clearly, we have never followed such an approach. A standard of review frames the terms in which justification may be offered, and thus delineates the boundaries within which argument may take place. The use of differing levels of scrutiny proclaims that on some occasions official power must justify itself in a way that otherwise it need not. A relatively strict standard of review is a signal that a decree prohibiting a political demonstration on the basis of the participants' political beliefs is of more serious concern, and therefore will be scrutinized more closely, than a rule limiting the number of demonstrations that may take place downtown at noon.

Thus, even if the absolute nature of the deprivation may be taken into account in the Court's formulation, it makes a difference that this is merely one factor in determining if official conduct is "reasonable." Once we provide such an elastic and deferential principle of justification, "[t]he principle . . . lies about like a loaded weapon ready for the hand of any authority that can bring forth a plausible claim of an urgent need. Every repetition imbeds that principle more deeply in our law and thinking and expands it to new purposes." *Korematsu v. United States* (Jackson, J., dissenting). Mere assertions of exigency have a way of providing a colorable defense for governmental deprivation, and we should be especially wary of expansive delegations of power to those who wield it on the margins of society. Prisons are too often shielded from public view; there is no need to make them virtually invisible.

An approach better suited to the sensitive task of protecting the constitutional rights of inmates is laid out by Judge Kaufman in *Abdul Wali v. Coughlin*. That approach maintains that the degree of scrutiny of prison regulations should depend on "the nature of the right being asserted by prisoners, the type of activity in which they seek to engage, and whether the challenged restriction works a total deprivation (as opposed to a mere limitation) on the exercise of that right." *Id.* Essentially, if the activity in which inmates seek to engage is presumptively dangerous, or if a regulation merely restricts the time, place, or manner in which prisoners may exercise a right, a prison regulation will be invalidated only if there is no reasonable justification for official action. Where exercise of the asserted right is not presumptively dangerous, however, and where the prison has completely deprived an inmate of that right, then prison officials must show that "a particular restriction is necessary to further an important governmental interest, and that the limitations on freedoms occasioned by the restrictions are no greater than necessary to effectuate the governmental objective involved." *Id.*

The court's analytical framework in *Abdul Wali* recognizes that in many instances it is inappropriate for courts "to substitute our judgments for those of trained professionals with years of firsthand experience." It would thus apply a standard of review identical to the Court's "reasonableness" standard in a significant percentage of cases. At the same time, the *Abdul Wali* approach takes seriously the Constitution's function of requiring that official power be called to account when it completely deprives a person of a right that society regards as basic. In this limited number of cases, it would require more than a demonstration of "reasonableness" to justify such infringement. To the extent that prison is meant to inculcate a respect for social and legal norms, a requirement that prison officials persuasively demonstrate the need for the absolute deprivation of inmate rights is consistent with that end. Furthermore, prison officials are in control of the evidence that is essential to establish the superiority of such deprivation over other alternatives. It is thus only fair for these officials to be held to a stringent standard of review in such extreme cases.

The prison in this case has completely prevented respondent inmates from attending the central religious service of their Muslim faith. I would therefore hold prison officials to the standard articulated in *Abdul Wali*, and would find their proffered justifications wanting. The State has neither demonstrated that the restriction is necessary to further an important objective nor proved that less extreme measures may not serve its purpose. Even if I accepted the Court's standard of review, however, I could not conclude on this record that prison officials have proved that it is reasonable to preclude respondents from attending Jumu'ah. Petitioners have provided mere unsubstantiated assertions that the plausible alternatives proposed by respondents are infeasible.

II

*** The Court in this case acknowledges that "respondents' sincerely held religious beliefs compe[l] attendance at Jumu'ah," and concedes that there are "no alternative means of attending Jumu'ah." Nonetheless, the Court finds that prison policy does not work a complete deprivation of respondents' asserted religious right, because respondents have the opportunity to participate in other religious activities. This analysis ignores the fact that, as the District Court found, Jumu'ah is the central religious ceremony of Muslims * * * [that] provides a special time in which Muslims "assert their identity as a community covenanted to God." As a result:

> unlike other Muslim prayers which are performed individually and can be made up if missed, the Jumu'ah is obligatory, cannot be made up, and must be performed in congregation. The Jumu'ah is therefore regarded as the central service of the Muslim religion, and the obligation to attend is commanded by the Qur'an, the central book of the Muslim religion.

Jumu'ah therefore cannot be regarded as one of several essentially fungible religious practices. The ability to engage in other religious activities cannot obscure the fact that the denial at issue in this case is absolute: respondents are completely foreclosed from participating in the core ceremony that reflects their membership in a particular religious community. If a Catholic prisoner were prevented from attending Mass on Sunday, few would regard that deprivation as anything but absolute, even if the prisoner were afforded other opportunities to pray, to discuss the Catholic faith with others, and even to avoid eating meat on Friday if that were a preference. Prison officials in this case therefore cannot show that " 'other avenues' remain available for the exercise of the asserted right." *Turner v. Safley* (quoting *Jones v. North Carolina Prisoners' Union*).

* * * [T]he infliction of an absolute deprivation should require more than mere assertion that such a deprivation is necessary. In particular, "the existence of obvious, easy alternatives may be evidence that the regulation is not reasonable, but is an 'exaggerated response' to prison concerns." In this case, petitioners have not established the reasonableness of their policy, because they have provided only bare assertions that the proposals for accommodation offered by respondents are infeasible. * * *

That Muslim inmates are able to participate in Jumu'ah throughout the entire federal prison system suggests that the practice is, under normal circumstances, compatible with the demands of prison administration. Indeed, the Leesburg State Prison permitted participation in this ceremony for five years, and experienced no threats to security or safety as a result. In light of both standard federal prison practice and Leesburg's own past practice, a reasonableness test in this case demands at least minimal substantiation by prison officials that alternatives that would permit participation in Jumu'ah are infeasible. * * *

IV

* * *

Incarceration by its nature denies a prisoner participation in the larger human community. To deny the opportunity to affirm membership in a spiritual community, however, may extinguish an inmate's last source of hope for dignity and redemption. Such a denial requires more justification than mere assertion that any other course of action is infeasible. While I would prefer that this case be analyzed under the approach set out in Part I, I would at a minimum remand to the District Court for an analysis of respondents' claims in accordance with the standard enunciated by the Court in * * * this case. I therefore dissent.

❀ 3 ❀

ALONE AGAINST THE STATE

The preceding two chapters concerned individual rights that are, at least in some sense, also collective rights. Communication requires two: a writer and a reader, a speaker and listener, a protestor and an observer. Similarly, while religious beliefs are to some extent profoundly personal, they also normally imply the existence of a community of people who share those beliefs.

This chapter, however, explores those situations when an individual is alone against the state, and therefore most vulnerable. This occurs most commonly when an individual is accused of a crime. Yet it can also occur whenever the state musters its vast resources against one person, such as when an individual is threatened with commitment to a mental hospital. Even when the state seeks merely to terminate the public assistance that a welfare recipient needs for survival, the confrontation involves a powerful and often uncompromising state against a solitary individual.

When the Supreme Court looked at these issues, it often placed great weight on institutional concerns and administrative burdens. Justice Brennan was cognizant of such considerations, yet he never failed to view the matter from the perspective of the individual as well. Throughout his tenure on the Court, Brennan never lost sight of or empathy for the predicament of such individuals. The Court often assumed that the person in these settings either needed no assistance, as in *United States v. Ash*, or had adequate allies, as in *Parham v. J.R.* Brennan knew better.

Many object to Brennan's expansive view of individual rights. While recognizing that the Bill of Rights was designed to protect "the people" from "the government," they argue that when the state acts legislatively, through the electorate's representatives, it is "the people" who are acting. In such instances, they insist, courts should defer to the will of the majority.

Brennan believed that majorities could take care of themselves through the legislative process. He was less convinced that solitary human beings, particularly those marginalized by society, could do so. From his perspective, the Bill of Rights requires that the rights of individuals, including—and sometimes, especially—the rights of criminal defendants, be safeguarded against possible overreaching by the majority. To ensure adequate protection for individuals, in his view, the Court is obliged on some occasions to interpret the Bill of Rights broadly. The Court has this unique role in upholding the constitutional rights of the individual because there is no one else.

SCHMERBER V. CALIFORNIA

June 20, 1966

Although Justice Brennan is renowned for his opinions protecting the rights of individuals against the state, he was not hostile to the reasonable and legitimate needs of government. Nor did he blindly assume that every asserted civil rights claim was valid. In this case, Brennan did not side with the individual. Instead he authored the opinion for the 5-4 majority permitting the warrantless extraction of blood from a drunk driving suspect over the driver's objection.

The driver in this case argued that the forcible extraction of his blood violated his Fourth Amendment right to be free from unreasonable searches and seizures. He also claimed that using the results of the involuntary blood test in his criminal prosecution infringed on his Fifth Amendment right against self-incrimination.

Brennan easily dismissed the driver's unreasonable search claim by noting that probable cause existed for the action and by concluding that requiring the police officer in charge to procure a warrant from a judicial official was impractical. This is because "the percentage of alcohol in the blood begins to diminish shortly after drinking stops," and because there would be no time for the police to seek out a magistrate while also investigating the accident scene and transporting those injured—including the accused—to a hospital. This analysis is quite consistent with both prior and subsequent Supreme Court jurisprudence in the area and, while certainly notable, is fairly unremarkable.

The action Brennan and the Court took with respect to the self-incrimination claim was far more significant. Two years earlier, Brennan wrote the Court's opinion in *Malloy v. Hogan* (1964), which held the Fifth Amendment's mandate that "no person shall be compelled in any criminal case to be a witness against himself" applies in state court proceedings. Just the previous week, the Court issued its landmark opinion in *Miranda v. Arizona* (1966), which required that criminal suspects be informed of their right to remain silent while in police custody and undergoing interrogation. That ruling effectively applied the privilege against self-incrimination to pretrial, investigatory proceedings. The decision here, however, severely limits the right against self-incrimination.

In *Malloy*, Brennan was concerned that criminal defendants without a privilege against self-incrimination would be faced with a "cruel trilemma": provide incriminating testimony, commit perjury, or refuse to testify and risk being cited for contempt, each of which subject the defendant to incarceration. In this case, however, because the driver's blood and not his testimony was being extracted, that trilemma was not present. Thus the principal rationale for the privilege was absent. Similarly, one of the primary considerations underlying *Miranda*, the unreliability of coerced confessions, also was inapplicable. The Court therefore concluded that the police may conduct involuntary blood tests of drunk driving suspects.

In dissent, Justices Black and Douglas criticized both Brennan's restriction of the privilege against self-incrimination to the accused's own statements and his conclusion that physical evidence is not communicative. They maintained that while blood test results are not oral testimony, some results "can certainly 'communicate' to a court and jury the fact of guilt." As Justice Brennan noted, however, prohibiting use of the blood-test results on self-incrimination grounds would have raised serious concerns about the propriety of many traditional police investigatory techniques, such as fingerprinting, photographing, line-ups, and the comparison of handwriting and voice samples—techniques long upheld by courts at all levels.

Thirty years later, *Schmerber* continues to articulate the limits of the Fifth Amendment's privilege against self-incrimination. Scientific advances have made DNA and other newer types of tests a routine part of many criminal investigations. The principles expressed in *Schmerber* have allowed the results of those tests to be used at trial, enhancing the likelihood of conviction for those—and only those—truly guilty.

Justice Brennan wrote the majority opinion, joined by Justices Clark, Harlan, Stewart, and White. Chief Justice Warren and Justices Black, Douglas, and Fortas dissented.

✧　✧　✧

Mr. Justice BRENNAN delivered the opinion of the Court.

Petitioner was convicted in Los Angeles Municipal Court of the criminal offense of driving an automobile while under the influence of intoxicating liquor. He had been arrested at a hospital while receiving treatment for injuries suffered in an accident involving the automobile that he had apparently been driving. At the direction of a police officer, a blood sample was then withdrawn from petitioner's body by a physician at the hospital. The chemical analysis of this sample revealed a percent by weight of alcohol in his blood at the time of the offense which indicated intoxication, and the report of this analysis was admitted in evidence at the trial. Petitioner objected to receipt of this evidence of the analysis on the ground that the blood had been withdrawn despite his refusal, on the advice of his counsel, to consent to the test. He contended that in that circumstance the withdrawal of the blood and the admission of the analysis in evidence denied him due process of law under the Fourteenth Amendment, [by infringing upon the following] specific guarantees of the Bill of Rights secured against the States by that Amendment: his privilege against self-incrimination under the Fifth Amendment. * * * The Appellate Department of the California Superior Court rejected these contentions and affirmed the conviction. * * * We affirm.

* * *

THE PRIVILEGE AGAINST SELF-INCRIMINATION CLAIM

* * * [We] must now decide whether the withdrawal of the blood and admission in evidence of the analysis involved in this case violated petitioner's privilege. We hold that the privilege protects an accused only from being compelled to testify against himself, or otherwise provide the State with evidence of a testimonial or communicative nature, and that the withdrawal of blood and use of the analysis in question in this case did not involve compulsion to these ends.

It could not be denied that in requiring petitioner to submit to the withdrawal and chemical analysis of his blood the State compelled him to submit to an attempt to discover evidence that might be used to prosecute him for a criminal offense. He submitted only after the police officer rejected his objection and directed the physician to proceed. The officer's direction to the physician to administer the test over petitioner's objection constituted compulsion for the purposes of the privilege. The critical question, then, is whether petitioner was thus compelled "to be a witness against himself."

If the scope of the privilege coincided with the complex of values it helps to protect, we might be obliged to conclude that the privilege was violated. In *Miranda v. Arizona*, the Court said of the interests protected by the privilege:

> All these policies point to one overriding thought: the constitutional foundation underlying the privilege is the respect a government—state or federal—must accord to the dignity and integrity of its citizens. To maintain a "fair state-individual balance," to require the government "to shoulder the entire load," . . . to respect the inviolability of the human personality, our accusatory system of criminal justice demands that the government seeking to punish an individual produce the evidence against him by its own independent labors, rather than by the cruel, simple expedient of compelling it from his own mouth.

The withdrawal of blood necessarily involves puncturing the skin for extraction, and the percent by weight of alcohol in that blood, as established by chemical analysis, is evidence of criminal guilt. Compelled submission fails on one view to respect the "inviolability of the human personality." Moreover, since it enables the State to rely on evidence forced from the accused, the compulsion violates at least one meaning of the requirement that the State procure the evidence against an accused "by its own independent labors."

As the passage in *Miranda* implicitly recognizes, however, the privilege has never been given the full scope which the values it helps to protect suggest. History and a long line of authorities in lower courts have consistently limited its protection to situations in which the State seeks to submerge those values by obtaining the evidence against an accused through "the cruel, simple expedient of compelling it from his own mouth. . . . In sum, the privilege is fulfilled only when the person is guaranteed the right to remain silent unless he chooses to speak in the unfettered exercise of his own will." *Id.* The leading case in this Court is *Holt v. United States.* There the question was whether evidence was admissible that the accused, prior to trial and over his protest, put on a blouse that fitted him. It was contended that compelling the accused to submit to the demand that he model the blouse violated the privilege. Mr. Justice Holmes, speaking for the Court, rejected the argument as "based upon an extravagant extension of the Fifth Amendment," and went on to say:

[T]he prohibition of compelling a man in a criminal court to be witness against himself is a prohibition of the use of physical or moral compulsion to extort communications from him, not an exclusion of his body as evidence when it may be material. The objection in principle would forbid a jury to look at a prisoner and compare his features with a photograph in proof.

It is clear that the protection of the privilege reaches an accused's communications, whatever form they might take, and the compulsion of responses which are also communications, for example, compliance with a subpoena to produce one's papers. On the other hand, both federal and state courts have usually held that it offers no protection against compulsion to submit to fingerprinting, photographing, or measurements, to write or speak for identification, to appear in court, to stand, to assume a stance, to walk, or to make a particular gesture. The distinction which has emerged, often expressed in different ways, is that the privilege is a bar against compelling "communications" or "testimony," but that compulsion which makes a suspect or accused the source of "real or physical evidence" does not violate it.

Although we agree that this distinction is a helpful framework for analysis, we are not to be understood to agree with past applications in all instances. There will be many cases in which such a distinction is not readily drawn. Some tests seemingly directed to obtain "physical evidence," for example, lie detector tests measuring changes in body function during interrogation, may actually be directed to eliciting responses which are essentially testimonial. To compel a person to submit to testing in which an effort will be made to determine his guilt or innocence on the basis of physiological responses, whether willed or not, is to evoke the spirit and history of the Fifth Amendment. Such situations call to mind the principle that the protection of the privilege "is as broad as the mischief against which it seeks to guard." *Counselman v. Hitchcock*.

In the present case, however, no such problem of application is presented. Not even a shadow of testimonial compulsion upon or enforced communication by the accused was involved either in the extraction or in the chemical analysis. Petitioner's testimonial capacities were in no way implicated; indeed, his participation, except as a donor, was irrelevant to the results of the test, which depend on chemical analysis and on that alone.[9] Since the blood test evidence, although an incriminating product of compulsion, was neither petitioner's testimony nor evidence relating to some communicative act or writing by the petitioner, it was not inadmissible on privilege grounds.

* * *

Affirmed.

---

9. This conclusion would not necessarily govern had the State tried to show that the accused had incriminated himself when told that he would have to be tested. Such incriminating evidence may be an unavoidable by-product of the compulsion to take the test, especially for an individual who fears the extraction or opposes it on religious grounds. If it wishes to compel persons to submit to such attempts to discover evidence, the State may have to forgo the advantage of any *testimonial* products of administering the test—products which would fall within the privilege. Indeed, there may be circumstances in which the pain, danger, or severity of an operation would almost inevitably cause a person to prefer confession to undergoing the "search," and nothing we say today should be taken as establishing the permissibility of compulsion in that case. But no such situation is presented in this case. * * *

GOLDBERG V. KELLY

March 23, 1970

Justice Brennan's majority opinion in this case is a classic illustration of his approach to constitutional decision making. The legal issue presented was whether welfare recipients are entitled to both notice and a hearing before the state terminates their public assistance. Under the Fourteenth Amendment, no state may "deprive a person of life, liberty, or property without due process of law." This language, whose origins date back to the Magna Carta, directs the government to comply with proper procedures in dealing with its people. The plaintiffs claimed that their due process rights were violated when the government, here the State of New York, cut off their aid before notifying them or affording them a meaningful opportunity to be heard.

Brennan did not approach the issue from a textualist's perspective. He did not dwell on whether welfare benefits qualify as a "property" interest protected by the Fourteenth Amendment. He readily determined that this financial aid was a statutory entitlement for persons who qualify. Instead, Brennan defined the issue as a larger question of essential fairness.

To Brennan and the other members of the majority, it was inappropriate to deprive human beings of their sole source of income without prior warning or an opportunity to contest the decision. Instead of focusing on a narrow and sterile legal issue, Brennan looked at the impact of the government's action on people's lives. The overriding consideration was that a basic societal commitment to human dignity and well-being is breached when an individual is deprived of the means to acquire basic subsistence such as food, clothing, and shelter while the person's eligibility for such aid remains contested and undetermined. By requiring a pre-termination hearing, Brennan recognized that the state will incur greater expense, yet he concluded that the interests of both the individual and the state in avoiding an erroneous termination outweigh the fiscal and administrative burden.

When discussing this case in a 1987 address titled "Reason, Passion, and the 'Progress of Law,'" Justice Brennan stressed the importance of passion and empathy—in addition to reason—in governmental decision making. He credited this decision with starting a national discussion about "the responsibilities of the bureaucratic state to its citizens." Now, almost two decades later, that discussion has taken a decidedly different turn; state and federal legislation enacted in the 1990s may well have ended welfare as we know it. Yet the changing status of public assistance programs may actually underscore the importance of Brennan's commitment to ensuring that human dignity is maintained when the government acts.

Justice Brennan wrote the opinion of the Court, joined by Justices Douglas, Harlan, White, and Marshall. Chief Justice Warren and Justices Black and Stewart dissented.

✿   ✿   ✿

MR. JUSTICE BRENNAN delivered the opinion of the Court.

The question for decision is whether a State that terminates public assistance payments to a particular recipient without affording him the opportunity for an evidentiary hearing prior to termination denies the recipient procedural due process in violation of the Due Process Clause of the Fourteenth Amendment.

This action was brought in the District Court for the Southern District of New York by residents of New York City receiving financial aid under the federally assisted program of Aid to Families with Dependent Children (AFDC) or under New York State's general Home Relief program. Their complaint alleged that the New York State and New York City officials administering these programs terminated, or were about to terminate, such aid without prior notice and hearing, thereby denying them due process of law. At the time the suits were filed there was no requirement of prior notice or hearing of any kind before termination of financial aid. However, the State and city adopted procedures for notice and hearing after the suits were brought, and the plaintiffs, appellees here, then challenged the constitutional adequacy of those procedures.

* * *

I

The constitutional issue to be decided, therefore, is the narrow one whether the Due Process Clause requires that the recipient be afforded an evidentiary hearing *before* the termination of benefits.[7] The District

---

7. Appellant does not question the recipient's due process right to evidentiary review after termination. * * *

Court held that only a pre-termination evidentiary hearing would satisfy the constitutional command, and rejected the argument of the
state and city officials that the combination of the post-termination
"fair hearing" with the informal pre-termination review disposed of all
due process claims. * * * We affirm.

Appellant does not contend that procedural due process is not applicable to the termination of welfare benefits. Such benefits are a matter
of statutory entitlement for persons qualified to receive them. Their
termination involves state action that adjudicates important rights. The
constitutional challenge cannot be answered by an argument that public assistance benefits are "a 'privilege' and not a 'right.'" *Shapiro v.
Thompson*. Relevant constitutional restraints apply as much to the withdrawal of public assistance benefits as to disqualification for unemployment compensation, *Sherbert v. Verner*; or to denial of a tax exemption,
Speiser v. Randall; or to discharge from public employment. * * *

It is true, of course, that some governmental benefits may be admin-
istratively terminated without affording the recipient a pre-termination evidentiary hearing. But we agree with the District Court that
when welfare is discontinued, only a pre-termination evidentiary hearing provides the recipient with procedural due process. For qualified recipients, welfare provides the means to obtain essential food, clothing,
housing, and medical care. Thus the crucial factor in this context—a
factor not present in the case of the blacklisted government contractor,
the discharged government employee, the taxpayer denied a tax exemption, or virtually anyone else whose governmental entitlements are
ended—is that termination of aid pending resolution of a controversy
over eligibility may deprive an *eligible* recipient of the very means by
which to live while he waits. Since he lacks independent resources, his
situation becomes immediately desperate. His need to concentrate upon
finding the means for daily subsistence, in turn, adversely affects his
ability to seek redress from the welfare bureaucracy.

Moreover, important governmental interests are promoted by affording recipients a pre-termination evidentiary hearing. From its founding
the Nation's basic commitment has been to foster the dignity and well-
being of all persons within its borders. We have come to recognize that
forces not within the control of the poor contribute to their poverty.
This perception, against the background of our traditions, has significantly influenced the development of the contemporary public assistance system. Welfare, by meeting the basic demands of subsistence,
can help bring within the reach of the poor the same opportunities that

are available to others to participate meaningfully in the life of the community. At the same time, welfare guards against the societal malaise that may flow from a widespread sense of unjustified frustration and insecurity. Public assistance, then, is not mere charity, but a means to "promote the general Welfare, and secure the Blessings of Liberty to ourselves and our Posterity." The same governmental interests that counsel the provision of welfare, counsel as well its uninterrupted provision to those eligible to receive it; pre-termination evidentiary hearings are indispensable to that end.

Appellant does not challenge the force of these considerations but argues that they are outweighed by countervailing governmental interests in conserving fiscal and administrative resources. These interests, the argument goes, justify the delay of any evidentiary hearing until after discontinuance of the grants. Summary adjudication protects the public fisc by stopping payments promptly upon discovery of reason to believe that a recipient is no longer eligible. Since most terminations are accepted without challenge, summary adjudication also conserves both the fisc and administrative time and energy by reducing the number of evidentiary hearings actually held.

We agree with the District Court, however, that these governmental interests are not overriding in the welfare context. The requirement of a prior hearing doubtless involves some greater expense, and the benefits paid to ineligible recipients pending decision at the hearing probably cannot be recouped, since these recipients are likely to be judgment-proof. But the State is not without weapons to minimize these increased costs. Much of the drain on fiscal and administrative resources can be reduced by developing procedures for prompt pre-termination hearings and by skillful use of personnel and facilities. Indeed, the very provision for a post-termination evidentiary hearing in New York's Home Relief program is itself cogent evidence that the State recognizes the primacy of the public interest in correct eligibility determinations and therefore in the provision of procedural safeguards. Thus, the interest of the eligible recipient in uninterrupted receipt of public assistance, coupled with the State's interest that his payments not be erroneously terminated, clearly outweighs the State's competing concern to prevent any increase in its fiscal and administrative burdens. As the District Court correctly concluded, "[the] stakes are simply too high for the welfare recipient, and the possibility for honest error or irritable misjudgment too great, to allow termination of aid without giving the recipient a chance, if he so desires, to be fully informed of the case against him so that he may contest its basis and produce evidence in rebuttal."

II

We also agree with the District Court, however, that the pre-termination hearing need not take the form of a judicial or quasi-judicial trial. We bear in mind that the statutory "fair hearing" will provide the recipient with a full administrative review.[14] Accordingly, the pre-termination hearing has one function only: to produce an initial determination of the validity of the welfare department's grounds for discontinuance of payments in order to protect a recipient against an erroneous termination of his benefits. Thus, a complete record and a comprehensive opinion, which would serve primarily to facilitate judicial review and to guide future decisions, need not be provided at the pre-termination stage. We recognize, too, that both welfare authorities and recipients have an interest in relatively speedy resolution of questions of eligibility, that they are used to dealing with one another informally, and that some welfare departments have very burdensome caseloads. These considerations justify the limitation of the pre-termination hearing to minimum procedural safeguards, adapted to the particular characteristics of welfare recipients, and to the limited nature of the controversies to be resolved. We wish to add that we, no less than the dissenters, recognize the importance of not imposing upon the States or the Federal Government in this developing field of law any procedural requirements beyond those demanded by rudimentary due process.

"The fundamental requisite of due process of law is the opportunity to be heard." *Grannis v. Ordean.* The hearing must be "at a meaningful time and in a meaningful manner." *Armstrong v. Manzo.* In the present context these principles require that a recipient have timely and adequate notice detailing the reasons for a proposed termination, and an effective opportunity to defend by confronting any adverse witnesses and by presenting his own arguments and evidence orally. These rights are important in cases such as those before us, where recipients have challenged proposed terminations as resting on incorrect or misleading

14. Due process does not, of course, require two hearings. If, for example, a State simply wishes to continue benefits until after a "fair" hearing there will be no need for a preliminary hearing.

factual premises or on misapplication of rules or policies to the facts of particular cases.

We are not prepared to say that the seven-day notice currently provided by New York City is constitutionally insufficient *per se*, although there may be cases where fairness would require that a longer time be given. Nor do we see any constitutional deficiency in the content or form of the notice. * * * [However, t]he city's procedures presently do not permit recipients to appear personally with or without counsel before the official who finally determines continued eligibility. Thus a recipient is not permitted to present evidence to that official orally, or to confront or cross-examine adverse witnesses. These omissions are fatal to the constitutional adequacy of the procedures.

The opportunity to be heard must be tailored to the capacities and circumstances of those who are to be heard. It is not enough that a welfare recipient may present his position to the decision maker in writing or secondhand through his caseworker. Written submissions are an unrealistic option for most recipients, who lack the educational attainment necessary to write effectively and who cannot obtain professional assistance. * * * The second-hand presentation to the decisionmaker by the caseworker has its own deficiencies; since the caseworker usually gathers the facts upon which the charge of ineligibility rests, the presentation of the recipient's side of the controversy cannot safely be left to him. Therefore a recipient must be allowed to state his position orally. * * *

Affirmed.

FURMAN V. GEORGIA

June 29, 1972

In this 5-4 decision, which actually is a consolidation of three separate capital punishment cases, the Supreme Court issued a succinct statement striking down state death penalty statutes by declaring that "[t]he Court holds that the imposition and carrying out of the death penalty in these cases constitutes cruel and unusual punishment in violation of the eighth and fourteenth amendments." The brevity of this holding belies the overall length—261 pages in total—and the conflicts among the concurring and dissenting opinions. In fact, each Justice issued a separate opinion, and none joined the opinion of another. Nevertheless, there were recurring themes.

The primary consideration for Justices Douglas, Stewart, and White, who along with Justices Brennan and Marshall formed the majority, was what they saw as the arbitrary, capricious, and discriminatory manner in which the death penalty was administered. Unlike current capital punishment statutory schemes, sentencing procedures in 1972 provided little or no guidance to either judges or juries about what circumstances might merit the imposition of a death sentence.

For Brennan and Marshall, however, the arbitrary and discriminatory application of capital punishment was only part of its constitutional infirmity. In their view, the death penalty is in all circumstances a "cruel and unusual punishment."

In his concurring opinion, Brennan examined the meaning of the Cruel and Unusual Punishments Clause in the Eighth Amendment by looking to its plain meaning and past judicial interpretation. He determined that the phrase could not be precisely defined and that the intent of the Framers in including this provision in the Bill of Rights was unclear. More significant, he believed that its meaning must be drawn from the "evolving standards of decency that mark the progress of a maturing society." This willingness to interpret the Constitution as a living document is what distinguished Brennan's method of constitutional interpretation from that of many of his judicial colleagues.

Brennan's paramount concern was whether a challenged punishment "comports with human dignity," a concern that two years earlier had been an

139

underpinning of his majority opinion in *Goldberg v. Kelly* (p. 133). Punishments that did not comport with human dignity were, in his view, "cruel and unusual." Brennan set forth principles to aid in this determination, and concluded that the death penalty is constitutionally impermissible.

In response to this case, many state legislatures amended their sentencing procedures. In an appeal to the views of Justices Douglas, Stewart, and White, they attempted to "suitably direct and limit" the discretion of judges and juries without usurping their authority to determine the appropriate punishment in a particular case. As a result, four years later in *Gregg v. Georgia* (1976), the Court upheld the new approach by a vote of 7–2.

Having taken a firm stand in *Furman*, Brennan and Marshall dissented in *Gregg*, and they continued to do so for the remainder of their terms every time the Court refused to review a death penalty case, in all, on some 2,500 petitions. In a 1985 address at Hastings College of Law titled "In Defense of Dissents," Brennan explained the varied reasons why judges dissent. He presented his perspective on, as he characterized it, "a special kind of dissent: the repeated dissent in which a justice refuses to yield to the views of the majority although persistently rebuffed by them." He used the death penalty cases as an example. This sustained opposition, according to Brennan, is a form of legitimate line-drawing. Mindful of precedent, it remains beholden to a larger constitutional duty to expose the majority's departure from the essential meaning of a particular constitutional principle.

Brennan may not have convinced a significant number of his colleagues, much less a majority of the American people, of the correctness of his position, but there is evidence of at least some incremental movement in his direction. Justice Blackmun, who throughout his tenure on the Court consistently voted with the majority to uphold the death penalty, finally altered his stance shortly before he retired. In *Callins v. Collins* (1994), Blackmun announced that he was no longer willing to "tinker with the machinery of death." He proclaimed that the death penalty experiment had failed and that capital punishment "was fraught with arbitrariness, discrimination, caprice, and mistake."

Today, the United States stands alone among Western industrialized nations in its use of the death penalty. This fact may well be a gauge of the "evolving standards of decency" Brennan wrote about in *Furman*. While pressure from international and religious communities may ultimately effect a change in our country's social policy, current public sentiment appears as strongly supportive of capital punishment as it ever has been. Even conclusive evidence that some of those executed were in fact innocent has not moved the public to oppose the death penalty generally. Nevertheless, Brennan's consistent public pronouncements in opposition to the death penalty, an opposition that extended for a quarter century and grew even more forceful after his retirement, made him the conscience of the Court—and perhaps also of the community—on this issue.

Justices Douglas, Brennan, Stewart, White, and Marshall concurred in the judgment of the Court. Chief Justice Burger and Justices Blackmun, Powell, and Rehnquist dissented.

◌ ◌ ◌

Mr. Justice BRENNAN, concurring.

The question presented in these cases is whether death is today a punishment for crime that is "cruel and unusual" and consequently, by virtue of the Eighth and Fourteenth Amendments, beyond the power of the State to inflict.

Almost a century ago, this Court observed that "[d]ifficulty would attend the effort to define with exactness the extent of the constitutional provision which provides that cruel and unusual punishments shall not be inflicted." *Wilkerson v. Utah.* Less than 15 years ago, it was again noted that "[t]he exact scope of the constitutional phrase "cruel and unusual" has not been detailed by this Court." *Trop v. Dulles.* Those statements remain true today. The Cruel and Unusual Punishments Clause, like the other great clauses of the Constitution, is not susceptible of precise definition. Yet we know that the values and ideals it embodies are basic to our scheme of government. And we know also that the Clause imposes upon this Court the duty, when the issue is properly presented, to determine the constitutional validity of a challenged punishment, whatever that punishment may be. In these cases, "[t]hat issue confronts us, and the task of resolving it is inescapably ours." *Id.*

I

We have very little evidence of the Framers' intent in including the Cruel and Unusual Punishments Clause among those restraints upon the new Government enumerated in the Bill of Rights. * * * We know that the Framers' concern was directed specifically at the exercise of legislative power. They included in the Bill of Rights a prohibition upon "cruel and unusual punishments" precisely because the legislature would otherwise have had the unfettered power to prescribe punishments for crimes. Yet we cannot now know exactly what the Framers thought "cruel and unusual punishments" were. Certainly they intended to ban torturous punishments, but the available evidence does not support the further conclusion that *only* torturous punishments were to be outlawed. * * * Nor did they intend simply to forbid punishments considered "cruel and unusual" at the time. The "import" of the Clause is, indeed, "indefinite," and for good reason. A constitutional provision "is enacted, it is true, from an experience of evils, but its general language should not, therefore, be necessarily confined to the form that evil had theretofore taken. Time works changes, brings into existence new conditions and purposes. Therefore a principle, to be vital, must be capable of wider application than the mischief which gave it birth." *Weems v. United States.*

* * *

II

Ours would indeed be a simple task were we required merely to measure a challenged punishment against those that history has long condemned. That narrow and unwarranted view of the Clause, however, was left behind with the 19th century. Our task today is more complex. We know "that the words of the [Clause] are not precise, and that their scope is not static." We know, therefore, that the Clause "must draw its meaning from the evolving standards of decency that mark the progress of a maturing society." *Trop v. Dulles.* That knowledge, of course, is but the beginning of the inquiry.

* * * [T]he Cruel and Unusual Punishments Clause prohibits the infliction of uncivilized and inhuman punishments. The State, even as it punishes, must treat its members with respect for their intrinsic worth as human beings. A punishment is "cruel and unusual," therefore, if it does not comport with human dignity.

This formulation, of course, does not of itself yield principles for assessing the constitutional validity of particular punishments. Nevertheless, even though "[t]his Court has had little occasion to give precise content to the [Clause]," *id.*, there are principles recognized in our cases and inherent in the Clause sufficient to permit a judicial determination whether a challenged punishment comports with human dignity.

The primary principle is that a punishment must not be so severe as to be degrading to the dignity of human beings. Pain, certainly, may be a factor in the judgment. * * * More than the presence of pain, however, is comprehended in the judgment that the extreme severity of a punishment makes it degrading to the dignity of human beings. The barbaric punishments condemned by history, "punishments which inflict torture, such as the rack, the thumb-screw, the iron boot, the stretching of limbs, and the like," are, of course, "attended with acute pain and suffering." *O'Neil v. Vermont*, (Field, J., dissenting). When we consider why they have been condemned, however, we realize that the pain involved is not the only reason. The true significance of these punishments is that they treat members of the human race as nonhumans, as objects to be toyed with and discarded. They are thus inconsistent with the fundamental premise of the Clause that even the vilest criminal remains a human being possessed of common human dignity.

* * *

In determining whether a punishment comports with human dignity, we are aided also by a second principle inherent in the Clause—that the State must not arbitrarily inflict a severe punishment. This principle derives from the notion that the State does not respect human dignity when, without reason, it inflicts upon some people a severe punishment that it does not inflict upon others. Indeed, the very words "cruel and unusual punishments" imply condemnation of the arbitrary infliction of severe punishments. * * *

A third principle inherent in the Clause is that a severe punishment must not be unacceptable to contemporary society. Rejection by society, of course, is a strong indication that a severe punishment does not comport with human dignity. In applying this principle, however, we must make certain that the judicial determination is as objective as possible. * * * Accordingly, the judicial task is to review the history of a challenged punishment and to examine society's present practices with respect to its use. Legislative authorization, of course, does not establish acceptance. The acceptability of a severe punishment is measured, not by its availability, for it might become so offensive to society as never to be inflicted, but by its use.

The final principle inherent in the Clause is that a severe punishment must not be excessive. A punishment is excessive under this principle if it is unnecessary: The infliction of a severe punishment by the State cannot comport with human dignity when it is nothing more than the pointless infliction of suffering. If there is a significantly less severe punishment adequate to achieve the purposes for which the punishment is inflicted, the punishment inflicted is unnecessary and therefore excessive.

* * *

III

The punishment challenged in these cases is death. * * * The question, then, is whether the deliberate infliction of death is today consistent with the command of the Clause that the State may not inflict punishments that do not comport with human dignity. I will analyze the punishment of death in terms of the principles set out above and the cumulative test to which they lead: It is a denial of human dignity for the State arbitrarily to subject a person to an unusually severe punishment that society has indicated it does not regard as acceptable, and that cannot be shown to serve any penal purpose more effectively than a significantly less drastic punishment. Under these principles and this test, death is today a "cruel and unusual" punishment.

Death is a unique punishment in the United States. In a society that so strongly affirms the sanctity of life, not surprisingly the common view is that death is the ultimate sanction. This natural human feeling appears all about us. There has been no national debate about punishment, in general or by imprisonment, comparable to the debate about the punishment of death. No other punishment has been so continuously restricted, nor has any State yet abolished prisons, as some have abolished this punishment. And those States that still inflict death reserve it for the most heinous crimes. Juries, of course, have always treated death cases differently, as have governors exercising their commutation powers. * * * This Court, too, almost always treats death cases as a class apart. * * *

The only explanation for the uniqueness of death is its extreme severity. Death is today an unusually severe punishment, unusual in its pain, in its finality, and in its enormity. No other existing punishment is comparable to death in terms of physical and mental suffering. Although our information is not conclusive, it appears that there is no method available that guarantees an immediate and painless death. Since the discontinuance of flogging as a constitutionally permissible punishment, death remains as the only punishment that may involve the conscious infliction of physical pain. In addition, we know that mental pain is an inseparable part of our practice of punishing criminals by death, for the prospect of pending execution exacts a frightful toll during the inevitable long wait between the imposition of sentence and the actual infliction of death. * * *

Death is truly an awesome punishment. The calculated killing of a human being by the State involves, by its very nature, a denial of the executed person's humanity. The contrast with the plight of a person punished by imprisonment is evident. An individual in prison does not lose "the right to have rights." A prisoner retains, for example, the constitutional rights to the free exercise of religion, to be free of cruel and unusual punishments, and to treatment as a "person" for purposes of due process of law and the equal protection of the laws. A prisoner remains a member of the human family. Moreover, he retains the right of access to the courts. His punishment is not irrevocable. Apart from the common charge, grounded upon the recognition of human fallibility, that the punishment of death must inevitably be inflicted upon innocent men, we know that death has been the lot of men whose convictions were unconstitutionally secured in view of later, retroactively applied, holdings of this Court. The punishment itself may have been unconstitutionally inflicted, yet the finality of death precludes relief. An executed person has indeed "lost the right to have rights." As one 19th century proponent of punishing criminals by death declared, "When a man is hung, there is an end of our relations with him. His execution is a way of saying, 'You are not fit for this world, take your chance elsewhere.'"

In comparison to all other punishments today, then, the deliberate extinguishment of human life by the State is uniquely degrading to human dignity. I would not hesitate to hold, on that ground alone, that death is today a "cruel and unusual" punishment, were it not that death is a punishment of longstanding usage and acceptance in this country. I therefore turn to the second principle—that the State may not arbitrarily inflict an unusually severe punishment.

The outstanding characteristic of our present practice of punishing criminals by death is the infrequency with which we resort to it. The evidence is conclusive that death is not the ordinary punishment for any crime.

* * *

When a country of over 200 million people inflicts an unusually severe punishment no more than 50 times a year, the inference is strong that the punishment is not being regularly and fairly applied. To dispel it would indeed require a clear showing of nonarbitrary infliction.

Although there are no exact figures available, we know that thousands of murders and rapes are committed annually in States where death is an authorized punishment for those crimes. However the rate of infliction is characterized—as "freakishly" or "spectacularly" rare, or simply as rare—it would take the purest sophistry to deny that death is inflicted in only a minute fraction of these cases. How much rarer, after all, could the infliction of death be?

When the punishment of death is inflicted in a trivial number of the cases in which it is legally available, the conclusion is virtually inescapable that it is being inflicted arbitrarily. Indeed, it smacks of little more than a lottery system. The States claim, however, that this rarity is evidence not of arbitrariness, but of informed selectivity: Death is inflicted, they say, only in "extreme" cases.

Informed selectivity, of course, is a value not to be denigrated. Yet presumably the States could make precisely the same claim if there were 10 executions per year, or five, or even if there were but one. That there may be as many as 50 per year does not strengthen the claim. When the rate of infliction is at this low level, it is highly implausible that only the worst criminals or the criminals who commit the worst crimes are selected for this punishment. No one has yet suggested a rational basis that could differentiate in those terms the few who die from the many who go to prison. Crimes and criminals simply do not admit of a distinction that can be drawn so finely as to explain, on that ground, the execution of such a tiny sample of those eligible. Certainly the laws that provide for this punishment do not attempt to draw that distinction; all cases to which the laws apply are necessarily "extreme." Nor is the distinction credible in fact. If, for example, petitioner Furman or his crime illustrates the "extreme," then nearly all murderers and their murders are also "extreme."[48] Furthermore, our procedures in death cases, rather than resulting in the selection of "extreme" cases for this punishment, actually sanction an arbitrary selection. For this Court has held that juries may, as they do, make the decision whether to impose a death sentence wholly unguided by standards governing that decision. In other words, our procedures are not constructed to guard against the totally capricious selection of criminals for the punishment of death.

Although it is difficult to imagine what further facts would be necessary in order to prove that death is, as my Brother Stewart puts it, "wantonly and . . . freakishly" inflicted, I need not conclude that arbitrary infliction is patently obvious. I am not considering this punishment by the isolated light of one principle. The probability of arbitrariness is sufficiently substantial that it can be relied upon, in combination with the other principles, in reaching a judgment on the constitutionality of this punishment.

When there is a strong probability that an unusually severe and degrading punishment is being inflicted arbitrarily, we may well expect that society will disapprove of its infliction. I turn, therefore, to the third principle. An examination of the history and present operation of the American practice of punishing criminals by death reveals that this punishment has been almost totally rejected by contemporary society.

I cannot add to my Brother Marshall's comprehensive treatment of the English and American history of this punishment. I emphasize, however, one significant conclusion that emerges from that history. From the beginning of our Nation, the punishment of death has stirred acute public controversy. Although pragmatic arguments for and against the punishment have been frequently advanced, this longstanding and heated controversy cannot be explained solely as the result of differ-

---

48. The victim surprised Furman in the act of burglarizing the victim's home in the middle of the night. While escaping, Furman killed the victim with one pistol shot fired through the closed kitchen door from the outside. At the trial, Furman gave his version of the killing:

They got me charged with murder and I admit, I admit going to these folks' home and they did caught me in there and I was coming back out, backing up and there was a wire down there on the floor. I was coming out backwards and fell back and I didn't intend to kill nobody. I didn't know they was behind the door. The gun went off and I didn't know nothing about no murder until they arrested me, and when the gun went off I was down on the floor and I got up and ran. That's all to it.

The Georgia Supreme Court accepted that version.

ences over the practical wisdom of a particular government policy. At bottom, the battle has been waged on moral grounds. The country has debated whether a society for which the dignity of the individual is the supreme value can, without a fundamental inconsistency, follow the practice of deliberately putting some of its members to death. * * * Thus, although "the death penalty has been employed throughout our history," *Trop v. Dulles*, in fact the history of this punishment is one of successive restriction. What was once a common punishment has become, in the context of a continuing moral debate, increasingly rare. The evolution of this punishment evidences, not that it is an inevitable part of the American scene, but that it has proved progressively more troublesome to the national conscience. * * *

The final principle to be considered is that an unusually severe and degrading punishment may not be excessive in view of the purposes for which it is inflicted. This principle, too, is related to the others. When there is a strong probability that the State is arbitrarily inflicting an unusually severe punishment that is subject to grave societal doubts, it is likely also that the punishment cannot be shown to be serving any penal purpose that could not be served equally well by some less severe punishment.

The States' primary claim is that death is a necessary punishment because it prevents the commission of capital crimes more effectively than any less severe punishment. The first part of this claim is that the infliction of death is necessary to stop the individuals executed from committing further crimes. The sufficient answer to this is that if a criminal convicted of a capital crime poses a danger to society, effective administration of the State's pardon and parole laws can delay or deny his release from prison, and techniques of isolation can eliminate or minimize the danger while he remains confined.

The more significant argument is that the threat of death prevents the commission of capital crimes because it deters potential criminals who would not be deterred by the threat of imprisonment. The argument is not based upon evidence that the threat of death is a superior deterrent. Indeed, as my Brother Marshall establishes, the available evidence uniformly indicates, although it does not conclusively prove, that the threat of death has no greater deterrent effect than the threat of imprisonment. The States argue, however, that they are entitled to rely upon common human experience, and that experience, they say, supports the conclusion that death must be a more effective deterrent than any less severe punishment. Because people fear death the most, the argument runs, the threat of death must be the greatest deterrent.

It is important to focus upon the precise import of this argument. It is not denied that many, and probably most, capital crimes cannot be deterred by the threat of punishment. Thus the argument can apply only to those who think rationally about the commission of capital crimes. Particularly is that true when the potential criminal, under this argument, must not only consider the risk of punishment, but also distinguish between two possible punishments. The concern, then, is with a particular type of potential criminal, the rational person who will commit a capital crime knowing that the punishment is long-term imprisonment, which may well be for the rest of his life, but will not commit the crime knowing that the punishment is death. On the face of it, the assumption that such persons exist is implausible.

* * *

There is, however, another aspect to the argument that the punishment of death is necessary for the protection of society. The infliction of death, the States urge, serves to manifest the community's outrage at the commission of the crime. It is, they say, a concrete public expression of moral indignation that inculcates respect for the law and helps assure a more peaceful community. Moreover, we are told, not only does the punishment of death exert this widespread moralizing influence upon community values, it also satisfies the popular demand for grievous condemnation of abhorrent crimes and thus prevents disorder, lynching, and attempts by private citizens to take the law into their own hands.

The question, however, is not whether death serves these supposed purposes of punishment, but whether death serves them more effectively than imprisonment. There is no evidence whatever that utilization of imprisonment rather than death encourages private blood feuds and other disorders. Surely if there were such a danger, the execution of a handful of criminals each year would not prevent it. * * * Furthermore, it is certainly doubtful that the infliction of death by the State does in fact strengthen the community's moral code; if the deliberate extinguishment of human life has any effect at all, it more likely tends to lower our respect for life and brutalize our values. * * *

There is, then, no substantial reason to believe that the punishment of death, as currently administered, is necessary for the protection of society. The only other purpose suggested, one that is independent of protection for society, is retribution. Shortly stated, retribution in this context means that criminals are put to death because they deserve it.

∗ ∗ ∗ The claim that death is a just punishment necessarily refers to the existence of certain public beliefs. The claim must be that for capital crimes death alone comports with society's notion of proper punishment. As administered today, however, the punishment of death cannot be justified as a necessary means of exacting retribution from criminals. When the overwhelming number of criminals who commit capital crimes go to prison, it cannot be concluded that death serves the purpose of retribution more effectively than imprisonment. The asserted public belief that murderers and rapists deserve to die is flatly inconsistent with the execution of a random few. As the history of the punishment of death in this country shows, our society wishes to prevent crime; we have no desire to kill criminals simply to get even with them.

In sum, the punishment of death is inconsistent with all four principles: Death is an unusually severe and degrading punishment; there is a strong probability that it is inflicted arbitrarily; its rejection by contemporary society is virtually total; and there is no reason to believe that it serves any penal purpose more effectively than the less severe punishment of imprisonment. The function of these principles is to enable a court to determine whether a punishment comports with human dignity. Death, quite simply, does not.

IV

When this country was founded, memories of the Stuart horrors were fresh and severe corporal punishments were common. Death was not then a unique punishment. The practice of punishing criminals by death, moreover, was widespread and by and large acceptable to society. Indeed, without developed prison systems, there was frequently no workable alternative. Since that time successive restrictions, imposed against the background of a continuing moral controversy, have drastically curtailed the use of this punishment. Today death is a uniquely and unusually severe punishment. When examined by the principles applicable under the Cruel and Unusual Punishments Clause, death stands condemned as fatally offensive to human dignity. The punishment of death is therefore "cruel and unusual," and the States may no longer inflict it as a punishment for crimes. ∗ ∗ ∗

I concur in the judgments of the Court.

UNITED STATES V. ASH

June 21, 1973

In writing for the Court in *Schmerber* (p. 127), Justice Brennan rejected Fifth
Amendment self-incrimination and Fourth Amendment search and seizure
claims against the mandatory blood testing of drunk driving suspects. In a
single paragraph, he also ruled that such a procedure does not violate the
Sixth Amendment right to counsel. There was, after all, nothing an attorney could do to help the suspect, since the suspect was not free to refuse the
blood test.

Yet in other contexts the Court has been most protective of the Sixth
Amendment's guarantee that "[i]n all criminal prosecutions, the accused
shall . . . have the assistance of counsel for his defense." Most notably, in its
ruling in *Gideon v. Wainwright* (1963), the Court required states to provide
defendants with legal counsel at state expense in all felony trials. Without
such representation, indigent defendants would be at a severe disadvantage.

In 1967, Brennan authored three of the Court's opinions holding that the
Sixth Amendment applies even to pretrial activities and requires that a suspect's attorney be permitted to attend police lineups. At such proceedings,
prosecutors and police may—intentionally or unintentionally—do things
that prompt a witness to identify the suspect, who may lack the opportunity
or expertise that counsel presumably would have to discover these suggestive practices. Because witnesses who have identified a suspect at a suggestive
lineup are unlikely to recant that identification at trial, the Court concluded
that lineups without counsel create a real risk of "irreparable misidentification." Therefore, a witness who identifies a suspect at a lineup conducted outside the presence of an attorney will not be permitted to make the identification in court unless the prosecution can demonstrate that the identification
has a basis independent of the possibly suggestive lineup.

Five years later, after three members of Brennan's majority coalition had
retired, the Court began to retrench. In *Kirby v. Illinois* (1972), a new majority
determined that the right to counsel did not arise until the suspect had been
indicted. Prior to indictment, so the Court ruled, the proceedings are not at
a "critical stage."

In the case excerpted here, the majority retreated further. It concluded that there is no right to counsel at all at photographic arrays, another common form of pretrial identification. Perhaps fearing that a contrary decision would interfere too greatly with traditional police practices, the Court noted that, unlike a lineup, a photographic array can easily be reconstructed later, minimizing the risk of improper suggestiveness and irreparable misidentification.

Brennan stood firm, apparently regarding this case as a natural corollary to the Court's earlier decisions. He chastised the majority for disingenuously ignoring the fact that the identification could easily be tainted by the actions of police officers, a principal reason underlying the Court's decisions in the original trilogy.

Justice Blackmun authored the opinion of the Court, joined by Chief Justice Burger and Justices White, Powell, and Rehnquist. Justice Stewart concurred in the Court's judgment. Justices Douglas, Brennan, and Marshall dissented.

❂   ❂   ❂

Mr. Justice BRENNAN, with whom Mr. Justice DOUGLAS and Mr. Justice MARSHALL join, dissenting.

The Court holds today that a pretrial display of photographs to the witnesses of a crime for the purpose of identifying the accused, unlike a lineup, does not constitute a "critical stage" of the prosecution at which the accused is constitutionally entitled to the presence of counsel. In my view, today's decision is wholly unsupportable in terms of such considerations as logic, consistency, and, indeed, fairness. As a result, I must reluctantly conclude that today's decision marks simply another step towards the complete evisceration of the fundamental constitutional principles established by this Court, only six years ago, in *United States v. Wade*; *Gilbert v. California*; and *Stovall v. Denno*. I dissent.

I

On the morning of August 26, 1965, two men wearing stocking masks robbed the American Security and Trust Co. in Washington, D.C. The robbery lasted only about three or four minutes and, on the day of the crime, none of the four witnesses was able to give the police a description of the robbers' facial characteristics. Some five months later, on February 3, 1966, an FBI agent showed each of the four witnesses a group of black and white mug shots of the faces of five black males, including respondent, all of generally the same age, height, and weight. Respondent's photograph was included because of information received from a Government informant charged with other crimes. None of the witnesses was able to make a "positive" identification of respondent.

On April 1, 1966, an indictment was returned charging respondent and a codefendant in five counts relating to the robbery of the American Security and Trust Co. Trial was finally set for May 8, 1968, almost three years after the crime and more than two years after the return of the indictment. During the entire two-year period between indictment and trial, although one of the witnesses expressly sought an opportunity to see respondent in person, the Government never attempted to arrange a corporeal lineup for the purposes of identification. Rather, *less than 24 hours before trial*, the FBI agent, accompanied by the prosecutor, showed five color photographs to the witnesses, three of whom identified the picture of respondent.

At trial, all four witnesses made incourt identifications of respondent, but only one of these witnesses was "positive" of her identification. The fact that three of the witnesses had previously identified respondent from the color photographs, and the photographs themselves, were also admitted into evidence. The only other evidence implicating respondent in the crime was the testimony of the Government informant.[4] On the basis of this evidence, respondent was convicted on all counts of the indictment.

On appeal, the United States Court of Appeals for the District of Columbia Circuit, sitting en banc, reversed respondent's conviction. Noting that "the dangers of mistaken identification from uncounseled lineup identifications . . . are applicable in large measure to photographic as well as corporeal identifications," the Court of Appeals reasoned that this Court's decisions in *Wade, Gilbert,* and *Stovall,* compelled the conclusion that a pretrial photographic identification, like a lineup, is a "critical" stage of the prosecution at which the accused is constitutionally entitled to the attendance of counsel. Accordingly, the Court of Appeals held that respondent was denied his Sixth Amendment right to "the Assistance of Counsel for his defence" when his attorney was not given an opportunity to attend the display of the color

---

4. As the Court of Appeals noted, this testimony was of at least questionable credibility.

photographs on the very eve of trial. In my view, both the reasoning and conclusion of the Court of Appeals were unimpeachably correct, and I would therefore affirm.

II

In June 1967, this Court decided a trilogy of "lineup" cases which brought into sharp focus the problems of pretrial identification. *See United States v. Wade; Gilbert v. California; Stovall v. Denno.* In essence, those decisions held (1)that a pretrial lineup is a "critical stage" in the criminal process at which the accused is constitutionally entitled to the presence of counsel; (2)that evidence of an identification of the accused at such an uncounseled lineup is *per se* inadmissible; and (3)that evidence of a subsequent in-court identification of the accused is likewise inadmissible unless the Government can demonstrate by clear and convincing evidence that the in-court identification was based upon observations of the accused independent of the prior uncounseled lineup identification. The considerations relied upon by the Court in reaching these conclusions are clearly applicable to photographic as well as corporeal identifications. Those considerations bear repeating here in some detail, for they touch upon the very heart of our criminal justice system—the right of an accused to a fair trial, including the effective "Assistance of Counsel for his defence."

At the outset, the Court noted that "identification evidence is peculiarly riddled with innumerable dangers and variable factors which might seriously, even crucially, derogate from a fair trial." *United States v. Wade.* Indeed, "[t]he vagaries of eyewitness identification are well-known; the annals of criminal law are rife with instances of mistaken identification." *Id.* Apart from "the dangers inherent in eyewitness identification," such as unreliable memory or perception, the Court pointed out that "[a] major factor contributing to the high incidence of miscarriage of justice from mistaken identification has been the degree of suggestion inherent in the manner in which the prosecution presents the suspect to witnesses for pretrial identification." *Id.* The Court recognized that the dangers of suggestion are not necessarily due to "police procedures intentionally designed to prejudice an accused." On the contrary, "[s]uggestion can be created intentionally or unintentionally in many subtle ways." *Id.* And the "fact that the police themselves have, in a given case, little or no doubt that the man put up for identification has committed the offense . . . involves a danger that this persuasion may communicate itself even in a doubtful case to the witness in some way. . . . " *Id.*

The Court also expressed concern over the possibility that a mistaken identification at a pretrial line-up might itself be conclusive on the question of identity, thereby resulting in the conviction of an innocent man. The Court observed that "once a witness has picked out the accused at the lineup, he is not likely to go back on his word later on, so that in practice the issue of identity may (in the absence of other relevant evidence) for all practical purposes be determined there and then, before the trial." *Id.*

Moreover, "the defense can seldom reconstruct the manner and mode of lineup identification for judge or jury at trial." *Id.* For "as is the case with secret interrogations, there is serious difficulty in depicting what transpires at lineups. . . . " *Id.* Although the accused is present at such corporeal identifications, he is hardly in a position to detect many of the more subtle "improper influences" that might infect the identification.[7] In addition, the Court emphasized that "neither witnesses nor lineup participants are apt to be alert for conditions prejudicial to the suspect. And, if they were, it would likely be of scant benefit to the suspect since neither witnesses nor lineup participants are likely to be schooled in the detection of suggestive influences." As a result, "even though cross-examination is a precious safeguard to a fair trial, it cannot [in this context] be viewed as an absolute assurance of accuracy and reliability."

With these considerations in mind, the Court reasoned that "the accused's inability effectively to reconstruct at trial any unfairness that occurred at the lineup may deprive him of his only opportunity meaningfully to attack the credibility of the witness' courtroom identification." And "[i]nsofar as the accused's conviction may rest on a courtroom identification in fact the fruit of a suspect pretrial identification which the accused is helpless to subject to effective scrutiny at trial, the accused is deprived of that right of cross-examination which is an es-

---

7. The Court pointed out that

[i]mproper influences may go undetected by a suspect, guilty or not, who experiences the emotional tension which we might expect in one being confronted with potential accusers. Even when he does observe abuse, if he has a criminal record he may be reluctant to take the stand and open up the admission of prior convictions. Moreover, any protestations by the suspect of the fairness of the lineup made at trial are likely to be in vain; the jury's choice is between the accused's unsupported version and that of the police officers present.

sential safeguard to his right to confront the witnesses against him." Thus, noting that "presence of counsel [at the lineup] can often avert prejudice and assure a meaningful confrontation at trial," the Court concluded that a pretrial corporeal identification is "a critical stage of the prosecution is which [the accused is] as much entitled to such aid [of counsel] . . . as at the trial itself."

III

As the Court of Appeals recognized, "the dangers of mistaken identification . . . set forth in *Wade* are applicable in large measure to photographic as well as corporeal identifications." To the extent that misidentification may be attributable to a witness' faulty memory or perception, or inadequate opportunity for detailed observation during the crime, the risks are obviously as great at a photographic display as at a lineup.

* * *

Moreover, as in the lineup situation, the possibilities for impermissible suggestion in the context of a photographic display are manifold. Such suggestion, intentional or unintentional, may derive from three possible sources. First, the photographs themselves might tend to suggest which of the pictures is that of the suspect. For example, differences in age, pose, or other physical characteristics of the persons represented, and variations in the mounting, background, lighting, or markings of the photographs all might have the effect of singling out the accused.

Second, impermissible suggestion may inhere in the manner in which the photographs are displayed to the witness. The danger of misidentification is, of course, "increased if the police display to the witness . . . the pictures of several persons among which the photograph of a single such individual recurs or is in some way emphasized." *Simmons v. United States*. And, if the photographs are arranged in an asymmetrical pattern, or if they are displayed in a time sequence that tends to emphasize a particular photograph, "any identification of the photograph which stands out from the rest is no more reliable than an identification of a single photograph, exhibited alone." P. Wall, Eyewitness Identification in Criminal Cases 81.

Third, gestures or comments of the prosecutor at the time of the display may lead an otherwise uncertain witness to select the "correct" photograph. For example, the prosecutor might "indicate to the witness that (he has) other evidence that one of the persons pictured committed the crime," *Simmons v. United States*, and might even point to a particular photograph and ask whether the person pictured "looks familiar." More subtly, the prosecutor's inflection, facial expressions, physical motions, and myriad other almost imperceptible means of communication might tend, intentionally or unintentionally, to compromise the witness' objectivity. Thus, as is the case with lineups, "[i]mproper photographic identification procedures, . . . by exerting a suggestive influence upon the witnesses, can often lead to an erroneous identification." P. Wall, *supra*, at 89.[12] And "[r]egardless of how the initial misidentification comes about, the witness thereafter is apt to retain in his memory the image of the photograph rather than of the person actually seen." *Simmons v. United States.* As a result, "the issue of identity may (in the absence of other relevant evidence) for all practical purposes by determined there and then, before the trial." *United States v. Wade.*

Moreover, as with lineups, the defense can "seldom reconstruct" at trial the mode and manner of photographic identification. It is true, of course, that the photographs used at the pretrial display might be preserved for examination at trial. But * * * preservation of the photographs affords little protection to the unrepresented accused. For, although retention of the photographs may mitigate the dangers of misidentification due to the suggestiveness of the photographs themselves, it cannot in any sense reveal to defense counsel the more subtle, and therefore more dangerous, suggestiveness that might derive from the manner in which he photographs were displayed or any accompanying comments or gestures. Moreover, the accused cannot rely upon the witnesses themselves to expose these latter sources of suggestion, for the witnesses are not "apt to be alert for conditions prejudicial to the suspect. And if they were, it would likely be of scant benefit to the suspect" since the witnesses are hardly "likely to be schooled in the detection of suggestive influences." *Id.*

---

12. The Court maintains that "the ethical responsibility of the prosecutor" is in itself a sufficient 'safeguard' against impermissible suggestion at a photographic display. The same argument might, of course, be made with respect to lineups. Moreover, it is clear that the "prosecutor" is not always present at such pretrial displays. Indeed, in this very case, one of the four eye-witnesses was shown the color photographs on the morning of trial by an agent of the FBI, not in the presence of the "prosecutor." And even though "the ethical responsibility of the prosecutor" might be an adequate "safeguard" against *intentional* suggestion, it can hardly be doubted that a "prosecutor" is, after all, only human. His behavior may be fraught with wholly *unintentional* and indeed unconscious nuances that might effectively suggest the "proper" response. * * *

Finally, and *unlike* the lineup situation, the accused himself is not even present at the photographic identification, thereby reducing the likelihood that irregularities in the procedures will ever come to light.
* * *

IV

Ironically, the Court does not seriously challenge the proposition that presence of counsel at a pretrial photographic display is essential to preserve the accused's right to a fair trial on the issue of identification. Rather, in what I can only characterize a triumph of form over substance, the Court seeks to justify its result by engrafting a wholly unprecedented—and wholly unsupportable—limitation on the Sixth Amendment right of "the accused . . . to have the Assistance of Counsel for his defence." Although apparently conceding that the right to counsel attaches, not only at the trial itself, but at all "critical stages" of the prosecution, the Court holds today that, in order to be deemed "critical," the particular "stage of the prosecution" under consideration must, at the very least, involve the physical "presence of the accused," at a "trial-like confrontation" with the Government, at which the accused requires the "guiding hand of counsel." According to the Court a pretrial photographic identification does not, of course, meet these criteria.

In support of this rather crabbed view of the Sixth Amendment, the Court cites our decisions in [various cases]. * * * [However, t]he fundamental premise underlying *all* of [these] decisions holding the right to counsel applicable at "critical" pretrial proceedings, is that a "stage" of the prosecution must be deemed "critical" for the purposes of the Sixth Amendment if it is one at which the presence of counsel is necessary "to protect the fairness of *the trial itself." Schneckloth v. Bustamonte* (emphasis added). Thus, in *Hamilton v. Alabama,* for example, we made clear that an arraignment under Alabama law is a "critical stage" of the prosecution, not only because the accused at such an arraignment requires "the guiding hand of counsel," but, more broadly, because "[w]hat happens there may affect the whole trial." * * *

Thus, contrary to the suggestion of the Court, the conclusion in *Wade* that a pretrial lineup is a "critical stage" of the prosecution did not in any sense turn on the fact that a lineup involves the physical "presence of the accused" at a "trial-like confrontation" with the Government. And that conclusion most certainly did not turn on the notion that presence of counsel was necessary so that counsel could offer legal advice or "guidance" to the accused at the lineup. On the contrary, *Wade* envisioned counsel's function at the lineup to be primarily that of a trained observer, able to detect the existence of any suggestive influences and capable of understanding the legal implications of the events that transpire. Having witnessed the proceedings, counsel would then be in a position effectively to reconstruct at trial any unfairness that occurred at the lineup, thereby preserving the accused's fundamental right to a fair trial on the issue of identification.

There is something ironic about the Court's conclusion today that a pretrial lineup identification is a "critical stage" of the prosecution because counsel's presence can help to compensate for the accused's deficiencies as an observer, but that a pretrial photographic identification is not a "critical stage" of the prosecution because the accused is not able to observe at all. In my view, there simply is no meaningful difference, in terms of the need for attendance of counsel, between corporeal and photographic identifications. And applying established and well-reasoned Sixth Amendment principles, I can only conclude that a pretrial photographic display, like a pretrial lineup, is a "critical stage" of the prosecution at which the accused is constitutionally entitled to the presence of counsel.

PARHAM V. J.R.

June 20, 1979

In this opinion, Justice Brennan again showed his concern for individuals who are disempowered in the legal system and in society at large. His empathetic approach to the plight of children facing commitment to a mental institution contrasts markedly with the opinion of the Court, which seemed removed and distant about the prospect that the children might be wrongfully confined.

In *Parham*, the Court reviewed the constitutionality of a Georgia statute, typical of many state statutory schemes, that failed to provide a hearing to juveniles before they were committed to hospitals for mental health treatment. Children admitted to the hospital by their parents or by state guardians were viewed as "voluntary" patients, even though they may have been totally uninvolved in, or even opposed to, the placement decision.

Writing for the majority, Chief Justice Burger held that a child's liberty interests are adequately protected if a neutral fact finder, such as the admitting physician, determines that statutory admission criteria are met. There need be no hearing or judicial review, either before or after the juvenile's confinement in the hospital. This decision was a striking departure from earlier cases in which the Court ruled that the Constitution required safeguards for adults who were civilly committed and for children accused of delinquent acts.

More significant than the Court's holding in Parham was its perspective on family relationships and the mental health system. The Court's view of parental involvement in the juvenile commitment process, and the role of mental health providers, could be characterized as "benevolent pragmatism." According to Burger, the "natural bonds of affection lead parents to act in the best interests of their children," and the use of adversarial proceedings might exacerbate family conflicts or deter parents from seeking necessary treatment for their children. Mental health professionals, whom Burger characterized as "competent, conscientious, and dedicated," want, as a practical matter, to limit costly medical facilities to the neediest cases. To Burger, this reduced the risk of erroneous commitment. The majority concluded that questions surrounding hospital admission were "essentially medical in character," thus further obviating the need for an adversarial hearing or judicial oversight. The Court provided no social science data to support its assumptions about human behavior or relationships.

Brennan's opinion begins in a formalistic way by reviewing the Court's prior decisions involving the commitment of adults with mental health disabilities. Against this backdrop, he suggested that juveniles may be entitled to more protection than adults because confinement, particularly erroneous confinement, has more tragic consequences. In this sense, Brennan's approach is similar to what he would later do in *O'Lone v. Estate of Shabazz* (p. 118). In that case, the fact that the constitutional claimants were incarcerated convicts—generally subject to the state's control—was all the more reason to protect their rights. In *Parham*, Brennan treated the fact that children were normally subject to their parents' control as increased justification for interceding on the children's behalf. Thus, unlike the majority opinion, which emphasized parental autonomy and the expertise of medical personnel, Brennan's focus remained with the effects of the process on the child. Viewing the experience through the eyes of the child, he determined that treating children fairly throughout the process not only has constitutional implications but may also produce more effective therapeutic results.

Brennan wrote of the possibly devastating impact of the majority's decision on "children abandoned by their supposed protectors to the rigors of institutional confinement." He also noted the potential impact of the Court's language about parent-child relationships, directly challenging the foundation of the majority's opinion by stating that "it ignores reality to assume blindly that parents act in their children's best interests when making commitment decisions and when waiving their children's due process rights." He similarly urged that medical determinations not go unchecked, since the mental health providers may have reasons unrelated to the health of the child to support confinement.

The legacy of *Parham* is manifest in areas wholly unrelated to the commitment of children. Subsequent cases have cited the "natural bonds of affection" as the motivation for parents to act appropriately on behalf of their children without interference from the state or any other interested party. Courts also have demonstrated an increased willingness to defer to medical expertise and to uphold the legitimacy of non-judicial fact-finders in varied contexts. Brennan's caution in *Parham* against dispensing with procedural protections, where the basic liberty interests of our most vulnerable citizens were at stake, was foreboding. Yet his warning, much like the voices of the hospitalized children, has not been heard.

Chief Justice Burger wrote the opinion of the Court, joined by Justices White, Blackmun, Powell, and Rehnquist. Justice Stewart concurred in the Court's judgment. Justices Brennan, Marshall, and Stevens dissented.

○ ○ ○

MR. JUSTICE BRENNAN, with whom MR. JUSTICE MARSHALL and MR. JUSTICE STEVENS join, concurring in part and dissenting in part.

I agree with the Court that the commitment of juveniles to state mental hospitals by their parents or by state officials acting *in loco parentis* involves state action that impacts upon constitutionally protected interests and therefore must be accomplished through procedures consistent with the constitutional mandate of due process of law. I agree also that the District Court erred in interpreting the Due Process Clause to require preconfinement commitment hearings in all cases in which parents wish to hospitalize their children. I disagree, however, with the Court's decision to pretermit questions concerning the postadmission procedures due Georgia's institutionalized juveniles. While the question of the frequency of postadmission review hearings may properly be deferred, the right to at least one postadmission hearing can and should be affirmed now. I also disagree with the Court's conclusion concerning the procedures due juvenile wards of the State of Georgia.
* * *

I

RIGHTS OF CHILDREN COMMITTED TO MENTAL INSTITUTIONS

Commitment to a mental institution necessarily entails a "massive curtailment of liberty," *Humphrey v. Cady*, and inevitably affects "fundamental rights." Persons incarcerated in mental hospitals are not only deprived of their physical liberty, they are also deprived of friends, family, and community. Institutionalized mental patients must live in unnatural surroundings under the continuous and detailed control of strangers. They are subject to intrusive treatment which, especially if unwarranted, may violate their right to bodily integrity. Such treatment modalities may include forced administration of psychotropic medication, aversive conditioning, convulsive therapy, and even psychosurgery. Furthermore, as the Court recognizes, persons confined in mental institutions are stigmatized as sick and abnormal during confinement and, in some cases, even after release.

Because of these considerations, our cases have made clear that commitment to a mental hospital "is a deprivation of liberty which the State cannot accomplish without due process of law." *O'Connor v. Donaldson* (Burger, C.J., concurring). In the absence of a voluntary, knowing, and intelligent waiver, adults facing commitment to mental institutions are entitled to full and fair adversary hearings in which the necessity for their commitment is established to the satisfaction of a neutral tribunal. At such hearings they must be accorded the right to "be present with counsel, have an opportunity to be heard, be confronted with witnesses against [them], have the right to cross-examine, and to offer evidence of [their] own." *Specht v. Patterson.*

These principles also govern the commitment of children. "Constitutional rights do not mature and come into being magically only when one attains the state-defined age of majority. Minors, as well as adults, are protected by the Constitution and possess constitutional rights." *Planned Parenthood of Central Missouri v. Danforth.*

Indeed, it may well be argued that children are entitled to more protection than are adults. The consequences of an erroneous commitment decision are more tragic where children are involved. Children, on the average, are confined for longer periods than are adults. Moreover, childhood is a particularly vulnerable time of life and children erroneously institutionalized during their formative years may bear the scars for the rest of their lives. Furthermore, the provision of satisfactory institutionalized mental care for children generally requires a substantial financial commitment that too often has not been forthcoming. * * *

In addition, the chances of an erroneous commitment decision are particularly great where children are involved. Even under the best of circumstances psychiatric diagnosis and therapy decisions are fraught with uncertainties. These uncertainties are aggravated when, as under the Georgia practice, the psychiatrist interviews the child during a period of abnormal stress in connection with the commitment, and without adequate time or opportunity to become acquainted with the patient. These uncertainties may be further aggravated when economic and social class separate doctor and child, thereby frustrating the accurate diagnosis of pathology.

These compounded uncertainties often lead to erroneous commitments since psychiatrists tend to err on the side of medical caution and therefore hospitalize patients for whom other dispositions would be more beneficial. The National Institute of Mental Health recently found that only 36% of patients below age 20 who were confined at St. Elizabeths Hospital actually required such hospitalization. Of particular relevance to this case, a Georgia study Commission on Mental Health Services for Children and Youth concluded that more than half of the State's institutionalized children were not in need of confinement if other forms of care were made available or used.

II
RIGHTS OF CHILDREN COMMITTED BY THEIR PARENTS

A

Notwithstanding all this, Georgia denies hearings to juveniles institutionalized at the behest of their parents. Georgia rationalizes this practice on the theory that parents act in their children's best interests and therefore may waive their children's due process rights. Children incarcerated because their parents wish them confined, Georgia contends, are really voluntary patients. I cannot accept this argument.

In our society, parental rights are limited by the legitimate rights and interests of their children. "Parents may be free to become martyrs themselves. But it does not follow they are free, in identical circumstances, to make martyrs of their children before they have reached the age of full and legal discretion when they can make that choice for themselves." *Prince v. Massachusetts.* This principle is reflected in the variety of statutes and cases that authorize state intervention on behalf of neglected or abused children and that, *inter alia*, curtail parental authority to alienate their children's property, to withhold necessary medical treatment, and to deny children exposure to ideas and experiences they may later need as independent and autonomous adults.

This principle is also reflected in constitutional jurisprudence. Notions of parental authority and family autonomy cannot stand as absolute and invariable barriers to the assertion of constitutional rights by children. * * *

Additional considerations counsel against allowing parents unfettered power to institutionalize their children without cause or without any hearing to ascertain that cause. The presumption that parents act in their children's best interests, while applicable to most child-rearing decisions, is not applicable in the commitment context. Numerous studies reveal that parental decisions to institutionalize their children often are the results of dislocation in the family unrelated to the children's mental condition. Moreover, even well-meaning parents lack the expertise necessary to evaluate the relative advantages and disadvantages of inpatient as opposed to outpatient psychiatric treatment. Parental decisions to waive hearings in which such questions could be explored, therefore, cannot be conclusively deemed either informed or intelligent. In these circumstances, I respectfully suggest, it ignores reality to assume blindly that parents act in their children's best interests when making commitment decisions and when waiving their children's due process rights.

B

This does not mean States are obliged to treat children who are committed at the behest of their parents in precisely the same manner as other persons who are involuntarily committed. The demands of due process are flexible and the parental commitment decision carries with it practical implications that States may legitimately take into account. While as a general rule due process requires that commitment hearings precede involuntary hospitalization, when parents seek to hospitalize their children special considerations militate in favor of postponement of formal commitment proceedings and against mandatory adversary preconfinement commitment hearings.

First, the prospect of an adversary hearing prior to admission might deter parents from seeking needed medical attention for their children. Second, the hearings themselves might delay treatment of children whose home life has become impossible and who require some form of immediate state care. Furthermore, because adversary hearings at this juncture would necessarily involve direct challenges to parental authority, judgment, or veracity, preadmission hearings may well result in pitting the child and his advocate against the parents. This, in turn, might traumatize both parent and child and make the child's eventual return to his family more difficult.

Because of these special considerations, I believe that States may legitimately postpone formal commitment proceedings when parents seek inpatient psychiatric treatment for their children. Such children may be admitted, for a limited period, without prior hearing, so long as the admitting psychiatrist first interviews parent and child and concludes that short-term inpatient treatment would be appropriate.

* * *

C

* * * Although Georgia may postpone formal commitment hearings, when parents seek to commit their children, the State cannot dispense with such hearings altogether. Our cases make clear that, when protected interests are at stake, the "fundamental requirement of due process is the opportunity to be heard 'at a meaningful time and in a meaningful manner.'" *Mathews v. Eldridge*, quoting in part from *Armstrong v. Manzo*. Whenever prior hearings are impracticable, States must provide reasonably prompt postdeprivation hearings.

The informal postadmission procedures that Georgia now follows are simply not enough to qualify as hearings—let alone reasonably prompt hearings. The procedures lack all the traditional due process safeguards. Commitment decisions are made *ex parte*. Georgia's institutionalized juveniles are not informed of the reasons for their commitment; nor do they enjoy the right to be present at the commitment determination, the right to representation, the right to be heard, the right to be confronted with adverse witnesses, the right to cross-examine, or the right to offer evidence of their own. By any standard of due process, these procedures are deficient. I cannot understand why the Court pretermits condemnation of these *ex parte* procedures which operate to deny Georgia's institutionalized juveniles even "some form of hearing," before they are condemned to suffer the rigors of long-term institutional confinement.

The special considerations that militate against preadmission commitment hearings when parents seek to hospitalize their children do not militate against reasonably prompt postadmission commitment hearings. In the first place, postadmission hearings would not delay the commencement of needed treatment. Children could be cared for by the State pending the disposition decision.

Second, the interest in avoiding family discord would be less significant at this stage since the family autonomy already will have been fractured by the institutionalization of the child. * * *

As a consequence, the prospect of a postadmission hearing is unlikely to deter parents from seeking medical attention for their children and the hearing itself is unlikely so to traumatize parent and child as to make the child's eventual return to the family impracticable.

Nor would postadmission hearings defeat the primary purpose of the state juvenile mental health enterprise. Under the present juvenile commitment scheme, Georgia parents do not enjoy absolute discretion to commit their children to public mental hospitals. Superintendents of state facilities may not accept children for long-term treatment unless they first determine that the children are mentally ill and will likely benefit from long-term hospital care. If the superintendent determines either condition is unmet, the child must be released or refused admission, regardless of the parents' desires. No legitimate state interest would suffer if the superintendent's determinations were reached through fair proceedings with due consideration of fairly presented opposing viewpoints rather than through the present practice of secret, *ex parte* deliberations.[22]

* * *

IV

Children incarcerated in public mental institutions are constitutionally entitled to a fair opportunity to contest the legitimacy of their confinement. They are entitled to some champion who can speak on their behalf and who stands ready to oppose a wrongful commitment. Georgia should not be permitted to deny that opportunity and that champion simply because the children's parents or guardians wish them to be confined without a hearing. The risk of erroneous commitment is simply too great unless there is some form of adversary review. And fairness demands that children abandoned by their supposed protectors to the rigors of institutional confinement be given the help of some separate voice.

---

22. Indeed, postadmission hearings may well advance the purposes of the state enterprise. First, hearings will promote accuracy and ensure that the superintendent diverts children who do not require hospitalization to more appropriate programs. Second, the hearings themselves may prove therapeutic. Children who feel that they have received a fair hearing may be more likely to accept the legitimacy of their confinement, acknowledge their illness, and cooperate with those attempting to give treatment. This, in turn, would remove a significant impediment to successful therapy.

UNITED STATES V. LEON

July 5, 1984

The Fourth Amendment to the United States Constitution protects people from unreasonable searches and seizures, both of their persons and their property. It also requires that warrants to search be issued only upon a showing that there is probable cause to believe that contraband or evidence of criminal activity will be found in the area to be searched.

In 1914, the Supreme Court initiated what would become an ongoing struggle between liberal and conservative viewpoints over the meaning of the Fourth Amendment's prohibition against unreasonable searches and seizures. In *Weeks v. United States*, the Court ruled that evidence obtained by police illegally, that is in violation of a suspect's Fourth Amendment rights, could not be used in a federal criminal prosecution. This prohibition, known as the "exclusionary rule," was made applicable to state court proceedings in *Mapp v. Ohio* in 1961.

Supporters of the exclusionary rule—both within and outside the Court—have provided three justifications for it. First, the "personal rights" theory, which holds that a right without an effective remedy is really not a right at all, only a meaningless paper promise. Under this theory, the exclusionary rule is needed to give effect to the right against unreasonable searches and seizures that the Framers carved into the constitutional foundation of our society. Second, the "deterrence" theory, which assumes that exclusion of evidence is necessary both to deter police misconduct in each individual investigation and to act as a check on the law enforcement system overall. Finally, the "judicial integrity" theory, which seeks to avoid tainting judicial proceedings with illegally obtained evidence and which demands that judges avoid implicitly condoning unlawful police conduct by permitting the use of such evidence in court.

Detractors of the exclusionary rule tend to focus on those cases where application of the rule has resulted in obviously guilty defendants being freed on a "technicality." They often argue that two wrongs—the defendant's criminal action and the police's illegal investigatory techniques—do not make a right; rather both wrongs should be punished. Some also suggest that the deterrence theory is flawed because it presumes that the goal of police is

168

always a criminal conviction. They note that sometimes officers merely wish to seize contraband to get it off the streets, and the exclusionary rule does nothing to deter such conduct.

In reality, the exclusionary rule results in suppression of evidence in only about one percent of all criminal prosecutions. Of course, the exclusion of critical evidence in even one case can have a devastating effect if, for example, a dangerous defendant is thereby acquitted and then commits another violent crime.

Conscious of the need to balance the requirements of law enforcement against the rights of the individual, a bloc of Justices on the Court began to chip away at the exclusionary rule by creating exceptions to its application. The 1984 decision in this case established the so-called "good faith" exception to the exclusionary rule and still represents the deepest inroad into the rule itself. In the decision, the Court held that evidence seized by police officers who reasonably rely on a warrant issued by a neutral and detached magistrate is admissible at trial even if a reviewing court subsequently determines that there was insufficient cause to issue the warrant and conduct the search. Justice White, who had never supported the exclusionary rule and had strenuously and repeatedly urged adoption of a "good faith" exception, was the logical choice to author the opinion of the Court. Justice Brennan's lengthy dissent is an eloquent plea to preserve the protections that he had helped to put in place.

From White's perspective, the exclusionary rule is not a constitutional mandate, but a judicially created remedial device whose purpose is to counterbalance unlawful police conduct. Under that view, the Fourth Amendment requires the use of a test in which the benefits of deterrence are weighed against the costs of excluding incriminating evidence and possibly freeing guilty perpetrators. To White, the deterrence rationale carries no force if the police officer has a good faith belief in the validity of a warrant and if the cost of excluding evidence would be the dismissal of the case or acquittal after trial.

In his dissenting opinion, Brennan explored the origins of the exclusionary rule and determined that, while there is no explicit textual basis for barring illegally seized evidence, it is a rule that is constitutionally required. He chided the majority for focusing solely on deterring the misconduct of individual officers. He maintained that in using a cost-benefit analysis to bolster its position, the majority lost sight that the Fourth Amendment, not the exclusionary rule, is what exacts the cost because of its proscription against unreasonable searches and seizures. This cost that the Fourth Amendment exacts is the "price" our society must pay for enjoying the freedom and privacy safeguarded by the Fourth Amendment.

It is difficult to assess the accuracy of the predictions at the end of Brennan's dissenting opinion about the unfortunate consequences of adopting the "good faith" exception. The Court certainly has continued to ease the requirements for issuing a warrant and conducting a search. Whether, as Brennan feared, the "good faith" exception has encouraged law enforcement officials to cut corners in the performance of their routine duties is less clear.

Nevertheless, in one sense Brennan was prescient, or at least persuasive. Supreme Court decisions interpreting the United States Constitution establish a floor rather than a ceiling for constitutional rights. States may, if they choose, be more protective of individual freedoms. In a 1977 *Harvard Law Review* article titled "State Constitutions and the Protection of Individual Rights," Brennan urged advocates and judges to use state constitutions to provide this greater protection. Several state courts have done just that, relying on the reasoning expressed in Brennan's dissent in *Leon* to reject a "good faith" exception to the exclusionary rule. This response to Brennan's "invitation for state courts to step into the breach" left by the federal judiciary may well be his most lasting contribution to the law of search and seizure.

Justice White wrote the opinion of the Court, joined by Chief Justice Burger and Justices Powell, Rehnquist, and O'Connor. Justice Blackmun concurred in the Court's judgment. Justices Brennan, Marshall, and Steven dissented.

◊   ◊   ◊

Justice BRENNAN, with whom Justice MARSHALL joins, dissenting.

Ten years ago in *United States v. Calandra*, I expressed the fear that the Court's decision "may signal that a majority of my colleagues have positioned themselves to reopen the door [to evidence secured by official lawlessness] still further and abandon altogether the exclusionary rule in search-and-seizure cases." Since then, in case after case, I have witnessed the Court's gradual but determined strangulation of the rule. It now appears that the Court's victory over the Fourth Amendment is complete. That today's decision represents the *pièce de résistance* of the Court's past efforts cannot be doubted, for today the Court sanctions the use in the prosecution's case-in-chief of illegally obtained evidence against the individual whose rights have been violated—a result that had previously been thought to be foreclosed.

The Court seeks to justify this result on the ground that the "costs" of adhering to the exclusionary rule in cases like those before us exceed the "benefits." But the language of deterrence and of cost/benefit analysis, if used indiscriminately, can have a narcotic effect. It creates an illusion of technical precision and ineluctability. It suggests that not only constitutional principle but also empirical data supports the majority's result. When the Court's analysis is examined carefully, however, it is clear that we have not been treated to an honest assessment of the merits of the exclusionary rule, but have instead been drawn into a curious world where the "costs" of excluding illegally obtained evidence loom to exaggerated heights and where the "benefits" of such exclusion are made to disappear with a mere wave of the hand.

The majority ignores the fundamental constitutional importance of what is at stake here. While the machinery of law enforcement and indeed the nature of crime itself have changed dramatically since the Fourth Amendment became part of the Nation's fundamental law in 1791, what the Framers understood then remains true today—that the task of combatting crime and convicting the guilty will in every era seem of such critical and pressing concern that we may be lured by the temptations of expediency into forsaking our commitment to protecting individual liberty and privacy. It was for that very reason that the Framers of the Bill of Rights insisted that law enforcement efforts be permanently and unambiguously restricted in order to preserve personal freedoms. In the constitutional scheme they ordained, the sometimes unpopular task of ensuring that the government's enforcement efforts remain within the strict boundaries fixed by the Fourth Amendment was entrusted to the courts. * * *

I

The Court holds that physical evidence seized by police officers reasonably relying upon a warrant issued by a detached and neutral magistrate is admissible in the prosecution's case-in-chief, even though a reviewing court has subsequently determined either that the warrant was defective, or that those officers failed to demonstrate when applying for the warrant that there was probable cause to conduct the search. I have no doubt that these decisions will prove in time to have been a grave mistake. But, as troubling and important as today's new doctrine may be for the administration of criminal justice in this country, the mode of analysis used to generate that doctrine also requires critical examination, for it may prove in the long run to pose the greater threat to our civil liberties.

A

At bottom, the Court's decision turns on the proposition that the exclusionary rule is merely a "judicially created remedy designed to safeguard Fourth Amendment rights generally through its deterrent effect, rather than a personal constitutional right." The germ of that idea is found in *Wolf v. Colorado*, and although I had thought that such a narrow conception of the rule had been forever put to rest by our decision in *Mapp v. Ohio*, it has been revived by the present Court and reaches full flower with today's decision. The essence of this view, as expressed initially in the *Calandra* opinion and as reiterated today, is that the sole "purpose of the Fourth Amendment is to prevent unreasonable governmental intrusions into the privacy of one's person, house, papers, or effects. The wrong condemned is the unjustified governmental invasion of these areas of an individual's life. That wrong . . . is *fully accomplished* by the original search without probable cause." (emphasis added). This reading of the Amendment implies that its proscriptions are directed solely at those government agents who may actually invade an individual's constitutionally protected privacy. The courts are not subject to any direct constitutional duty to exclude illegally obtained evidence, because the question of the admissibility of such evidence is not addressed by the Amendment. This view of the scope of the Amendment relegates the judiciary to the periphery. Because the only constitutionally cognizable injury has already been "fully accomplished" by the police by the time a case comes before the courts, the Constitution is not itself violated if the judge decides to admit the tainted evidence. Indeed, the most the judge *can* do is wring his hands and hope that perhaps by excluding such evidence he can deter future transgressions by the police.

Such a reading appears plausible, because, as critics of the exclusionary rule never tire of repeating, the Fourth Amendment makes no express provision for the exclusion of evidence secured in violation of its commands. A short answer to this claim, of course, is that many of the Constitution's most vital imperatives are stated in general terms and the task of giving meaning to these precepts is therefore left to subsequent judicial decision-making in the context of concrete cases. The nature of our Constitution, as Chief Justice Marshall long ago explained, "requires that only its great outlines should be marked, its important objects designated, and the minor ingredients which compose those objects be deduced from the nature of the objects themselves." *McCulloch v. Maryland.*

A more direct answer may be supplied by recognizing that the Amendment, like other provisions of the Bill of Rights, restrains the power of the govenment as a whole; it does not specify only a particular agency and exempt all others. The judiciary is responsible, no less than the executive, for ensuring that constitutional rights are respected.

When that fact is kept in mind, the role of the courts and their possible involvement in the concerns of the Fourth Amendment comes into sharper focus. Because seizures are executed principally to secure evidence, and because such evidence generally has utility in our legal system only in the context of a trial supervised by a judge, it is apparent that the admission of illegally obtained evidence implicates the same constitutional concerns as the initial seizure of that evidence. Indeed, by admitting unlawfully seized evidence, the judiciary becomes a part of what is in fact a single governmental action prohibited by the terms of the Amendment. Once that connection between the evidence-gathering role of the police and the evidence-admitting function of the courts is acknowledged, the plausibility of the Court's interpretation becomes more suspect. Certainly nothing in the language or history of the Fourth Amendment suggests that a recognition of this evidentiary link between the police and the courts was meant to be foreclosed. It is difficult to give any meaning at all to the limitations imposed by the Amendment if they are read to proscribe only certain conduct by the police but to allow other agents of the same government to take advantage of evidence secured by the police in violation of its requirements. The Amendment therefore must be read to condemn not only the initial unconstitutional invasion of privacy—which is done, after all, for the purpose of securing evidence—but also the subsequent use of any evidence so obtained.

The Court evades this principle by drawing an artificial line between the constitutional rights and responsibilities that are engaged by actions of the police and those that are engaged when a defendant appears before the courts. According to the Court, the substantive protections of the Fourth Amendment are wholly exhausted at the moment when police unlawfully invade an individual's privacy and thus no substantive force remains to those protections at the time of trial when the government seeks to use evidence obtained by the police.

I submit that such a crabbed reading of the Fourth Amendment casts aside the teaching of those Justices who first formulated the exclusionary rule, and rests ultimately on an impoverished understanding of judicial responsibility in our constitutional scheme. For my part, "[t]he right of the people to be secure in their persons, houses, papers and effects, against unreasonable searches and seizures" comprises a personal right to exclude all evidence secured by means of unreasonable searches and seizures. The right to be free from the initial invasion of privacy and the right of exclusion are coordinate components of the central embracing right to be free from unreasonable searches and seizures.

Such a conception of the rights secured by the Fourth Amendment was unquestionably the original basis of what has come to be called the exclusionary rule when it was first formulated in *Weeks v. United States.* * * *

The heart of the *Weeks* opinion, and for me the beginning of wisdom about the Fourth Amendment's proper meaning, is found in the following passage:

> If letters and private documents can . . . be seized and held and used in evidence against a citizen accused of an offense, the protection of the Fourth Amendment declaring his right to be secure against such searches and seizures is of no value, and, so far as those thus placed are concerned, might as well be stricken from the Constitution. The efforts of the courts and [federal] officials to bring the guilty to punishment, praiseworthy as they are, are not to be aided by the sacrifice of those great principles established by years of endeavor and suffering which have resulted in their embodiment in the fundamental law of the land. * * *

What this passage succinctly captures is the essential recognition, ignored by the present Court, that seizures are generally executed for the purpose of bringing "proof to the aid of the Government," that the utility of such evidence in a criminal prosecution arises ultimately in the context of the courts, and that the courts therefore cannot be absolved of responsibility for the means by which evidence is obtained. As the Court in *Weeks* clearly recognized, the obligations cast upon government by the Fourth Amendment are not confined merely to the police. * * *

That conception of the rule, in my view, is more faithful to the meaning and purpose of the Fourth Amendment and to the judiciary's role as the guardian of the people's constitutional liberties. In contrast to the present Court's restrictive reading, the Court in *Weeks* recognized that, if the Amendment is to have any meaning, police and the courts cannot be regarded as constitutional strangers to each other; because the evidence-gathering role of the police is directly linked to the evidence-admitting function of the courts, an individual's Fourth Amendment rights may be undermined as completely by one as by the other.

B

From the foregoing, it is clear why the question whether the exclusion of evidence would deter future police misconduct was never considered a relevant concern in the early cases ***. In those formative decisions, the Court plainly understood that the exclusion of illegally obtained evidence was compelled not by judicially fashioned remedial purposes, but rather by a direct constitutional command. * * *

Despite this clear pronouncement, however, the Court since *Calandra* has gradually pressed the deterrence rationale for the rule back to center stage. The various arguments advanced by the Court in this campaign have only strengthened my conviction that the deterrence theory is both misguided and unworkable. First, the Court has frequently bewailed the "cost" of excluding reliable evidence. In large part, this criticism rests upon a refusal to acknowledge the function of the Fourth Amendment itself. If nothing else, the Amendment plainly operates to disable the government from gathering information and securing evidence in certain ways. In practical terms, of course, this restriction of official power means that some incriminating evidence inevitably will go undetected if the government obeys these constitutional restraints. It is the loss of that evidence that is the "price" our society pays for enjoying the freedom and privacy safeguarded by the Fourth Amendment. Thus, some criminals will go free *not*, in Justice (then Judge) Cardozo's misleading epigram, "because the constable has blundered," *People v. Defore*, but rather because official compliance with Fourth Amendment requirements makes it more difficult to catch criminals. Understood in this way, the Amendment directly contemplates that some reliable and incriminating evidence will be lost to the government; therefore, it is not the exclusionary rule, but the Amendment itself that has imposed this cost.

* * *

III

Even if I were to accept the Court's general approach to the exclusionary rule, I could not agree with today's result. There is no question that in the hands of the present Court the deterrence rationale has proved to be a powerful tool for confining the scope of the rule. * * * First there is the ritual incantation of the "substantial social costs" exacted by the exclusionary rule, followed by the virtually foreordained conclusion that, given the marginal benefits, application of the rule in the circumstances of these cases is not warranted. Upon analysis, however, such a result cannot be justified even on the Court's own terms.

At the outset, the Court suggests that society has been asked to pay a high price—in terms either of setting guilty persons free or of impeding the proper functioning of trials—as a result of excluding relevant physical evidence in cases where the police, in conducting searches and seizing evidence, have made only an "objectively reasonable" mistake concerning the constitutionality of their actions. But what evidence is there to support such a claim?

Significantly, the Court points to none, and, indeed, as the Court acknowledges, recent studies have demonstrated that the "costs" of the exclusionary rule—calculated in terms of dropped prosecutions and lost convictions—are quite low. * * *

What then supports the Court's insistence that this evidence be admitted? Apparently, the Court's only answer is that even though the costs of exclusion are not very substantial, the potential deterrent effect in these circumstances is so marginal that exclusion cannot be justified. The key to the Court's conclusion in this respect is its belief that the prospective deterrent effect of the exclusionary rule operates only in those situations in which police officers, when deciding whether to go forward with some particular search, have reason to know that their planned conduct will violate the requirements of the Fourth Amendment. If these officers in fact understand (or reasonably should understand because the law is well-settled) that their proposed conduct will offend the Fourth Amendment and that, consequently, any evidence they seize will be suppressed in court, they will refrain from conducting the planned search. In those circumstances, the incentive system created by the exclusionary rule will have the hoped-for deterrent effect. But in situations where police officers reasonably (but mistakenly) believe that their planned conduct satisfies Fourth Amendment requirements—presumably either (a) because they are acting on the basis of an apparently valid warrant, or (b) because their conduct is only later determined to be invalid as a result of a subsequent change in the law or the resolution of an unsettled question of law—then such officers will have no reason to refrain from conducting the search and the exclusionary rule will have no effect.

At first blush, there is some logic to this position. Undoubtedly, in the situation hypothesized by the Court, the existence of the exclusionary rule cannot be expected to have any deterrent effect on the particular officers at the moment they are deciding whether to go forward with the search. Indeed, the subsequent exclusion of any evidence seized under such circumstances appears somehow "unfair" to the particular officers involved. As the Court suggests, these officers have acted in what they thought was an appropriate and constitutionally authorized manner, but then the fruit of their efforts is nullified by the application of the exclusionary rule.

The flaw in the Court's argument, however, is that its logic captures only one comparatively minor element of the generally acknowledged deterrent purposes of the exclusionary rule. To be sure, the rule operates to some extent to deter future misconduct by individual officers who have had evidence suppressed in their own cases. But what the Court overlooks is that the deterrence rationale for the rule is not designed to be, nor should it be thought of as, a form of "punishment" of individual police officers for their failures to obey the restraints imposed by the Fourth Amendment. Instead, the chief deterrent function of the rule is its tendency to promote institutional compliance with Fourth Amendment requirements on the part of law enforcement agencies generally. Thus, as the Court has previously recognized, "over the long term, [the] demonstration [provided by the exclusionary rule] that our society attaches serious consequences to violation of constitutional rights is thought to encourage those who formulate law enforcement policies, and the officers who implement them, to incorporate Fourth Amendment ideals into their value system." *Stone v. Powell*. It is only through such an institution-wide m echanism that information concerning Fourth Amendment standards can be effectively communicated to rank and file officers.

If the overall educational effect of the exclusionary rule is considered, application of the rule to even those situations in which individual police officers have acted on the basis of a reasonable but mistaken belief that their conduct was authorized can still be expected to have a considerable long-term deterrent effect. If evidence is consistently excluded in these circumstances, police departments will surely be prompted to instruct their officers to devote greater care and attention to providing sufficient information to establish probable cause when applying for a warrant, and to review with some attention the form of the warrant that they have been issued, rather than automatically assuming that whatever document the magistrate has signed will necessarily comport with Fourth Amendment requirements.

After today's decision, however, that institutional incentive will be lost. Indeed, the Court's "reasonable mistake" exception to the exclusionary rule will tend to put a premium on police ignorance of the law. Armed with the assurance provided by today's decision that evidence will always be admissible whenever an officer has "reasonably" relied upon a warrant, police departments will be encouraged to train officers that if a warrant has simply been signed, it is reasonable, without more, to rely on it. Since in close cases there will no longer be any incentive to err on the side of constitutional behavior, police would have every reason to adopt a "let's-wait-until-its-decided" approach in situations in which there is a question about a warrant's validity or the basis for its issuance.

Although the Court brushes these concerns aside, a host of grave consequences can be expected to result from its decision to carve this new exception out of the exclusionary rule. A chief consequence of today's decision will be to convey a clear and unambiguous message to magistrates that their decisions to issue warrants are now insulated from subsequent judicial review. Creation of this new exception for good faith reliance upon a warrant implicitly tells magistrates that they need not take much care in reviewing warrant applications, since their mistakes will from now on have virtually no consequence: If their decision to issue a warrant was correct, the evidence will be admitted; if their decision was incorrect but the police relied in good faith on the warrant, the evidence will also be admitted. Inevitably, the care and attention devoted to such an inconsequential chore will dwindle. Although the Court is correct to note that magistrates do not share the same stake in the outcome of a criminal case as the police, they nevertheless need to appreciate that their role is of some moment in order to continue performing the important task of carefully reviewing warrant applications. Today's decision effectively removes that incentive.

Moreover, the good faith exception will encourage police to provide only the bare minimum of information in future warrant applications. The police will now know that if they can secure a warrant, so long as the circumstances of its issuance are not "entirely unreasonable," all police conduct pursuant to that warrant will be protected from further judicial review. The clear incentive that operated in the past to establish probable cause adequately because reviewing courts would examine the magistrate's judgment carefully has now been so completely vitiated that the police need only show that it was not "entirely unreasonable" under the circumstances of a particular case for them to believe that the warrant they were issued was valid. The long-run effect unquestionably will be to undermine the integrity of the warrant process.

* * *

IV

When the public, as it quite properly has done in the past as well as in the present, demands that those in government increase their efforts to combat crime, it is all too easy for those government officials to seek expedient solutions. In contrast to such costly and difficult measures as building more prisons, improving law enforcement methods, or hiring more prosecutors and judges to relieve the overburdened court systems in the country's metropolitan areas, the relaxation of Fourth Amendment standards seems a tempting, costless means of meeting the public's demand for better law enforcement. In the long run, however, we as a society pay a heavy price for such expediency, because as Justice Jackson observed, the rights guaranteed in the Fourth Amendment "are not mere second-class rights but belong in the catalog of indispensable freedoms." *Brinegar v. United States* (dissenting opinion). Once lost, such rights are difficult to recover. There is hope, however, that in time this or some later Court will restore these precious freedoms to their rightful place as a primary protection for our citizens against overreaching officialdom.

I dissent.

UNITED STATES V. VERDUGO-URQUIDEZ

February 28, 1990

This case concerned a search by the United States Drug Enforcement Agency of a Mexican citizen's residence in Mexico and the seizure of some of his papers. DEA agents were aided by Mexican officials and apparently complied with all the relevant requirements of Mexican law. They did not, however, obtain a warrant from either a Mexican or U.S. magistrate. Such a warrant is, almost without exception, a requirement for searching a home in the United States. When the homeowner later was brought to trial in the United States, he sought to exclude the evidence seized during the warrantless search of his Mexican residence.

The Supreme Court ruled against the defendant. It concluded that while acting outside the boundaries of the United States, federal authorities need not comply with the Fourth Amendment. Writing for the Court, Chief Justice Rehnquist ruled that foreign nationals living abroad were not among "the people" protected by the Bill of Rights because they were not part of a "national community" and did not have "sufficient connection" to the United States. Although the majority did not address the issue, federal authorities acting abroad presumably have to comply with the law of the jurisdiction in which their actions occur. However, any additional protection afforded by United States law would be unnecessary, since resident citizens of a foreign country have no greater expectation of privacy than that which their own domestic law affords.

As the first paragraph of Justice Brennan's dissent indicates, he saw some irony in the fact that foreign nationals are required to abide by United States law while in their own countries, but that agents of the United States in those countries did not have to comply with traditional constitutional requirements when acting in their official capacities.

More significant, though, the different opinions reveal starkly different views of what the Constitution and the Bill of Rights are. For the Court, the Bill of Rights prohibits governmental interference with individual rights, but only the rights of certain people. For Brennan, restricting the constitutional protections for individual rights to a select group is an anathema. The Constitution, in his view, is a limited grant of authority to the federal government, and the Bill of Rights helps set the limits on that federal power. In short, Brennan treated the Bill of Rights as an integral part of the Constitution's grant of limited authority, whereas the Court separated the two documents and treated the Bill of Rights as an affirmative grant of rights to a limited group of people.

The holding in this case will, by its nature, have no direct impact on citizens of the United States. However, the Court's willingness to disassociate the Bill of Rights from the Constitution which it amended and to which it is attached may have profound effects in ways that no one can foresee. Justice Brennan's unwillingness to accept the Court's vision of our founding documents may prove to be an important declaration that judges in the future use to restore the protections of the Bill of Rights to all people.

Chief Justice Rehnquist wrote the opinion of the Court, joined by Justices White, O'Connor, Scalia, and Kennedy. Justice Stevens concurred in the Court's judgment. Justices Brennan, Marshall, and Blackmun dissented.

           ○ ○ ○

Justice BRENNAN, with whom Justice MARSHALL joins, dissenting.

Today the Court holds that although foreign nationals must abide by our laws even when in their own countries, our Government need not abide by the Fourth Amendment when it investigates them for violations of our laws. I respectfully dissent.

I

Particularly in the past decade, our Government has sought, successfully, to hold foreign nationals criminally liable under federal laws for conduct committed entirely beyond the territorial limits of the United States that nevertheless has effects in this country. Foreign nationals must now take care not to violate our drug laws, our antitrust laws, our securities laws, and a host of other federal criminal statutes. The enormous expansion of federal criminal jurisdiction outside our Nation's boundaries has led one commentator to suggest that our country's three largest exports are now "rock music, blue jeans, and United States law." Grundman, *The New Imperialism: The Extraterritorial Application of United States Law.*

The Constitution is the source of Congress' authority to criminalize conduct, whether here or abroad, and of the Executive's authority to investigate and prosecute such conduct. But the same Constitution also prescribes limits on our Government's authority to investigate, prosecute, and punish criminal conduct, whether foreign or domestic. As a plurality of the Court noted in *Reid v. Covert*: "The United States is entirely a creature of the Constitution. Its power and authority have no other source. It can only act in accordance with all the limitations imposed by the Constitution." * * * The Court today creates an antilogy: the Constitution authorizes our Government to enforce our criminal laws abroad, but when Government agents exercise this authority, the Fourth Amendment does not travel with them. This cannot be. At the very least, the Fourth Amendment is an unavoidable correlative of the Government's power to enforce the criminal law.

A

The Fourth Amendment guarantees the right of "the people" to be free from unreasonable searches and seizures and provides that a warrant shall issue only upon presentation of an oath or affirmation demonstrating probable cause and particularly describing the place to be searched and the persons or things to be seized. According to the majority, the term "the people" refers to "a class of persons who are part of a national community or who have otherwise developed sufficient connection with this country to be considered part of that community." The Court admits that "the people" extends beyond the citizenry, but leaves the precise contours of its "sufficient connection" test unclear. At one point the majority hints that aliens are protected by the Fourth Amendment only when they come within the United States and develop "substantial connections" with our country. At other junctures, the Court suggests that an alien's presence in the United States must be voluntary and that the alien must have "accepted some societal obligations."[6] At yet other points, the majority implies that respondent would

---

6. In this discussion, the Court implicitly suggests that the Fourth Amendment may not protect illegal aliens in the United States. Numerous lower courts, however, have held that illegal aliens in the United States are protected by the Fourth Amendment, and not a single lower court has held to the contrary.

be protected by the Fourth Amendment if the place searched were in the United States.[7]

What the majority ignores, however, is the most obvious connection between Verdugo-Urquidez and the United States: he was investigated and is being prosecuted for violations of United States law and may well spend the rest of his life in a United States prison. The "sufficient connection" is supplied not by Verdugo-Urquidez, but by the Government. Respondent is entitled to the protections of the Fourth Amendment because our Government, by investigating him and attempting to hold him accountable under United States criminal laws, has treated him as a member of our community for purposes of enforcing our laws. He has become, quite literally, one of the governed. Fundamental fairness and the ideals underlying our Bill of Rights compel the conclusion that when we impose "societal obligations," such as the obligation to comply with our criminal laws, on foreign nationals, we in turn are obliged to respect certain correlative rights, among them the Fourth Amendment.

By concluding that respondent is not one of "the people" protected by the Fourth Amendment, the majority disregards basic notions of mutuality. If we expect aliens to obey our laws, aliens should be able to expect that we will obey our Constitution when we investigate, prosecute, and punish them. We have recognized this fundamental principle of mutuality since the time of the Framers. James Madison, universally recognized as the primary architect of the Bill of Rights, emphasized the importance of mutuality when he spoke out against the Alien and Sedition Acts less than a decade after the adoption of the Fourth Amendment:

---

7. The Fourth Amendment contains no express or implied territorial limitations, and the majority does not hold that the Fourth Amendment is inapplicable to searches outside the United States and its territories. It holds that respondent is not protected by the Fourth Amendment because he is not one of "the people." Indeed, the majority's analysis implies that a foreign national who had developed sufficient connection with this country to be considered part of [our] community" would be protected by the Fourth Amendment regardless of the location of the search. Certainly nothing in the Court's opinion questions the validity of the rule, accepted by every Court of Appeals to have considered the question, that the Fourth Amendment applies to searches conducted by the United States Government against United States citizens abroad. A warrantless, unreasonable search and seizure is no less a violation of the Fourth Amendment because it occurs in Mexicali, Mexico, rather than Calexico, California.

[I]t does not follow, because aliens are not parties to the Constitution, as citizens are parties to it, that, whilst they actually conform to it, they have no right to its protection. Aliens are no more parties to the laws than they are parties to the Constitution; yet it will not be disputed that, as they owe, on one hand, a temporary obedience, they are entitled, in return, to their protection and advantage.

Mutuality is essential to ensure the fundamental fairness that underlies our Bill of Rights. Foreign nationals investigated and prosecuted for alleged violations of United States criminal laws are just as vulnerable to oppressive government behavior as are United States citizens investigated and prosecuted for the same alleged violations. Indeed, in a case such as this where the Government claims the existence of an international criminal conspiracy, citizens and foreign nationals may be co-defendants, charged under the same statutes for the same conduct and facing the same penalties if convicted. They may have been investigated by the same agents pursuant to the same enforcement authority. When our Government holds these co-defendants to the same standards of conduct, the Fourth Amendment, which protects the citizen from unreasonable searches and seizures, should protect the foreign national as well.

Mutuality also serves to inculcate the values of law and order. By respecting the rights of foreign nationals, we encourage other nations to respect the rights of our citizens. Moreover, as our Nation becomes increasingly concerned about the domestic effects of international crime, we cannot forget that the behavior of our law enforcement agents abroad sends a powerful message about the rule of law to individuals everywhere. As Justice Brandeis warned [in his dissenting opinion] in *Olmstead v. United States*:

> If the Government becomes a lawbreaker, it breeds contempt for law; it invites every man to become a law unto himself; it invites anarchy. To declare that in the administration of the criminal law the end justifies the means . . . would bring terrible retribution. Against that pernicious doctrine, this Court should resolutely set its face.

This principle is no different when the United States applies its rules of conduct to foreign nationals. If we seek respect for law and order, we must observe these principles ourselves. Lawlessness breeds lawlessness.

Finally, when United States agents conduct unreasonable searches, whether at home or abroad, they disregard our Nation's values. For over 200 years, our country has considered itself the world's foremost protector of liberties. The privacy and sanctity of the home have been primary tenets of our moral, philosophical, and judicial beliefs.[8] Our national interest is defined by those values and by the need to preserve our own just institutions. We take pride in our commitment to a government that cannot, on mere whim, break down doors and invade the most personal of places. We exhort other nations to follow our example. How can we explain to others—and to ourselves—that these long cherished ideals are suddenly of no consequence when the door being broken belongs to a foreigner?

* * *

B

In its effort to establish that respondent does not have sufficient connection to the United States to be considered one of "the people" protected by the Fourth Amendment, the Court relies on the text of the Amendment, historical evidence, and cases refusing to apply certain constitutional provisions outside the United States. None of these, however, justifies the majority's cramped interpretation of the Fourth Amendment's applicability.

The majority looks to various constitutional provisions and suggests that "'the people' seems to have been a term of art." But the majority admits that its "textual exegesis is by no means conclusive." One Member of the majority even states that he "cannot place any weight on the reference to 'the people' in the Fourth Amendment as a source of restricting its protections." The majority suggests a restrictive interpretation of those with "sufficient connection" to this country to be considered among "the people," but the term "the people" is better understood as a rhetorical counterpoint to "the government," such that rights that were reserved to "the people" were to protect all those subject to "the government." "The people" are "the governed."

In drafting both the Constitution and the Bill of Rights, the Framers strove to create a form of government decidedly different from their

---

8. President John Adams traced the origins of our independence from England to James Otis' impassioned argument in 1761 against the British writs of assistance, which allowed revenue officers to search American homes wherever and whenever they wanted. Otis argued that "[a] man's house is his castle," and Adams declared that "[t]hen and there the child Independence was born."

British heritage. Whereas the British Parliament was unconstrained, the Framers intended to create a government of limited powers. The colonists considered the British government dangerously omnipotent. After all, the British declaration of rights in 1688 had been enacted not by the people, but by Parliament. Americans vehemently attacked the notion that rights were matters of "favor and grace," given *to* the people *from* the government.

Thus, the Framers of the Bill of Rights did not purport to "create" rights. Rather, they designed the Bill of Rights to prohibit our Government from infringing rights and liberties presumed to be pre-existing. *See, e.g.,* U.S. Const. Amend. 9 ("The enumeration in the Constitution of certain rights, shall not be construed to deny or disparage others retained by the people"). The Fourth Amendment, for example, does not create a new right of security against unreasonable searches and seizures. It states that "[t]he right of the people to be secure in their persons, houses, papers, and effects, against unreasonable searches and seizures, *shall not be violated.*" The focus of the Fourth Amendment is on *what* the Government can and cannot do, and *how* it may act, not on *against whom* these actions may be taken. Bestowing rights and delineating protected groups would have been inconsistent with the drafters' fundamental conception of a Bill of Rights as a limitation on the Government's conduct with respect to all whom it seeks to govern. It is thus extremely unlikely that the Framers intended the narrow construction of the term "the people" presented today by the majority.

The drafting history of the Fourth Amendment also does not support the majority's interpretation of "the people." First, the drafters chose not to limit the right against unreasonable searches and seizures in more specific ways. They could have limited the right to "citizens," "freemen," "residents," or "the American people." The conventions called to ratify the Constitution in New York and Virginia, for example, each recommended an amendment stating, "That every freeman has a right to be secure from all unreasonable searches and seizures." But the drafters of the Fourth Amendment rejected this limitation and instead provided broadly for "[t]he right of the people to be secure in their persons, houses, papers, and effects." Second, historical materials contain no evidence that the drafters intended to limit the availability of the right expressed in the Fourth Amendment. The Amendment was introduced on the floor of Congress, considered by Committee, debated by the House of Representatives and the Senate, and submitted to the 13

States for approval. Throughout that entire process, no speaker or commentator, pro or con, referred to the term "the people" as a limitation.

* * *

III

* * * When we tell the world that we expect all people, wherever they may be, to abide by our laws, we cannot in the same breath tell the world that our law enforcement officers need not do the same. Because we cannot expect others to respect our laws until we respect our Constitution, I respectfully dissent.

◦ 4 ◦

DIFFERENT BUT EQUAL

The Declaration of Independence states that the equality of all men is a self-evident truth. Clearly, though, its drafters did not mean that all men have equivalent talents and capabilities, rather that they stand equally before the law.

How, then, is a government that is committed to the principle of equality to deal with the real differences among people? Put another way, when people are not in similar situations, is it even possible to treat them equally without treating them differently? More significant, how is our nation to confront the fact that its statement affirming the equality of men excludes half the population—women—and was written at a time when the government authorized the enslavement of one-fifth of the people within its borders?

These are not easy questions to answer. They are not easy for policymakers or legislators to address and they are not easy for judges who must resolve the disputes brought to them.

The opinions excerpted in this chapter deal with six attributes that can differentiate people: residency, marital status, gender, race, illegal immigrant status, and illegitimacy. In each case, a person claimed that one of these differences was something that the government was required to ignore; that it had to treat people equally despite these differences.

All of these claims were rooted, at least indirectly, in the Fourteenth Amendment to the United States Constitution. That Amendment provides that the government may not "deny to any person within its jurisdiction the equal protection of the laws." When the Supreme Court reviews equal protection claims, typically it passes judgment on a legislative scheme that classifies individuals into separate groups and then treats people in one group differently from people in another. The Court, therefore, is put potentially in conflict with the people's elected representatives, whether in Congress or in one of the state legislatures.

Cognizant of its own unrepresentative nature, and of the undemocratic effect of invalidating a legislative enactment, the Court struggles to balance the democratic will of the majority with the rights of all people to be treated equally before the law. To do this, the Court over time has created different standards to review various claims of unequal treatment. In most instances, the Court merely inquires whether the legislative classification has a *rational connection* to a *legitimate* governmental objective. Thus, for example, a welfare rule that provides benefits only to people whose income is below a certain level would be upheld, since it is rationally related to the legitimate goal of assisting the poor. Under this low level of scrutiny, almost all governmental classifications are upheld. After all, it is difficult for a court to label legislation—and implicitly those who enacted it—as irrational.

When a "suspect classification" is involved, however, the Court applies a higher standard of scrutiny. This standard demands that the classification be *narrowly tailored* to serve a *compelling* governmental interest. Few legislative classifications survive such an exacting test. Race is considered a suspect classification, which is not surprising given that the Fourteenth Amendment, ratified as part of Reconstruction following the Civil War, was designed in large measure to protect people of color, specifically those recently freed from slavery. However, the Court has implied that other "discrete and insular" minority groups, particularly those identified by an immutable characteristic and subject to an historical animus, might be deemed "suspect" as well.

Another justification the Court uses for strictly scrutinizing legislative enactments is when the legislation impinges upon a fundamental right. Thus for example, if a city zoning ordinance restricted families with young children to certain small residential areas—in an effort, say, to minimize the number of schools it had to build or the number and length of bus routes—that ordinance would infringe upon the rights to procreate and raise a family. While under a low level of scrutiny—the so-called "rational basis test"—the ordinance might be upheld, the Court undoubtedly would apply strict scrutiny, look for a strong relationship to a compelling governmental interest, and find the rule lacking.

The result of this methodology is that claims of inequality often lead to questions about whether certain activities involve a fundamental right. In that sense, we can all be affected by the Court's pronouncements in this area.

Justice Brennan's approach in equal protection cases was consistent with his focus in other areas of the law. That is, he looked to the impact on the person or group subjected to discrimination. For him, whether lawmakers intended to discriminate is secondary, almost irrelevant. Instead, the Court's greatest responsibility lies in scrutinizing practices that disproportionately affect a class of persons who have been traditionally oppressed, such as racial and ethnic minorities, women, and illegitimate children. Brennan's ability to identify with litigants whose personal characteristics or life circumstances differed radically from his own is manifested in this chapter's opinions.

SHAPIRO V. THOMPSON

April 21, 1969

The right to travel, to relocate from state to state without restriction, is one of the freedoms Americans value. It is a part of our mythology that one can move to a new place, start over and then do so again and again. Indeed, many early European settlers were doing just that when they immigrated to this continent. While it is now common to mourn the breakdown of insular neighborhoods and communities, the fact is our society always has been a highly mobile one.

The United States Constitution contemplates the unimpeded movement of people and goods across state lines. It gives Congress the power to regulate interstate commerce, thereby ensuring that individual states do not erect trade barriers, horde goods or resources, or restrict freedom of movement. Moreover, it guarantees the privileges and immunities of each citizen, thus preventing the government of one state from treating a resident of another as a foreign national.

Still, there is no single, identifiable provision in the Constitution that directly protects the right to travel. As with other basic rights, such as the right to privacy, the question is whether the right is viewed as so fundamental that it did not warrant specific mention, is adequately protected inferentially by other provisions, or was not intended by the Framers to be guaranteed at all.

The case excerpted here involved three state statutes that conditioned certain welfare benefits on residency within the state for at least one year. These statutes thus created two classes of people: those in residence for less than one year, and those residing in the state for one year or more. This triggered an equal protection problem for the court to resolve.

Justice Brennan, writing for the Court, disregarded the uncertain origins of the right to travel. Instead, he referred to previous cases and concluded, somewhat to the surprise of the dissenters, that the Court had consistently viewed the right to travel as fundamental. Having determined that the statutes infringed upon a fundamental freedom, Brennan, proceeded to apply the strict scrutiny standard to them. The states therefore were faced with the arduous task of showing that the classification was necessary to achieve a compelling state objective. The Court decided that merely protecting the public fisc does not rise to that level and it recommended other less restrictive means to resolve the states' other objectives.

As in many of his other opinions, Brennan personalized the issue by recounting the circumstances of one of the plaintiffs, a pregnant teen mother with a small child who moved from Massachusetts to Connecticut to be near her family. He concluded that limiting welfare assistance, thereby deterring indigents such as "a mother seeking to make a new life for herself and her children" from moving into a state, is constitutionally impermissible.

Justice Harlan, in his dissenting opinion, broadly criticized the use of strict scrutiny for classifications that affect a fundamental right. He also took specific issue with the Court's characterization of the right to travel as fundamental. However, Brennan's view carried the day and directly influenced the outcome in subsequent cases involving the right to travel for much of the next two decades.

Justice Brennan wrote the opinion of the Court, joined by Justices Douglas, Stewart, White, and Marshall. Chief Justice Warren and Justices Black and Harlan dissented.

○ ○ ○

MR. JUSTICE BRENNAN delivered the opinion of the Court.

* * * Each [of these consolidated cases] is an appeal from a decision of a three-judge District Court holding unconstitutional a State or District of Columbia statutory provision which denies welfare assistance to residents of the State or District who have not resided within their jurisdictions for at least one year immediately preceding their applications for such assistance. We affirm. * * *

I

In [one of the cases], the Connecticut Welfare Department invoked § 17-2d of the Connecticut General Statutes to deny the application of appellee Vivian Marie Thompson for assistance under the program for Aid to Families with Dependent Children (AFDC). She was a 19-year-old unwed mother of one child and pregnant with her second child when she changed her residence in June 1966 from Dorchester, Massachusetts, to Hartford, Connecticut, to live with her mother, a Hartford resident. She moved to her own apartment in Hartford in August 1966, when her mother was no longer able to support her and her infant son.

Because of her pregnancy, she was unable to work or enter a work training program. Her application for AFDC assistance, filed in August, was denied in November solely on the ground that, as required by § 17-2d, she had not lived in the State for a year before her application was filed. She brought this action in the District Court for the District of Connecticut where a three-judge court, one judge dissenting, declared § 17-2d unconstitutional. The majority held that the waiting-period requirement is unconstitutional because it "has a chilling effect on the right to travel." The majority also held that the provision was a violation of the Equal Protection Clause of the Fourth Amendment because the denial of relief to those resident in the State for less than a year is not based on any per-missible purpose but is solely designed, as "Connecticut states quite frankly," "to protect its fisc by discouraging entry of those who come needing relief." * * *

[Similar descriptions of the cases arising out of Pennsylvania and the District of Columbia followed—ed.]

II

There is no dispute that the effect of the waiting-period requirement in each case is to create two classes of needy resident families indistinguishable from each other except that one is composed of residents who have resided a year or more, and the second of residents who have resided less than a year, in the jurisdiction. On the basis of this sole difference the first class is granted and the second class is denied welfare aid upon which may depend the ability of the families to obtain the very means to subsist—food, shelter, and other necessities of life. In each case, the District Court found that appellees met the test for residence in their jurisdictions, as well as all other eligibility requirements except the requirement of residence for a full year prior to their applications. On reargument, appellees' central contention is that the statutory prohibition of benefits to residents of less than a year creates a classification which constitutes an invidious discrimination denying them equal protection of the laws.[6] We agree. The interests which appellants assert are promoted by the classification either may not constitutionally be promoted by government or are not compelling governmental interests.

---

6. This constitutional challenge cannot be answered by the argument that public assistance benefits are a "privilege" and not a "right." See Sherbert v. Verner.

III

Primarily, appellants justify the waiting-period requirement as a protective device to preserve the fiscal integrity of state public assistance programs. It is asserted that people who require welfare assistance during their first year of residence in a State are likely to become continuing burdens on state welfare programs. Therefore, the argument runs, if such people can be deterred from entering the jurisdiction by denying them welfare benefits during the first year, state programs to assist long-time residents will not be impaired by a substantial influx of indigent newcomers.

* * *

We do not doubt that the one-year waiting-period device is well suited to discourage the influx of poor families in need of assistance. An indigent who desires to migrate, resettle, find a new job, and start a new life will doubtless hesitate if he knows that he must risk making the move without the possibility of falling back on state welfare assistance during his first year of residence, when his need may be most acute. But the purpose of inhibiting migration by needy persons into the State is constitutionally impermissible.

This Court long ago recognized that the nature of our Federal Union and our constitutional concepts of personal liberty unite to require that all citizens be free to travel throughout the length and breadth of our land uninhibited by statutes, rules, or regulations which unreasonably burden or restrict this movement. * * *

We have no occasion to ascribe the source of this right to travel interstate to a particular constitutional provision. It suffices that, as Mr. Justice Stewart said for the Court in *United States v. Guest*:

> The constitutional right to travel from one State to another . . . occupies a position fundamental to the concept of our Federal Union. It is a right that has been firmly established and repeatedly recognized. * * *

Thus, the purpose of deterring the in-migration of indigents cannot serve as justification for the classification created by the one-year waiting period, since that purpose is constitutionally impermissible. If a law has "no other purpose . . . than to chill the assertion of constitutional rights by penalizing those who choose to exercise them, then it [is] patently unconstitutional." *United States v. Jackson*.

Alternatively, appellants argue that even if it is impermissible for a State to attempt to deter the entry of all indigents, the challenged classification may be justified as a permissible state attempt to discourage those indigents who would enter the State solely to obtain larger benefits. We observe first that none of the statutes before us is tailored to serve that objective. Rather, the class of barred newcomers is all-inclusive, lumping the great majority who come to the State for other purposes with those who come for the sole purpose of collecting higher benefits. * * *

More fundamentally, a State may no more try to fence out those indigents who seek higher welfare benefits than it may try to fence out indigents generally. Implicit in any such distinction is the notion that indigents who enter a State with the hope of securing higher welfare benefits are somehow less deserving than indigents who do not take this consideration into account. But we do not perceive why a mother who is seeking to make a new life for herself and her children should be regarded as less deserving because she considers, among others factors, the level of a State's public assistance. Surely such a mother is no less deserving than a mother who moves into a particular State in order to take advantage of its better educational facilities.

Appellants argue further that the challenged classification may be sustained as an attempt to distinguish between new and old residents on the basis of the contribution they have made to the community through the payment of taxes. We have difficulty seeing how long-term residents who qualify for welfare are making a greater present contribution to the State in taxes than indigent residents who have recently arrived. * * * Appellants' reasoning would logically permit the State to bar new residents from schools, parks, and libraries or deprive them of police and fire protection. Indeed it would permit the State to apportion all benefits and services according to the past tax contributions of its citizens. The Equal Protection Clause prohibits such an apportionment of state services.

We recognize that a State has a valid interest in preserving the fiscal integrity of its programs. It may legitimately attempt to limit its expenditures, whether for public assistance, public education, or any other program. But a State may not accomplish such a purpose by invidious distinctions between classes of its citizens. It could not, for example, reduce expenditures for education by barring indigent children from its schools. Similarly, in the cases before us, appellants must do more than show that denying welfare benefits to new residents saves money. The saving of welfare costs cannot justify an otherwise invidious classification.

In sum, neither deterrence of indigents from migrating to the State nor limitation of welfare benefits to those regarded as contributing to the State is a constitutionally permissible state objective.

* * *

Since the classification here touches on the fundamental right of interstate movement, its constitutionality must be judged by the stricter standard of whether it promotes a compelling state interest. Under this standard, the waiting-period requirement clearly violates the Equal Protection Clause.[21]

* * *

Accordingly, the judgments are

Affirmed.

---

21. We imply no view of the validity of waiting-period or residence requirements determining eligibility to vote, eligibility for tuition-free education, to obtain a license to practice a profession, to hunt or fish, and so forth. Such requirements may promote compelling state interests on the one hand, or, on the other, may not be penalties upon the exercise of the constitutional right of interstate travel.

EISENSTADT V. BAIRD

March 22, 1972

This case arose from the prosecution of a guest speaker at a private university for both displaying contraceptives in the course of a lecture and distributing one to an unmarried woman. Lower courts had invalidated the two charges on different grounds. One court concluded that the prosecution for displaying contraceptives violated the lecturer's freedom of speech. The other court ruled that the law's restriction on the distribution of contraceptives unconstitutionally infringed upon the "right to privacy," which the Supreme Court had recognized seven years earlier in *Griswold v. Connecticut* (1965).

Justice Brennan's opinion for the Court took a different tack. The *Griswold* decision had invalidated restrictions on the dissemination of birth control information to married adults. Here, since single persons—but not married persons—were statutorily prohibited from obtaining contraceptives for pregnancy prevention, the Supreme Court framed the constitutional issue as a question of equal protection.

As explained in footnote 7, Brennan's opinion did not directly address whether the statute infringed upon any fundamental right. The extent to which unmarried persons enjoy such a fundamental "right to privacy" in matters of sexuality was a broader question than the Court needed to explore because there was an alternate and narrower ground for making the decision: the "different treatment accorded married and unmarried persons."

Marital status is not considered a suspect classification entitled to receive the heightened scrutiny afforded to race or national origin. For this reason, the Court used the "rational basis" test, the most deferential toward legislative action, in reviewing the statute in question. Nevertheless, because the Commonwealth of Massachusetts failed to articulate the purpose behind the statute, the Court concluded that the law unjustifiably discriminated against single persons by preventing them from lawfully obtaining contraceptives.

The Court's emphasis on equal protection is somewhat misleading. The decision's significance has proven to be its discussion of the "right to privacy," particularly in the context of reproductive freedom. Brennan's language near the end of the opinion about unwarranted governmental intrusion into

197

decisions about childbearing foreshadowed what many view as the Supreme Court's most controversial ruling. For it was less than two years later that Justice Blackmun would be revered by some and reviled by others for his authorship of the opinion in *Roe v. Wade* (1973), establishing a woman's right to choose whether to terminate her pregnancy.

Justice Brennan wrote the opinion of the Court, joined by Justices Douglas, Stewart, and Marshall. Justices White and Blackmun concurred in the Court's judgment. Chief Justice Burger dissented.

✿   ✿   ✿

MR. JUSTICE BRENNAN delivered the opinion of the Court.

Appellee William Baird was convicted at a bench trial in the Massachusetts Superior Court under Massachusetts General Law, chapter 272, § 21, first, for exhibiting contraceptive articles in the course of delivering a lecture on contraception to a group of students at Boston University and, second, for giving a young woman a package of Emko vaginal foam at the close of his address. The Massachusetts Supreme Judicial Court unanimously set aside the conviction for exhibiting contraceptives on the ground that it violated Baird's First Amendment rights, but by a four-to-three vote sustained the conviction for giving away the foam. [Baird appealed and the Court of Appeals for the First Circuit reversed the distribution conviction.] This appeal by the Sheriff of Suffolk County, Massachusetts, followed, and we * * * affirm.

Massachusetts General Law, chapter 272, § 21, under which Baird was convicted, provides a maximum five-year term of imprisonment for "whoever . . . gives away . . . any drug, medicine, instrument or article whatever for the prevention of conception," except as authorized in § 21A. Under § 21A, "[a] registered physician may administer to or prescribe for any married person drugs or articles intended for the prevention of pregnancy or conception. [And a] registered pharmacist actually engaged in the business of pharmacy may furnish such drugs or articles to any married person presenting a prescription from a registered physician." As interpreted by the State Supreme Judicial Court, these provisions make it a felony for anyone, other than a registered physician or pharmacist acting in accordance with the terms of § 21A, to dispense any article with the intention that it be used for the prevention of conception. The statutory scheme distinguishes among three

distinct classes of distributees—first, married persons may obtain contraceptives to prevent pregnancy, but only from doctors or druggists
on prescription; second, single persons may not obtain contraceptives
from anyone to prevent pregnancy; and, third, married or single persons may obtain contraceptives from anyone to prevent not pregnancy,
but the spread of disease. * * *

The legislative purposes that the statute is meant to serve are not altogether clear. In [its decision below], the Supreme Judicial Court noted
only the State's interest in protecting the health of its citizens: "[T]he
prohibition in § 21," the court declared, "is directly related to" the State's
goal of "preventing the distribution of articles designed to prevent conception which may have undesirable, if not dangerous, physical consequences." In a subsequent decision, the court, however, found "a second
and more compelling ground for upholding the statute"—namely, to
protect morals through "regulating the private sexual lives of single
persons." The Court of Appeals, for reasons that will appear, did not
consider the promotion of health or the protection of morals through
the deterrence of fornication to be the legislative aim. Instead, the court
concluded that the statutory goal was to limit contraception in and of
itself—a purpose that the court held conflicted "with fundamental human rights" under *Griswold v. Connecticut*, where this Court struck
down Connecticut's prohibition against the use of contraceptives as an
unconstitutional infringement of the right of marital privacy.

We agree that the goals of deterring premarital sex and regulating the
distribution of potentially harmful articles cannot reasonably be regarded as legislative aims of §§ 21 and 21A. And we hold that the statute,
viewed as a prohibition on contraception *per se*, violates the rights of
single persons under the Equal Protection Clause of the Fourteenth
Amendment.

* * *

II

The basic principles governing application of the Equal Protection
Clause of the Fourteenth Amendment are familiar. As the Chief Justice
only recently explained in *Reed v. Reed*:

In applying that clause, this Court has consistently recognized that the
Fourteenth Amendment does not deny to States the power to treat dif-

ferent classes of persons in different ways. The Equal Protection Clause of that amendment does, however, deny to States the power to legislate that different treatment be accorded to persons placed by a statute into different classes on the basis of criteria wholly unrelated to the objective of that statute. A classification must be reasonable, not arbitrary, and must rest upon some ground of difference having a fair and substantial relation to the object of the legislation, so that all persons similarly circumstanced shall be treated alike.

The question for our determination in this case is whether there is some ground of difference that rationally explains the different treatment accorded married and unmarried persons under §§ 21 and 21A.[7] For the reasons that follow, we conclude that no such ground exists.

First—Section 21 stems from [an 1879 statute], which prohibited, without exception, distribution of articles intended to be used as contraceptives. [T]he Massachusetts Supreme Judicial Court explained that the [original] law's "plain purpose is to protect purity, to preserve chastity, to encourage continence and self restraint, to defend the sanctity of the home, and thus to engender in the State and nation a virile and virtuous race of men and women." Although the State clearly abandoned that purpose with the enactment of § 21A, at least insofar as the illicit sexual activities of married persons are concerned, the court reiterated that the object of the legislation is to discourage premarital sexual intercourse. Conceding that the State could, consistently with the Equal Protection Clause, regard the problems of extramarital and premarital sexual relations as "[e]vils . . . of different dimensions and proportions, requiring different remedies," *Williamson v. Lee Optical Co.*, we cannot agree that the deterrence of premarital sex may reasonably be regarded as the purpose of the Massachusetts law.

It would be plainly unreasonable to assume that Massachusetts has prescribed pregnancy and the birth of an unwanted child as punishment for fornication, which is a misdemeanor under Massachusetts [Law]. Aside from the scheme of values that assumption would attribute to the State, it is abundantly clear that the effect of the ban on dis-

---

7. Of course, if we were to conclude that the Massachusetts statute impinges upon fundamental freedoms under *Griswold*, the statutory classification would have to be not merely rationally related to a valid public purpose but necessary to the achievement of a compelling state interest. But just as in *Reed v. Reed*, we do not have to address the statute's validity under that test because the law fails to satisfy even the more lenient equal protection standard.

tribution of contraceptives to unmarried persons has at best a marginal relation to the proffered objective. What Mr. Justice Goldberg said in *Griswold v. Connecticut* (concurring opinion), concerning the effect of Connecticut's prohibition on the use of contraceptives in discouraging extramarital sexual relations, is equally applicable here. "The rationality of this justification is dubious, particularly in light of the admitted widespread availability to all persons in the State of Connecticut, unmarried as well as married, of birth-control devices for the prevention of disease, as distinguished from the prevention of conception." Like Connecticut's laws, §§ 21 and 21A do not at all regulate the distribution of contraceptives when they are to be used to prevent not pregnancy, but the spread of disease. Nor, in making contraceptives available to married persons without regard to their intended use, does Massachusetts attempt to deter married persons from engaging in illicit sexual relations with unmarried persons. Even on the assumption that the fear of pregnancy operates as a deterrent to fornication, the Massachusetts statute is thus so riddled with exceptions that deterrence of premarital sex cannot reasonably be regarded as its aim.

Moreover, §§ 21 and 21A on their face have a dubious relation to the State's criminal prohibition on fornication. As the Court of Appeals explained, "Fornication is a misdemeanor [in Massachusetts], entailing a thirty dollar fine, or three months in jail. Violation of the present statute is a felony, punishable by five years in prison. We find it hard to believe that the legislature adopted a statute carrying a five-year penalty for its possible, obviously by no means fully effective, deterrence of the commission of a ninety-day misdemeanor." Even conceding the legislature a full measure of discretion in fashioning means to prevent fornication, and recognizing that the State may seek to deter prohibited conduct by punishing more severely those who facilitate than those who actually engage in its commission, we, like the Court of Appeals, cannot believe that in this instance Massachusetts has chosen to expose the aider and abetter who simply *gives away* a contraceptive to *20* times the *90-day* sentence of the offender himself. The very terms of the State's criminal statutes, coupled with the *de minimis* effect of §§ 21 and 21A in deterring fornication, thus compel the conclusion that such deterrence cannot reasonably be taken as the purpose of the ban on distribution of contraceptives to unmarried persons.

Second—Section 21A was added to the Massachusetts General Laws by [a 1966 statute]. The Supreme Judicial Court [below] held that the purpose of the amendment was to serve the health needs of the community by regulating the distribution of potentially harmful articles. It is plain that Massachusetts had no such purpose in mind before the enactment of § 21A. As the Court of Appeals remarked, "Consistent with the fact that the statute was contained in a chapter dealing with 'Crimes Against Chastity, Morality, Decency and Good Order,' it was cast only in terms of morals. A physician was forbidden to prescribe contraceptives even when needed for the protection of health. Nor did the Court of Appeals "believe that the legislature [in enacting § 21A] suddenly reversed its field and developed an interest in health. Rather, it merely made what it thought to be the precise accommodation necessary to escape the *Griswold* ruling."

Again, we must agree with the Court of Appeals. If health were the rationale of § 21A, the statute would be both discriminatory and overboard. Dissenting [below], Justices Whittemore and Cutter stated that they saw "in § 21 and § 21A, read together, no public health purpose. If there is need to have a physician prescribe (and a pharmacist dispense) contraceptives, that need is as great for unmarried persons as for married persons." The Court of Appeals added: "If the prohibition [on distribution to unmarried persons] . . . is to be taken to mean that the same physician who can prescribe for married patients does not have sufficient skill to protect the health of patients who lack a marriage certificate, or who may be currently divorced, it is illogical to the point of irrationality." Furthermore, we must join the Court of Appeals in noting that not all contraceptives are potentially dangerous. As a result, if the Massachusetts statute were a health measure, it would not only invidiously discriminate against the unmarried, but also be overbroad with respect to the married, a fact that the Supreme Judicial Court itself seems to have conceded where it noted that "it may well be that certain contraceptive medication and devices constitute no hazard to health, in which event it could be argued that the statute swept too broadly in its prohibition." "In this posture," as the Court of Appeals concluded, "it is impossible to think of the statute as intended as a health measure for the unmarried, and it is almost as difficult to think of it as so intended even as to the married."

But if further proof that the Massachusetts statute is not a health measure is necessary, the argument of Justice Spiegel, who also dissented [below], is conclusive: "It is at best a strained conception to say that the Legislature intended to prevent the distribution of articles which may have undesirable, if not dangerous, physical consequences. If that was the Legislature's goal, § 21 is not required" in view of the federal and state laws already regulating the distribution of harmful drugs. We conclude, accordingly, that, despite the statute's superficial earmarks as a health measure, health, on the face of the statute, may no more reasonably be regarded as its purpose than the deterrence of premarital sexual relations.

Third—If the Massachusetts statute cannot be upheld as a deterrent to fornication or as a health measure, may it, nevertheless, be sustained simply as a prohibition on contraception? * * * We need not and do not, however, decide that important question in this case because, whatever the rights of the individual to access to contraceptives may be, the rights must be the same for the unmarried and the married alike.

If under *Griswold* the distribution of contraceptives to married persons cannot be prohibited, a ban on distribution to unmarried persons would be equally impermissible. It is true that in *Griswold* the right of privacy in question inhered in the marital relationship. Yet the marital couple is not an independent entity with a mind and heart of its own, but an association of two individuals each with a separate intellectual and emotional makeup. If the right of privacy means anything, it is the right of the individual, married or single, to be free from unwarranted governmental intrusion into matters so fundamentally affecting a person as the decision whether to bear or beget a child.

On the other hand, if *Griswold* is no bar to a prohibition on the distribution of contraceptives, the State could not, consistently with the Equal Protection Clause, outlaw distribution to unmarried but not to married persons. In each case the evil, as perceived by the State, would be identical, and the under inclusion would be invidious. Mr. Justice Jackson, concurring in *Railway Express Agency v. New York*, made the point:

The framers of the Constitution knew, and we should not forget today, that there is no more effective practical guaranty against arbitrary and unreasonable government than to require that the principles of law which officials would impose upon a minority must be imposed generally. Conversely, nothing opens the door to arbitrary action so effectively as to allow those officials to pick and choose only a few to whom they will apply legislation and thus to escape the political retribution that might be visited upon them if larger numbers were affected. Courts can take no better measure to assure that laws will be just than to require that laws be equal in operation.

Although Mr. Justice Jackson's comments had reference to administrative regulations, the principle he affirmed has equal application to the legislation here. We hold that by providing dissimilar treatment for married and unmarried persons who are similarly situated, §§ 21 and 21A violate the Equal Protection Clause. The judgment of the Court of Appeals is

Affirmed.

FRONTIERO V. RICHARDSON

May 14, 1973

Claims of sex discrimination present a unique and difficult problem. The Fourteenth Amendment requires equal protection of the laws to all persons within the government's jurisdiction. This language, coupled with the immutability of sex, would seem an appropriate basis for strictly scrutinizing sex-based legal classifications.

However, when the Fourteenth Amendment was ratified in 1868, the principal goal of its Equal Protection Clause was to eliminate discrimination based on race and national origin. Discrimination based on sex was simply not an issue. Indeed, in the mid-nineteenth century women were deprived of most civil liberties and generally denied participation in public life. The notion of a so-called "separate spheres" ideology was pervasive throughout American society and culture: women were to focus on the private sphere, including the home and domestic concerns; men were to emphasize matters of the public sphere, such as paid employment and participation in community affairs. The laws reflected and reinforced this gender-role stereotyping. Moreover, since women were denied the vote except in a handful of western territories, they were powerless to use the legislative process to change their legal status. Thus, although the principle of equality would seem to apply across gender lines, women apparently were not among the persons intended to be protected by the Fourteenth Amendment.

Passage of the Nineteenth Amendment in 1920, which granted women the right to vote, ostensibly made women full partners in the political system. However, women and women's rights advocates were unable to capitalize on this new political clout by writing a protection for gender equality into the Constitution. Beginning in 1923, some form of an equal rights amendment—to expressly protect the rights of women—was introduced into every session of Congress for fifty years. None passed. The national electorate, through its mostly male representatives, was apparently not willing to embrace such a departure from historical practices.

In this context, what is the appropriate standard for reviewing gender-based legal rules? In 1971, the United States Supreme Court for the first time used the Equal Protection Clause to strike down a law that discriminated based on sex. In that case, *Reed v. Reed*, the Court held that an Idaho law that gave preference to men over women as administrators of probate estates violated equal protection. Under that law, if both the mother and father of a deceased child applied to serve as the administrator of the child's estate, the father would be automatically selected. The State of Idaho argued that this rule served administrative convenience by eliminating the need to make a choice between the two applicants. It also argued that its preference for male administrators was reasonable because men were "as a rule more conversant with business affairs . . . than women," an argument accepted by the Idaho Supreme Court in its review of the case at the state level. Chief Justice Burger, writing for the Court, recognized the legitimacy of the state's goal of its probate courts' workload, but nevertheless concluded that a classification scheme that grants a mandatory preference to either sex "is to make the very kind of arbitrary legislative choice forbidden by the Equal Protection Clause."

The standard of review was somewhat unclear because the Court purported to apply a "rational basis" standard but also used language suggesting a more intensive level of scrutiny. The decision thus set the stage for a more definite pronouncement by the Court on the status of equal protection challenges involving sex-based classifications.

Before that could happen, Congress passed an Equal Rights Amendment and sent it to the states for ratification. The text of the proposed amendment provided that "[e]quality of rights under the law shall not be denied or abridged by the United States or any State on account of sex." One purpose of that proposal was to ensure that sex-based classifications would be subjected to the same strict scrutiny standard applicable to race-based classifications. While the ratification effort was still ongoing, the case of *Frontiero v. Richardson* made its way to the Supreme Court.

In *Frontiero*, the plaintiff contended that federal military regulations providing certain benefits for dependents discriminated against female service personnel in violation of the constitution.* Ruth Bader Ginsburg, who would later take a seat on the Supreme Court, argued on behalf of the plaintiff that "strict scrutiny" should apply: sex-based classifications should be acceptable

---

*Technically, the Equal Protection Clause of the Fourteenth Amendment applies only to actions by states, not actions by the federal government. However, the Supreme Court has long held that the Due Process Clause of the Fifth Amendment, which requires that the federal government not deny any person due process of the laws, forbids unjustifiable discrimination. Thus, if a state classification would be invalid under the Equal Protection Clause of the Fourteenth Amendment, a similar federal classification would be inconsistent with the due process requirement of the Fifth Amendment.

only if they are narrowly tailored to serve a compelling governmental inter-est. Justice Brennan announced the judgment of the Court. Acknowledging that "women still face pervasive, although at times more subtle, discrimina-tion in our educational institutions, in the job market, and, perhaps most conspicuously, in the political arena," he adopted the strict scrutiny standard. However, he wrote only on behalf of a plurality of four. Four other justices agreed to strike down the regulations but declined to adopt a strict level of scrutiny. Justice Powell, speaking for himself, Chief Justice Burger, and Jus-tice Blackmun, expressed reluctance to determine the appropriate level of scrutiny while the ERA ratification effort was still pending. He conceded that the Court sometimes resolves issues without waiting for a legislative man-date, but said that in this situation it was not appropriate "to pre-empt by judicial action a major political decision."

The effort to ratify the ERA, although fueled in part by skepticism that the Court would ever apply strict scrutiny to sex-based classifications, neverthe-less failed. The time limit on ratification that Congress had imposed, and then extended, expired while the Amendment was still one state short. It is not hard to see a measure of irony in the fact that the effort of women's rights advocates to enact an Equal Rights Amendment may actually have under-mined Brennan's effort to forge a consensus on the use of strict scrutiny to review gender-based classifications.

In fact, *Frontiero* proved to be the closest the Court has ever come to adopt-ing a strict standard of review for sex-based classifications. In the 1976 case of *Craig v. Boren*, the Court nullified an Oklahoma statute that permitted women, but not men, between the ages of 18 and 21 to purchase 3.2% beer. Brennan, writing for the Court, had to settle for an intermediate level of re-view. Under this standard, gender is viewed as a "quasi-suspect" classifica-tion, and sex-based rules are upheld only if *substantially related* to the achieve-ment of an *important* governmental objective. Thus, while strict scrutiny usually leads to the invalidation of a classification and the rational basis test normally leads to the opposite conclusion, gender-based classifications are left in a much more ambiguous zone. The difficulty of applying that impre-cise standard is intensified by the fact that there are real biological differences between men and women. Thus, application of the Equal Protection Clause to gender-based rules and resolution of sexual equality issues generally re-main an ongoing struggle for the Court, the Congress, and society at large.

The legal significance of Brennan's plurality opinion in *Frontiero* has thus been minimized. Nevertheless, the opinion, particularly its description of the challenges women face in modern life, remains a lingering testament to Brennan's views about equality and the equal treatment of women.

Justice Brennan announced the judgment of the Court and delivered an opinion joined by Justices Douglas, White, and Marshall. Justice Stewart concurred in the judgment. Justice Powell also concurred in the judgment and filed an opinion joined by Chief Justice Burger and Justice Blackmun. Justice Rehnquist dissented.

o   o   o

Mr. Justice BRENNAN announced the judgment of the Court in an opinion in which Mr. Justice DOUGLAS, Mr. Justice WHITE, and Mr. Justice MARSHALL join.

The question before us concerns the right of a female member of the uniformed services[1] to claim her spouse as a "dependent" for the purposes of obtaining increased quarters allowances and medical and dental benefits on an equal footing with male members. Under [the applicable] statutes, a serviceman may claim his wife as a "dependent" without regard to whether she is in fact dependent upon him for any part of her support. A servicewoman, on the other hand, may not claim her husband as a "dependent" under these programs unless he is in fact dependent upon her for over one-half of his support. Thus, the question for decision is whether this difference in treatment constitutes an unconstitutional discrimination against servicewomen in violation of the Due Process Clause of the Fifth Amendment. * * *

I

In an effort to attract career personnel through reenlistment, Congress established a scheme for the provision of fringe benefits to members of the uniformed services on a competitive basis with business and industry. Thus, a member of the uniformed services with dependents is entitled to an increased "basic allowence for quarters" and a member's dependents are provided comprehensive medical and dental care.

Appellant Sharron Frontiero, a lieutenant in the United States Air

---

1. The "uniformed services" include the Army, Navy, Air Force, Marine Corps, Coast Guard, Environmental Science Services Administration, and Public Health Service.

Force, sought increased quarters allowances, and housing and medical benefits for her husband, appellant Joseph Frontiero, on the ground that he was her "dependent." Although such benefits would automatically have been granted with respect to the wife of a male member of the uniformed services, appellant's application was denied because she failed to demonstrate that her husband was dependent on her for more than one-half of his support.[4] Appellants then commenced this suit, contending that, by making this distinction, the statutes unreasonably discriminate on the basis of sex in violation of the Due Process Clause of the Fifth Amendment. In essence, appellants asserted that the discriminatory impact of the statutes is twofold: first, as a procedural matter, a female member is required to demonstrate her spouse's dependency, while no such burden is imposed upon male members; and, second, as a substantive matter, a male member who does not provide more than one-half of his wife's support receives benefits, while a similarly situated female member is denied such benefits. Appellants therefore sought a permanent injunction against the continued enforcement of these statutes and an order directing the appellees to provide Lieutenant Frontiero with the same housing and medical benefits that a similarly situated male member would receive.

Although the legislative history of these statutes sheds virtually no light on the purposes underlying the differential treatment accorded male and female members, a majority of the three-judge District Court surmised that Congress might reasonably have concluded that, since the husband in our society is generally the "breadwinner" in the family—and the wife typically the "dependent" partner—"it would be more economical to require married female members claiming husbands to prove actual dependency than to extend the presumption of dependency to such members." Indeed, given the fact that approximately 99% of all members of the uniformed services are male, the District Court speculated that such differential treatment might conceivably lead to a "considerable saving of administrative expense and manpower."

---

4. Appellant Joseph Frontiero is a full-time student at Huntingdon College in Montgomery, Alabama. According to the agreed stipulation of facts, his living expenses, including his share of the house-hold expenses, total approximately $354 per month. Since he receives $205 per month in veterans' benefits, it is clear that he is not dependent upon appellant Sharron Frontiero for more than one-half of his support.

II

At the outset, appellants contend that classifications based upon sex, like classifications based upon race, alienage, and national origin, are inherently suspect and must therefore be subjected to close judicial scrutiny. We agree and, indeed, find at least implicit support for such an approach in our unanimous decision only last Term in *Reed v. Reed.*

* * *

There can be no doubt that our Nation has had a long and unfortunate history of sex discrimination.[13] Traditionally, such discrimination was rationalized by an attitude of "romantic paternalism" which, in practical effect, put women, not on a pedestal, but in a cage. Indeed, this paternalistic attitude became so firmly rooted in our national consciousness that, 100 years ago, a distinguished Member of this Court was able to proclaim:

> Man is, or should be, women's protector and defender. The natural and proper timidity and delicacy which belongs to the female sex evidently unfits it for many of the occupations of civil life. The constitution of the family organization, which is founded in the divine ordinance, as well as in the nature of things, indicates the domestic sphere as that which properly belongs to the domain and functions of womanhood. * * * The paramount destiny and mission of woman are to fulfil the noble and benign offices of wife and mother. This is the law of the Creator.

Bradwell v. Illinois (Bradley, J. dissenting).

As a result of notions such as these, our statute books gradually became laden with gross, stereotyped distinctions between the sexes and, indeed, throughout much of the 19th century the position of women in our society was, in many respects, comparable to that of blacks under the pre–Civil War slave codes. Neither slaves nor women could hold office, serve on juries, or bring suit in their own names, and married women traditionally were denied the legal capacity to hold or convey property or to serve as legal guardians of their own children. And although blacks were guaranteed the right to vote in 1870, women were

---

13. Indeed, the position of women in this country at its inception is reflected in the view expressed by Thomas Jefferson that women should be neither seen nor heard in society's decisionmaking councils.

denied even that right—which is itself "preservative of other basic civil and political rights"—until adoption of the Nineteenth Amendment half a century later.

It is true, of course, that the position of women in America has improved markedly in recent decades. Nevertheless, it can hardly be doubted that, in part because of the high visibility of the sex characteristic, women still face pervasive, although at times more subtle, discrimination in our educational institutions, in the job market and, perhaps most conspicuously, in the political arena.[17]

Moreover, since sex, like race and national origin, is an immutable characteristic determined solely by the accident of birth, the imposition of special disabilities upon the members of a particular sex because of their sex would seem to violate "the basic concept of our system that legal burdens should bear some relationship to individual responsibility." And what differentiates sex from such non-suspect statuses as intelligence or physical disability, and aligns it with the recognized suspect criteria, is that the sex characteristic frequently bears no relation to ability to perform or contribute to society. As a result, statutory distinctions between the sexes often have the effect of invidiously relegating the entire class of females to inferior legal status without regard to the actual capabilities of its individual members.

* * *

With these considerations in mind, we can only conclude that classifications based upon sex, like classifications based upon race, alienage, or national origin, are inherently suspect, and must therefore be subjected to strict judicial scrutiny. Applying the analysis mandated by that stricter standard of review, it is clear that the statutory scheme now before us is constitutionally invalid.

III

The sole basis of the classification established in the challenged statutes is the sex of the individuals involved. Thus, a female member of

---

17. It is true, of course, that when viewed in the abstract, women do not constitute a small and powerless minority. Nevertheless, in part because of past discrimination, women are vastly underrepresented in this Nation's decisionmaking councils. There has never been a female President, nor a female member of this Court. Not a single woman presently sits in the United States Senate, and only 14 women hold seats in the House of Representatives. And, as appellants point out, this underrepresentation is present throughout all levels of our State and Federal Government.

212 DIFFERENT BUT EQUAL

the uniformed services seeking to obtain housing and medical benefits for her spouse must prove his dependency in fact, whereas no such burden is imposed upon male members. In addition, the statutes operate so as to deny benefits to a female member, such as appellant Sharron Frontiero, who provides less than one-half of her spouse's support, while at the same time granting such benefits to a male member who likewise provides less than one-half of his spouse's support. Thus, to this extent at least, it may fairly be said that these statutes command "dissimilar treatment for men and women who are . . . similarly situated." *Reed v. Reed.*

Moreover, the Government concedes that the differential treatment accorded men and women under these statutes serves no purpose other than mere "administrative convenience." In essence, the Government maintains that, as an empirical matter, wives in our society frequently are dependent upon their husbands, while husbands rarely are dependent upon their wives. Thus, the Government argues that Congress might reasonably have concluded that it would be both cheaper and easier simply conclusively to presume that wives of male members are financially dependent upon their husbands, while burdening female members with the task of establishing dependency in fact.[22]

The Government offers no concrete evidence, however, tending to support its view that such differential treatment in fact saves the Government any money. In order to satisfy the demands of strict judicial scrutiny, the Government must demonstrate, for example, that it is actually cheaper to grant increased benefits with respect to all male members, than it is to determine which male members are in fact entitled to such benefits and to grant increased benefits only to those members whose wives actually meet the dependency requirement. Here, however, there is substantial evidence that, if put to the test, many of the wives of male members would fail to qualify for benefits. And in light of the fact that the dependency determination with respect to the husbands of female members is presently made solely on the basis of affidavits rather than through the more costly hearing process, the Government's explanation of the statutory scheme is, to say the least, questionable.

---

22. It should be noted that these statutes are not in any sense designed to rectify the effects of past discrimination against women. On the contrary, these statutes seize upon a group—women—who have historically suffered discrimination in employment, and rely on the effects of this past discrimination as a justification for heaping on additional economic disadvantages.

In any case, our prior decisions make clear that, although efficacious administration of governmental programs is not without some importance, "the Constitution recognizes higher values than speed and efficiency." *Stanley v. Illinois.* And when we enter the realm of "strict judicial scrutiny," there can be no doubt that "administrative convenience" is not a shibboleth, the mere recitation of which dictates constitutionality. On the contrary, any statutory scheme which draws a sharp line between the sexes, solely for the purpose of achieving administrative convenience, necessarily commands "dissimilar treatment for men and women who are . . . similarly situated," and therefore involves the "very kind of arbitrary legislative choice forbidden by the [Constitution]." *Reed v. Reed.* We therefore conclude that, by according differential treatment to male and female members of the uniformed services for the sole purpose of achieving administrative convenience, the challenged statutes violate the Due Process Clause of the Fifth Amendment insofar as they require a female member to prove the dependency of her husband.

Reversed.

REGENTS OF THE UNIVERSITY OF CALIFORNIA V. BAKKE

June 28, 1978

It is tragic that a country founded on principles of freedom and equality was built in part on the backs of slave labor and financed in part through the slave trade. Even ratification of the Fourteenth Amendment, which granted all people equal protection of the law, made few meaningful inroads into the depths of the social and economic discrimination to which most Blacks were subjected in this country. That is because the Amendment prohibited only governmental discrimination, not discrimination by private parties such as employers, landlords, hotels, restaurants, common carriers, and private schools. Without real access to good jobs and good schools, even a century of freedom left Blacks in an impoverished and unequal condition.

Only with the enactment of the federal Civil Rights Act of 1964, almost two centuries after the country was founded and one century after the adoption of the Fourteenth Amendment, did the nation finally apply its promise of equality to persons of color. That Act prohibited discrimination in a full range of commercial and social activities, including education, employment, housing, and places of public accommodation. In doing so, it appeared to fulfill the dream of providing equal opportunity for all individuals, regardless of their race, color, creed, sex or national origin. Of course, no single piece of legislation could end overnight the cumulative effects of centuries of slavery and discrimination. More was needed to accomplish that. Enter affirmative action.

An affirmative action program or policy is one that grants—rather than denies—benefits to individuals based on their membership in an historically disadvantaged group. Through a series of Executive Orders, President Johnson imposed affirmative action obligations on many types of contractors doing business with the federal government. Some states and municipalities followed suit. Business and industry then struggled to implement programs to comply with these affirmative action mandates. Many colleges and universities, viewing their role in the educational process as essential to any individual or group seeking economic and social advancement, also adopted affirmative action plans.

The University of California at Davis was one such institution. It developed an affirmative action program to benefit members of minority groups. Under the school's plan, 16 out of the 100 places in each year's medical school class were set aside for disadvantaged applicants. Allan Bakke, a white male with better qualifications than most admitted minority students, was rejected two years in a row when he applied for admission to the medical school. He filed suit claiming that the special admission program violated both the equal protection guarantee of the Fourteenth Amendment and the educational equity provisions of the Civil Rights Act.

When Bakke's case reached the Supreme Court, it presented the Court its first chance to review a so-called "reverse discrimination" race-based program. Four members of the Court voted to strike down the medical school's program as a violation of the Civil Rights Act, avoiding the constitutional issue. Four members of the Court, including Justice Brennan, voted to uphold the medical school's approach. They determined that it was compatible with both the Act and the Equal Protection Clause. Justice Powell was the critical fifth vote, and he concluded that this particular program was a quota system, which violated equal protection. He was not, however, willing to prohibit all race-conscious programs. Thus, he agreed in principle with the Brennan faction that some types of affirmative action programs were constitutionally acceptable to remedy past discrimination and to achieve diversity among the student population.

One of the issues addressed by the Court's ruling in *Bakke* was the level of scrutiny to be applied to reverse discrimination claims. Usually, an equal protection claim comes from a member of an historically oppressed group who argues that a particular governmental action discriminates in an unconstitutional manner. When a claim of unequal treatment is brought by a member of a group that has benefitted from societal discrimination, strict scrutiny may not be appropriate. Yet using the same standard in every situation involving race-based claims, regardless of the race of the person complaining of unfair treatment, has some appeal: it is symmetrical and it appears to be color-blind. A majority of the Court's members adopted this approach.

Brennan, however, thought strict scrutiny did not adequately consider the country's history of race discrimination. For him, the Equal Protection Clause was designed primarily to safeguard the rights of persons who are members of a traditionally oppressed group. As a result, the level of scrutiny employed in cases involving "reverse" discrimination should not be as stringent as in cases involving discrimination against Black Americans. Rather, the Court should apply an intermediate level of scrutiny, as is used in reviewing claims of gender-based discrimination, which requires that the state demonstrate only that the means were substantially related to an important government objective.

In subsequent cases and for several years, the Court equivocated about the proper approach for dealing with affirmative action cases. Eventually, it concluded that strict scrutiny should be used to review affirmative action programs implemented by states or municipalities. Under this review, the only justification for such a program is to remedy past discrimination by the same entity that now wishes to benefit previously disadvantaged groups. In *F. C. C. v. Metro Broadcasting* (1990), Brennan convinced four of his colleagues that the lower, intermediate scrutiny standard was appropriate to review affirmative action plans mandated by Congress. This allowed the goal of remedying past discrimination in society generally to justify an affirmative action program. The opinion was one of the last he wrote before retiring from the Court, but his victory was short-lived. The Court overruled the *Metro Broadcasting* decision five years later, holding that strict scrutiny should be applied even to federal programs.

Although Brennan ultimately lost on the legal issue, his opinion in *Bakke* remains salient for its sensitivity to the condition of disadvantaged minorities. As with any affirmative action plan, the University of California's program represented a clash between the policy of social justice and the principle of equality. Some would argue that because the principle of equal treatment, not the policy of social justice, is codified in both the Constitution and the Civil Rights Act, the principle should take precedence. Brennan would have responded, no doubt, that equality without social justice is illusory.

Justice Powell wrote the opinion of the Court. Justices Brennan, White, Marshall, and Blackmun collectively wrote an opinion concurring in part and dissenting in part. Justice Stevens wrote an opinion concurring in part and dissenting in part, joined by Chief Justice Burger and Justices Stewart and Rehnquist.

❂   ❂   ❂

Opinion of MR. JUSTICE BRENNAN, MR. JUSTICE WHITE, MR. JUSTICE MARSHALL, and MR. JUSTICE BLACKMUN, concurring in the judgment in part and dissenting in part.

The Court today, in reversing in part the judgment of the Supreme Court of California, affirms the constitutional power of Federal and

State Governments to act affirmatively to achieve equal opportunity for all. The difficulty of the issue presented—whether government may use race-conscious programs to redress the continuing effects of past discrimination—and the mature consideration which each of our Brethren has brought to it have resulted in many opinions, no single one speaking for the Court. But this should not and must not mask the central meaning of today's opinions: Government may take race into account when it acts not to demean or insult any racial group, but to remedy disadvantages cast on minorities by past racial prejudice, at least when appropriate findings have been made by judicial, legislative, or administrative bodies with competence to act in this area.

* * *

I

Our Nation was founded on the principle that "all Men are created equal." Yet candor requires acknowledgment that the Framers of our Constitution, to forge the 13 Colonies into one Nation, openly compromised this principle of equality with its antithesis: slavery. The consequences of this compromise are well known and have aptly been called our "American Dilemma." Still, it is well to recount how recent the time has been, if it has yet come, when the promise of our principles has flowered into the actuality of equal opportunity for all regardless of race or color.

The Fourteenth Amendment, the embodiment in the Constitution of our abiding belief in human equality, has been the law of our land for only slightly more than half its 200 years. And for half of that half, the Equal Protection Clause of the Amendment was largely moribund * * *. Worse than desuetude, the Clause was early turned against those whom it was intended to set free, condemning them to a "separate but equal" status before the law, a status always separate but seldom equal. Not until 1954—only 24 years ago—was this odious doctrine interred by our decision in *Brown v. Board of Education* (*Brown I*), and its progeny, which proclaimed that separate schools and public facilities of all sorts were inherently unequal and forbidden under our Constitution. Even then inequality was not eliminated with "all deliberate speed." *Brown v. Board of Education* (*Brown II*). In 1968 and again in 1971, for example, we were forced to remind school boards of their obligation to eliminate racial discrimination root and branch. And a glance at our docket and at dockets of lower courts will show that even today officially sanctioned discrimination is not a thing of the past.

Against this background, claims that law must be "colorblind" or that the datum of race is no longer relevant to public policy must be seen as aspiration rather than as description of reality. This is not to denigrate aspiration; for reality rebukes us that race has too often been used by those who would stigmatize and oppress minorities. Yet we cannot— and, as we shall demonstrate, need not under our Constitution or [the Civil Rights Act], which merely extends the constraints of the Fourteenth Amendment to private parties who receive federal funds—let color blindness become myopia which masks the reality that many "created equal" have been treated within our lifetimes as inferior both by the law and by their fellow citizens.

* * *

III

B

Respondent argues that racial classifications are always suspect and, consequently, that this Court should weigh the importance of the objectives served by Davis' special admissions program to see if they are compelling. In addition, he asserts that this Court must inquire whether, in its judgment, there are alternatives to racial classifications which would suit Davis' purposes. Petitioner, on the other hand, states that our proper role is simply to accept petitioner's determination that the racial classifications used by its program are reasonably related to what it tells us are its benign purposes. We reject petitioner's view, but, because our prior cases are in many respects inapposite to that before us now, we find it necessary to define with precision the meaning of that inexact term, "strict scrutiny."

Unquestionably we have held that a government practice or statute which restricts "fundamental rights" or which contains "suspect classifications" is to be subjected to "strict scrutiny" and can be justified only if it furthers a compelling government purpose and, even then, only if no less restrictive alternative is available. But no fundamental right is involved here. Nor do whites as a class have any of the "traditional indicia of suspectness: the class is not saddled with such disabilities, or subjected to such a history of purposeful unequal treatment, or relegated to such a position of political powerlessness as to command extraordinary protection from the majoritarian political process." *San Antonio Independent School District v. Rodriguez.*[31]

Moreover, if the University's representations are credited, this is not a case where racial classifications are "irrelevant and therefore prohibited." *Hirabayashi v. United States.* Nor has anyone suggested that the University's purposes contravene the cardinal principle that racial classifications that stigmatize—because they are drawn on the presumption that one race is inferior to another or because they put the weight of government behind racial hatred and separatism—are invalid without more.

On the other hand, the fact that this case does not fit neatly into our prior analytic framework for race cases does not mean that it should be analyzed by applying the very loose rational-basis standard of review that is the very least that is always applied in equal protection cases. " '[T]he mere recitation of a benign, compensatory purpose is not an automatic shield which protects against any inquiry into the actual purposes underlying a statutory scheme.' " *Califano v. Webster,* quoting *Weinberger v. Wiesenfeld.* Instead, a number of considerations—developed in gender-discrimination cases but which carry even more force when applied to racial classifications—lead us to conclude that racial classifications designed to further remedial purposes " 'must serve important governmental objectives and must be substantially related to achievement of those objectives.' " *Califano v. Webster,* quoting *Craig v. Boren.*

First, race, like, "gender-based classifications too often [has] been inexcusably utilized to stereotype and stigmatize politically powerless segments of society." *Kahn v. Shevin* (dissenting opinion). While a carefully tailored statute designed to remedy past discrimination could avoid these vices, we nonetheless have recognized that the line between honest and thoughtful appraisal of the effects of past discrimination and paternalistic stereotyping is not so clear and that a statute based on the latter is patently capable of stigmatizing all women with a badge of inferiority. State programs designed ostensibly to ameliorate the effects of past racial discrimination obviously create the same hazard of stigma,

---

31. Of course, the fact that whites constitute a political majority in our Nation does not necessarily mean that active judicial scrutiny of racial classifications that disadvantage whites is inappropriate.

since they may promote racial separatism and reinforce the views of those who believe that members of racial minorities are inherently incapable of succeeding on their own.

Second, race, like gender and illegitimacy, is an immutable characteristic which its possessors are powerless to escape or set aside. While a classification is not per se invalid because it divides classes on the basis of an immutable characteristic, it is nevertheless true that such divisions are contrary to our deep belief that "legal burdens should bear some relationship to individual responsibility or wrongdoing," *Weber v. Aetna Casualty & Surety Co.*, and that advancement sanctioned, sponsored, or approved by the State should ideally be based on individual merit or achievement, or at the least on factors within the control of an individual.

* * *

In sum, because of the significant risk that racial classifications established for ostensibly benign purposes can be misused, causing effects not unlike those created by invidious classifications, it is inappropriate to inquire only whether there is any conceivable basis that might sustain such a classification. Instead, to justify such a classification an important and articulated purpose for its use must be shown. In addition, any statute must be stricken that stigmatizes any group or that singles out those least well represented in the political process to bear the brunt of a benign program. Thus, our review under the Fourteenth Amendment should be strict—not "'strict' in theory and fatal in fact," because it is stigma that causes fatality—but strict and searching nonetheless.

IV

Davis' articulated purpose of remedying the effects of past societal discrimination is, under our cases, sufficiently important to justify the use of race-conscious admissions programs where there is a sound basis for concluding that minority underrepresentation is substantial and chronic, and that the handicap of past discrimination is impeding access of minorities to the Medical School.

A

At least since [1968], it has been clear that a public body which has itself been adjudged to have engaged in racial discrimination cannot bring itself into compliance with the Equal Protection Clause simply by ending its unlawful acts and adopting a neutral stance. Three years later, * * * [we] reiterated that racially neutral remedies for past discrimination were inadequate where consequences of past discriminatory acts influence or control present decisions. And the Court further held both that courts could enter desegregation orders which assigned students and faculty by reference to race, and that local school boards could voluntarily adopt desegregation plans which made express reference to race if this was necessary to remedy the effects of past discrimination. Moreover, we stated that school boards, even in the absence of a judicial finding of past discrimination, could voluntarily adopt plans which assigned students with the end of creating racial pluralism by establishing fixed ratios of black and white students in each school. * * *

Thus, our cases * * * have held that, in order to achieve minority participation in previously segregated areas of public life, Congress may require or authorize preferential treatment for those likely disadvantaged by societal racial discrimination. Such legislation has been sustained even without a requirement of findings of intentional racial discrimination by those required or authorized to accord preferential treatment, or a case-by-case determination that those to be benefited suffered from racial discrimination. These decisions compel the conclusion that States also may adopt race-conscious programs designed to overcome substantial, chronic minority underrepresentation where there is reason to believe that the evil addressed is a product of past racial discrimination.

* * *

B

Properly construed, therefore, our prior cases unequivocally show that a state government may adopt race-conscious programs if the purpose of such programs is to remove the disparate racial impact its actions might otherwise have and if there is reason to believe that the disparate impact is itself the product of past discrimination, whether its own or that of society at large. There is no question that Davis' program is valid under this test.

Certainly, on the basis of the undisputed factual submissions before this Court, Davis had a sound basis for believing that the problem of underrepresentation of minorities was substantial and chronic and that the problem was attributable to handicaps imposed on minority applicants by past and present racial discrimination. Until at least 1973, the practice of medicine in this country was, in fact, if not in law, largely the prerogative of whites.[45] In 1950, for example, while Negroes constituted 10% of the total population, Negro physicians constituted only 2.2% of the total number of physicians. The overwhelming majority of these, moreover, were educated in two predominantly Negro medical schools, Howard and Meharry. By 1970, the gap between the proportion of Negroes in medicine and their proportion in the population had widened: The number of Negroes employed in medicine remained frozen at 2.2% while the Negro population had increased to 11.1%. The number of Negro admittees to predominantly white medical schools, moreover, had declined in absolute numbers during the years 1955 to 1964.

Moreover, Davis had very good reason to believe that the national pattern of underrepresentation of minorities in medicine would be perpetuated if it retained a single admissions standard. For example, the entering classes in 1968 and 1969, the years in which such a standard was used, included only 1 Chicano and 2 Negroes out of the 50 admittees for each year. Nor is there any relief from this pattern of underrepresentation in the statistics for the regular admissions program in later years.

Davis clearly could conclude that the serious and persistent underrepresentation of minorities in medicine depicted by these statistics is the result of handicaps under which minority applicants labor as a consequence of a background of deliberate, purposeful discrimination against minorities in education and in society generally, as well as in the medical profession. * * *

C

The second prong of our test—whether the Davis program stigmatizes any discrete group or individual and whether race is reasonably used in light of the program's objectives—is clearly satisfied by the Davis program.

---

45. According to 89 schools responding to a questionnaire sent to 112 medical schools (all of the then-accredited medical schools in the United States except Howard and Meharry), substantial efforts to admit minority students did not begin until 1968. That year was the earliest year of involvement for 34% of the schools; an additional 66% became involved during the years 1969 to 1973. These efforts were reflected in a significant increase in the percentage of minority M.D. graduates. The number of American Negro graduates increased from 2.2% in 1970 to 3.3% in 1973 and 5.0% in 1975. Significant percentage increases in the number of Mexican-American, American Indian, and mainland Puerto Rican graduates were also recorded during those years. * * *

It is not even claimed that Davis' program in any way operates to stigmatize or single out any discrete and insular, or even any identifiable, nonminority group. Nor will harm comparable to that imposed upon racial minorities by exclusion or separation on grounds of race be the likely result of the program. It does not, for example, establish an exclusive preserve for minority students apart from and exclusive of whites. Rather, its purpose is to overcome the effects of segregation by bringing the races together. True, whites are excluded from participation in the special admissions program, but this fact only operates to reduce the number of whites to be admitted in the regular admissions program in order to permit admission of a reasonable percentage—less than their proportion of the California population—of otherwise underrepresented qualified minority applicants.

Nor was Bakke in any sense stamped as inferior by the Medical School's rejection of him. Indeed, it is conceded by all that he satisfied those criteria regarded by the school as generally relevant to academic performance better than most of the minority members who were admitted. Moreover, there is absolutely no basis for concluding that Bakke's rejection as a result of Davis' use of racial preference will affect him throughout his life in the same way as the segregation of the Negro school-children in *Brown I* would have affected them. Unlike discrimination against racial minorities, the use of racial preferences for remedial purposes does not inflict a pervasive injury upon individual whites in the sense that wherever they go or whatever they do there is a significant likelihood that they will be treated as second-class citizens because of their color. * * *

In addition, there is simply no evidence that the Davis program discriminates intentionally or unintentionally against any minority group which it purports to benefit. The program does not establish a quota in the invidious sense of a ceiling on the number of minority applicants to be admitted. Nor can the program reasonably be regarded as stigmatizing the program's beneficiaries or their race as inferior. The Davis program does not simply advance less qualified applicants; rather, it com-pensates applicants, who it is uncontested are fully qualified to study medicine, for educational disadvantages which it was reasonable to conclude were a product of state-fostered discrimination. Once admitted, these students must satisfy the same degree requirements as regularly admitted students; they are taught by the same faculty in the same classes; and their performance is evaluated by the same standards by which regularly admitted students are judged. Under these circumstances, their performance and degrees must be regarded equally with the regularly admitted students with whom they compete for standing. Since minority graduates cannot justifiably be regarded as less well qualified than nonminority graduates by virtue of the special admissions program, there is no reasonable basis to conclude that minority graduates at schools using such programs would be stigmatized as inferior by the existence of such programs.

D

We disagree with the lower courts' conclusion that the Davis program's use of race was unreasonable in light of its objectives. First, as petitioner argues, there are no practical means by which it could achieve its ends in the foreseeable future without the use of race-conscious measures. With respect to any factor (such as poverty or family educational background) that may be used as a substitute for race as an indicator of past discrimination, whites greatly outnumber racial minorities simply because whites make up a far larger percentage of the total population and therefore far outnumber minorities in absolute terms at every socio-economic level. * * * Moreover, while race is positively correlated with differences in GPA and MCAT scores, economic disadvantage is not. Thus, it appears that economically disadvantaged whites do not score less well than economically advantaged whites, while economically advantaged blacks score less well than do disadvantaged whites. These statistics graphically illustrate that the University's purpose to integrate its classes by compensating for past discrimination could not be achieved by a general preference for the economically disadvantaged or the children of parents of limited education unless such groups were to make up the entire class.

* * *

E

Finally, Davis' special admissions program cannot be said to violate the Constitution simply because it has set aside a predetermined number of places for qualified minority applicants rather than using minority status as a positive factor to be considered in evaluating the applications of disadvantaged minority applicants. For purposes of constitutional adjudication, there is no difference between the two ap-

proaches. In any admissions program which accords special consideration to disadvantaged racial minorities, a determination of the degree
of preference to be given is unavoidable, and any given preference that
results in the exclusion of a white candidate is no more or less constitutionally acceptable than a program such as that at Davis. Furthermore, the extent of the preference inevitably depends on how many minority applicants the particular school is seeking to admit in any
particular year so long as the number of qualified minority applicants
exceeds that number. There is no sensible, and certainly no constitutional, distinction between, for example, adding a set number of points
to the admissions rating of disadvantaged minority applicants as an expression of the preference with the expectation that this will result in
the admission of an approximately determined number of qualified
minority applicants and setting a fixed number of places for such applicants as was done here.

* * *

V

Accordingly, we would reverse the judgment of the Supreme Court of
California holding the Medical School's special admissions program
unconstitutional and directing respondent's admission, as well as that
portion of the judgment enjoining the Medical School from according
any consideration to race in the admissions process.

PLYLER V. DOE

June 15, 1982

Beginning in the late 1970s, many states became frustrated with federal immigration policy. They were compelled to absorb the cost of providing services for new residents, some of whom had special needs as a result of their language and cultural differences. Believing that the federal government had been insensitive to the predicament of the overburdened states, even with regard to legal immigration policies, several states on the southern border passed legislation to limit expenditures for aliens, particularly those who entered the United States unlawfully.

This case originated from such a piece of legislation: a Texas statute that withheld state funds for the education of minors who were in the country illegally. The law also permitted local school districts to deny enrollment to them outright. Representatives of the immigrant children brought suit on the children's behalf, claiming that the act violated the Equal Protection Clause by discriminating against illegal aliens. Justice Brennan, writing for the Court, upheld the claim.

The difficulty for Brennan and the Court in reaching this result was in the standard of review. Back in *Shapiro v. Thompson* (p. 191), involving the right to travel, the Court had ruled that fiscal considerations were not the type of compelling governmental interest that could justify invidious discrimination. However, application of strict scrutiny was not called for here. Illegal immigrants were not a "suspect class." Furthermore, in the case of *San Antonio Independent School District v. Rodriguez* (1973), the Court had ruled that an education at public expense was not a "fundamental right." Despite these barriers, Brennan concluded that a statute which denies educational opportunities to undocumented children may be justified only by a showing that it furthers some "substantial state interest," and he ruled that Texas failed to make this showing.

Chief Justice Burger, writing for himself and three dissenting colleagues, characterized Brennan's analysis as judicial sleight-of-hand. As Burger put it, the Court's opinion was a patchwork of constitutional analysis which "spins out a theory custom-tailored to the facts of these cases." He complained that "[i]f ever a court were guilty of an unabashedly result-oriented approach, this case is a prime example."

While the dissent viewed Brennan's methodology as fabricated, it is worth noting that Justice Marshall had for years urged the Court to use a variable standard of review in equal protection cases. The Court's decision here is a variation on that theme.

Perhaps more important than the legal arguments made in the majority and dissenting opinions is their overall tenor. The dissenting Justices, while apparently sympathetic to the children's situation, evidenced greater concern for the government and its lawful citizens, whose only loss was the diversion of tax dollars. Brennan's opinion, on the other hand, displayed true compassion for the children. Noting that they may have entered the country involuntarily in their parent's custody, Brennan regarded it as fundamentally unjust to punish them for the illegal conduct of their parents.

There may also be something more, further below the surface. While most of the proponents of this legislation were undoubtedly motivated by fiscal concerns, others may have had less pure motives for this discriminatory legislation. Xenophobia seems curious in a relatively young nation whose population is readily traceable to scores of other countries and cultures. Nevertheless, it may have been this kind of irrational prejudice, conscious or not, that spurred the legislative action here. Brennan would have agreed with the sentiment, expressed by a task force on gender discrimination, that the Court's role should be to "reject—not reflect—society's irrational prejudices."

In the 15 years since the decision in this case, Congress has tightened the immigration laws and states have continued to struggle against providing services to lawful and unlawful aliens. Yet *Plyler* remains good law, at least in the area of public education for school children.

Justice Brennan wrote the opinion of the Court, joined by Justices White, Marshall, Blackmun, Powell, and Stevens. Chief Justice Burger and Justices Rehnquist and O'Connor dissented.

○ ○ ○

JUSTICE BRENNAN delivered the opinion of the Court.

The question presented by these cases is whether, consistent with the Equal Protection Clause of the Fourteenth Amendment, Texas may deny to undocumented school-age children the free public education that it provides to children who are citizens of the United States or legally admitted aliens.

I

Since the late 19th century, the United States has restricted immigration into this country. Unsanctioned entry into the United States is a crime, and those who have entered unlawfully are subject to deportation. But despite the existence of these legal restrictions, a substantial number of persons have succeeded in unlawfully entering the United States, and now live within various States, including the State of Texas.

In May 1975, the Texas Legislature revised [§ 21.031 of] its [E]ducation [Code] to withhold from local school districts any state funds for the education of children who were not "legally admitted" into the United States. The 1975 revision also authorized local school districts to deny enrollment in their public schools to children not "legally admitted" to the country. These cases involve constitutional challenges to those provisions.

* * *

III

The Equal Protection Clause directs that "all persons similarly circumstanced shall be treated alike." *F. S. Royster Guano Co. v. Virginia.* But so too, "[t]he Constitution does not require things which are different in fact or opinion to be treated in law as though they were the same." *Tigner v. Texas.* The initial discretion to determine what is "different" and what is "the same" resides in the legislatures of the States. A legislature must have substantial latitude to establish classifications that roughly approximate the nature of the problem perceived, that accommodate competing concerns both public and private, and that account for limitations on the practical ability of the State to remedy every ill. In applying the Equal Protection Clause to most forms of state action, we thus seek only the assurance that the classification at issue bears some fair relationship to a legitimate public purpose.

But we would not be faithful to our obligations under the Fourteenth Amendment if we applied so deferential a standard to every classification. The Equal Protection Clause was intended as a restriction on state legislative action inconsistent with elemental constitutional premises. Thus we have treated as presumptively invidious those classifications that disadvantage a "suspect class,"[14] or that impinge upon the exercise of a "fundamental right."[15] With respect to such classifications, it is appropriate to enforce the mandate of equal protection by requiring the State to demonstrate that its classification has been precisely tailored to serve a compelling governmental interest. In addition, we have recognized that certain forms of legislative classification, while not facially invidious, nonetheless give rise to recurring constitutional difficulties; in these limited circumstances we have sought the assurance that the classification reflects a reasoned judgment consistent with the ideal of equal protection by inquiring whether it may fairly be viewed as furthering a substantial interest of the State.[16] We turn to a consideration of the standard appropriate for the evaluation of § 21.031.

A

Sheer incapability or lax enforcement of the laws barring entry into this country, coupled with the failure to establish an effective bar to the employment of undocumented aliens, has resulted in the creation of a substantial "shadow population" of illegal migrants—numbering in the millions—within our borders. This situation raises the specter of a permanent caste of undocumented resident aliens, encouraged by some to remain here as a source of cheap labor, but nevertheless denied the

---

14. Several formulations might explain our treatment of certain classifications as "suspect." Some classifications are more likely than others to reflect deep-seated prejudice rather than legislative rationality in pursuit of some legitimate objective. Legislation predicated on such prejudice is easily recognized as incompatible with the constitutional understanding that each person is to be judged individually and is entitled to equal justice under the law. Classifications treated as suspect tend to be irrelevant to any proper legislative goal. Finally, certain groups, indeed largely the same groups, have historically been "relegated to such a position of political powerlessness as to command extraordinary protection from the majoritarian political process." San Antonio Indep. School Dist. v. Rodriguez. The experience of our Nation has shown that prejudice may manifest itself in the treatment of some groups. Our response to that experience is reflected in the Equal Protection Clause of the Fourteenth Amendment. Legislation imposing special disabilities upon groups disfavored by virtue of circumstances beyond their control suggests the kind of "class or caste" treatment that the Fourteenth Amendment was designed to abolish.

15. In determining whether a class-based denial of a particular right is deserving of strict scrutiny under the Equal Protection Clause, we look to the Constitution to see if the right infringed has its source, explicitly or implicitly, therein. But we have also recognized the fundamentality of participation in state "elections on an equal basis with other citizens in the jurisdiction," even though "the right to vote, per se, is not a constitutionally protected right." San Antonio Indep. School Dist. With respect to suffrage, we have explained the need for strict scrutiny as arising from the significance of the franchise as the guardian of all other rights.

16. See Craig v. Boren. This technique of "intermediate" scrutiny permits us to evaluate the rationality of the legislative judgment with reference to well-settled constitutional principles. ⋆ ⋆ ⋆

benefits that our society makes available to citizens and lawful residents. The existence of such an underclass presents most difficult problems for a Nation that prides itself on adherence to principles of equality under law.[19]

The children who are plaintiffs in these cases are special members of this underclass. Persuasive arguments support the view that a State may withhold its beneficence from those whose very presence within the United States is the product of their own unlawful conduct. These arguments do not apply with the same force to classifications imposing disabilities on the minor *children* of such illegal entrants. At the least, those who elect to enter our territory by stealth and in violation of our law should be prepared to bear the consequences, including, but not limited to, deportation. But the children of those illegal entrants are not comparably situated. Their "parents have the ability to conform their conduct to societal norms," and presumably the ability to remove themselves from the State's jurisdiction; but the children who are plaintiffs in these cases "can affect neither their parents' conduct nor their own status." *Trimble v. Gordon*. Even if the State found it expedient to control the conduct of adults by acting against their children, legislation directing the onus of a parent's misconduct against his children does not comport with fundamental conceptions of justice. * * *

Of course, undocumented status is not irrelevant to any proper legislative goal. Nor is undocumented status an absolutely immutable characteristic since it is the product of conscious, indeed unlawful, action. But § 21.031 is directed against children, and imposes its discriminatory burden on the basis of a legal characteristic over which children can have little control. It is thus difficult to conceive of a rational justification for penalizing these children for their presence within the United States. Yet that appears to be precisely the effect of § 21.031.

Public education is not a "right" granted to individuals by the Constitution. But neither is it merely some governmental "benefit" indistinguishable from other forms of social welfare legislation. Both the importance of education in maintaining our basic institutions, and the lasting impact of its deprivation on the life of the child, mark the dis-

---

19. We reject the claim that "illegal aliens" are a "suspect class." No case in which we have attempted to define a suspect class has addressed the status of persons unlawfully in our country. Unlike most of the classifications that we have recognized as suspect, entry into this class, by virtue of entry into this country, is the product of voluntary action. Indeed, entry into the class is itself a crime. * * *

tinction. The "American people have always regarded education and [the] acquisition of knowledge as matters of supreme importance." *Meyer v. Nebraska.* We have recognized "the public schools as a most vital civic institution for the preservation of a democratic system of government," *School District of Abington Township v. Schempp,* (Brennan, J., concurring), and as the primary vehicle for transmitting "the values on which our society rests." *Ambach v. Norwick.* "[A]s . . . pointed out early in our history, . . . some degree of education is necessary to prepare citizens to participate effectively and intelligently in our open political system if we are to preserve freedom and independence." *Wisconsin v. Yoder.* * * * In addition, education provides the basic tools by which individuals might lead economically productive lives to the benefit of us all. In sum, education has a fundamental role in maintaining the fabric of our society. We cannot ignore the significant social costs borne by our Nation when select groups are denied the means to absorb the values and skills upon which our social order rests.

In addition to the pivotal role of education in sustaining our political and cultural heritage, denial of education to some isolated group of children poses an affront to one of the goals of the Equal Protection Clause: the abolition of governmental barriers presenting unreasonable obstacles to advancement on the basis of individual merit. Paradoxically, by depriving the children of any disfavored group of an education, we foreclose the means by which that group might raise the level of esteem in which it is held by the majority. But more directly, "education prepares individuals to be self-reliant and self-sufficient participants in society." *Wisconsin v. Yoder.* Illiteracy is an enduring disability. The inability to read and write will handicap the individual deprived of a basic education each and every day of his life. The inestimable toll of that deprivation on the social, economic, intellectual, and psychological well-being of the individual, and the obstacle it poses to individual achievement, make it most difficult to reconcile the cost or the principle of a status-based denial of basic education with the framework of equality embodied in the Equal Protection Clause. * * *

B

These well-settled principles allow us to determine the proper level of deference to be afforded § 21.031. Undocumented aliens cannot be treated as a suspect class because their presence in this country in violation of federal law is not a "constitutional irrelevancy." Nor is education a fundamental right; a State need not justify by compelling necessity every variation in the manner in which education is provided to its population. But more is involved in these cases than the abstract question whether § 21.031 discriminates against a suspect class, or whether education is a fundamental right. Section 21.031 imposes a lifetime hardship on a discrete class of children not accountable for their disabling status. The stigma of illiteracy will mark them for the rest of their lives. By denying these children a basic education, we deny them the ability to live within the structure of our civic institutions, and foreclose any realistic possibility that they will contribute in even the smallest way to the progress of our Nation. In determining the rationality of § 21.031, we may appropriately take into account its costs to the Nation and to the innocent children who are its victims. In light of these countervailing costs, the discrimination contained in § 21.031 can hardly be considered rational unless it furthers some substantial goal of the State.

* * *

V

Appellants argue that the classification at issue furthers an interest in the "preservation of the state's limited resources for the education of its lawful residents." Of course, a concern for the preservation of resources standing alone can hardly justify the classification used in allocating those resources. The State must do more than justify its classification with a concise expression of an intention to discriminate. Apart from the asserted state prerogative to act against undocumented children solely on the basis of their undocumented status—an asserted prerogative that carries only minimal force in the circumstances of these cases—we discern three colorable state interests that might support § 21.031.

First, appellants appear to suggest that the State may seek to protect itself from an influx of illegal immigrants. While a State might have an interest in mitigating the potentially harsh economic effects of sudden shifts in population, § 21.031 hardly offers an effective method of dealing with an urgent demographic or economic problem. There is no evidence in the record suggesting that illegal entrants impose any significant burden on the State's economy. To the contrary, the available evidence suggests that illegal aliens underutilize public services, while contributing their labor to the local economy and tax money to the state fisc. The dominant incentive for illegal entry into the State of Texas is the availability of employment; few if any illegal immigrants come to this country, or presumably to the State of Texas, in order to avail themselves of a free education. Thus, even making the doubtful assumption that the net impact of illegal aliens on the economy of the State is negative, we think it clear that [as the District Court said] "[c]harging tuition to undocumented children constitutes a ludicrously ineffectual attempt to stem the tide of illegal immigration," at least when compared with the alternative of prohibiting the employment of illegal aliens.

Second, while it is apparent that a State may "not . . . reduce expenditures for education by barring [some arbitrarily chosen class of] children from its schools," *Shapiro v. Thompson*, appellants suggest that undocumented children are appropriately singled out for exclusion because of the special burdens they impose on the State's ability to provide high quality public education. But the record in no way supports the claim that exclusion of undocumented children is likely to improve the overall quality of education in the State. As the District Court noted, the State failed to offer any "credible supporting evidence that a proportionately small diminution of the funds spent on each child [which might result from devoting some State funds to the education of the excluded group] will have a grave impact on the quality of education." And, after reviewing the State's school financing mechanism, the District Court concluded that barring undocumented children from local schools would not necessarily improve the quality of education provided in those schools. Of course, even if improvement in the quality of education were a likely result of barring some *number* of children from the schools of the State, the State must support its selection of this group as the appropriate target for exclusion. In terms of educational cost and need, however, undocumented children are "basically indistinguishable" from legally resident alien children.

Finally, appellants suggest that undocumented children are appropriately singled out because their unlawful presence within the United States renders them less likely than other children to remain within the boundaries of the State, and to put their education to productive social or political use within the State. Even assuming that such an interest is legitimate, it is an interest that is most difficult to quantify. The State has no assurance that any child, citizen or not, will employ the education provided by the State within the confines of the State's borders. In any event, the record is clear that many of the undocumented children disabled by this classification will remain in this country indefinitely, and that some will become lawful residents or citizens of the United States. It is difficult to understand precisely what the State hopes to achieve by promoting the creation and perpetuation of a subclass of illiterates within our boundaries, surely adding to the problems and costs of unemployment, welfare, and crime. It is thus clear that whatever savings might be achieved by denying these children an education, they are wholly insubstantial in light of the costs involved to these children, the State, and the Nation.

VI

If the State is to deny a discrete group of innocent children the free public education that it offers to other children residing within its borders, that denial must be justified by a showing that it furthers some substantial state interest. No such showing was made here. Accordingly, the judgment of the Court of Appeals in each of these cases is

Affirmed.

MICHAEL H. V. GERALD D.

June 15, 1989

When Justice Brennan interpreted the Constitution, he often examined history but ultimately did not feel bound by the Framers' intent. He believed we could never really know what the Framers intended, even if we could identify who the relevant "Framers" were. Perhaps he also questioned whether the wishes and whims of a small and homogenous group of people long dead should control the meaning of the document that governs people of many races and cultures. Instead, Brennan regarded the Constitution as a "living document," one that established broad principles for Americans to live by. Only over time, as new and different conflicts arose involving these principles, could we fully realize the import and meaning of the fundamental tenets of our American creed. Moreover, as each successive generation reinterpreted our founding document, it would thereby adopt it unto itself and give the Constitution new and continuing legitimacy. Jefferson believed that no generation had the right to rule from the grave, and that each had the right to create its own government, by armed rebellion if necessary. Brennan followed, as his opinions document, a more peaceful—but perhaps no less revolutionary—approach, through constitutional reinterpretation. Perhaps more than any other, this case demonstrates Brennan's methodology.

The case involved Carole, an international model, who had an extended affair with her neighbor Michael. Carole gave birth to a daughter, Victoria, and listed her husband Gerald as the father on Victoria's birth certificate. Although Gerald always treated Victoria as his daughter, Carole informed Michael that she believed he was Victoria's true biological father. Blood tests confirmed this to a 98 percent certainty.

For the next several years, Carole's relationships with Gerald and Michael alternated. For a while, Carole and Michael lived together in St. Thomas, where Michael's primary business interests were located. During this time, Michael regarded Victoria as his daughter, and she called him "Daddy." Carole then moved in with Gerald and prevented Michael from seeing Victoria. Michael responded by filing suit in California to establish his paternity and to obtain visitation rights. A court-ordered psychological evaluation recommended continued contact between Victoria and Michael. The attorney representing Victoria's interests claimed that she was entitled to maintain a relationship with both men. While the case was pending, Carole returned with Victoria to live with Michael. Several months later, however, Carole permanently reconciled with Gerald, and subsequently had two more children with him. When Michael and Victoria sought visitation rights for Michael, Gerald intervened in the proceedings, claiming that he was Victoria's natural father.

Under California law, a child born to a married woman co-habiting with her husband is conclusively deemed to be the legitimate offspring of the husband. Applying this law, the California courts agreed with Gerald and refused to grant either Michael or Victoria an evidentiary hearing on the matter. Michael and Victoria challenged the California statute on the grounds that its refusal to recognize their father-daughter relationship or permit visitation violated their due process rights.

Actually, none of the opinions in this case dwelled on the Equal Protection Clause. For the litigants and the judges alike, the issue presented was whether Michael, Victoria, or both had a fundamental right—protected by the Due Process Clause of the Fourteenth Amendment—to a hearing on paternity and to maintain their relationship if they were indeed father and daughter. Yet all of the judges would agree that both Michael and Victoria would have such a fundamental right if he had been married to Carole or, perhaps, if Carole had not been married at all. Thus, the case can be viewed as an issue of equality for illegitimate children and their fathers.

In announcing the Court's judgment, Justice Scalia began by stating that "[t]he facts of this case are, we must hope, extraordinary." As an observation on numerous changes in the parties' relationships and jet-setting lifestyles, Scalia may have been correct. However, the statement also established Scalia's bias for what he regards as a "normal" family relationship deserving of constitutional protection. Throughout his opinion, he referred to Michael as the "adulterous natural father," evidencing the moral judgment underlying his legal analysis. Not surprisingly, therefore, he distinguished this case from the Court's previous decisions about the constitutional rights of unwed fathers by referring to the fact that none of the earlier cases arose from an adulterous relationship. He also paid little attention to any interest that Victoria might possess and disregarded the possible psychological benefit to her in maintaining a relationship with Michael. The end result of the Court's decision was that California was not required to conduct a hearing to determine paternity and could deny Michael and Victoria a relationship with each other.

Scalia defended his approach as true to the historical roots of the Fourteenth Amendment. In a lengthy footnote, he expounded on the propriety of using historical tradition to define the interests protected by the Due Process Clause. Deference to tradition was necessary, so Scalia argued, to restrain judges from inscribing their own social conscience into the Constitution. Only Chief Justice Rehnquist agreed with this argument. Justices O'Connor and Kennedy, while joining Scalia's plurality opinion, specifically disavowed his mode of historical analysis and refused to sign onto this controversial footnote.

Justice Brennan vehemently disagreed with both Scalia's conclusion and methodology. In doing so, he set forth a completely different vision of what the Constitution is and how it is to be interpreted. To him, it was Michael's fatherhood of Victoria, not his adultery with Carole, that really mattered. It was immaterial that the law had not historically recognized or respected the parental rights of fathers in the specific circumstances presented here, because courts at all levels had long protected the rights of fathers generally. In a moving final paragraph, he rebuked the Court for accepting into law the fiction that Michael was not Victoria's real father.

Justice Scalia wrote the opinion for the Court, joined by Chief Justice Rehnquist. Justices Stevens, O'Connor, and Kennedy concurred in part. Justices Brennan, White, Marshall, and Blackmun dissented.

❂   ❂   ❂

JUSTICE BRENNAN, with whom JUSTICE MARSHALL and JUSTICE BLACKMUN join, dissenting.

* * * [B]ecause the plurality opinion's exclusively historical analysis portends a significant and unfortunate departure from our prior cases and from sound constitutional decisionmaking, I devote a substantial portion of my discussion to it.

I

Once we recognized that the "liberty" protected by the Due Process Clause of the Fourteenth Amendment encompasses more than freedom from bodily restraint, today's plurality opinion emphasizes, the concept was cut loose from one natural limitation on its meaning. This innovation paved the way, so the plurality hints, for judges to substitute their own preferences for those of elected officials. Dissatisfied with this supposedly unbridled and uncertain state of affairs, the plurality casts about for another limitation on the concept of liberty.

It finds this limitation in "tradition." Apparently oblivious to the fact that this concept can be as malleable and as elusive as "liberty" itself, the plurality pretends that tradition places a discernible border around the Constitution. The pretense is seductive; it would be comforting to believe that a search for "tradition" involves nothing more idiosyncratic or complicated than poring through dusty volumes on American history. Yet, as Justice White observed in his dissent in *Moore v. East Cleveland*: "What the deeply rooted traditions of the country are is arguable." Indeed, wherever I would begin to look for an interest "deeply rooted in the country's traditions," one thing is certain: I would not stop (as does the plurality) at Bracton, or Blackstone, or Kent, or even the American Law Reports in conducting my search. Because reasonable people can disagree about the content of particular traditions, and because they can disagree even about which traditions are relevant to the definition of "liberty," the plurality has not found the objective boundary that it seeks.

Even if we could agree, moreover, on the content and significance of particular traditions, we still would be forced to identify the point at which a tradition becomes firm enough to be relevant to our definition of liberty and the moment at which it becomes too obsolete to be relevant any longer. The plurality supplies no objective means by which we might make these determinations. * * *

It is ironic that an approach so utterly dependent on tradition is so indifferent to our precedents. Citing barely a handful of this Court's numerous decisions defining the scope of the liberty protected by the Due Process Clause to support its reliance on tradition, the plurality acts as though English legal treatises and the American Law Reports always have provided the sole source for our constitutional principles. They have not. Just as common-law notions no longer define the "property" that the Constitution protects, neither do they circumscribe the "liberty" that it guarantees. On the contrary, " 'liberty' and 'property' are broad and majestic terms. They are among the 'great [constitutional] concepts . . . purposely left to gather meaning from experience. . . . They relate to the whole domain of social and economic fact, and the statesmen who founded this Nation knew too well that only a stagnant society remains unchanged.' " *Board of Regents of State Colleges v. Roth*, quoting *National Insurance Co. v. Tidewater Co.* (Frankfurter, J., dissenting).

It is not that tradition has been irrelevant to our prior decisions.

Throughout our decisionmaking in this important area runs the theme that certain interests and practices—freedom from physical restraint, marriage, childbearing, childrearing, and others—form the core of our definition of "liberty." Our solicitude for these interests is partly the result of the fact that the Due Process Clause would seem an empty promise if it did not protect them, and partly the result of the historical and traditional importance of these interests in our society. In deciding cases arising under the Due Process Clause, therefore, we have considered whether the concrete limitation under consideration impermissibly impinges upon one of these more generalized interests.

Today's plurality, however, does not ask whether parenthood is an interest that historically has received our attention and protection; the answer to that question is too clear for dispute. Instead, the plurality asks whether the specific variety of parenthood under consideration—a natural father's relationship with a child whose mother is married to another man—has enjoyed such protection.

If we had looked to tradition with such specificity in past cases, many a decision would have reached a different result. Surely the use of contraceptives by unmarried couples, *Eisenstadt v. Baird*, or even by married couples, *Griswold v. Connecticut*; the freedom from corporal punishment in schools, *Ingraham v. Wright*; the freedom from an arbitrary transfer from a prison to a psychiatric institution, *Vitek v. Jones*; and even the right to raise one's natural but illegitimate children, *Stanley v. Illinois*, were not "interest[s] traditionally protected by our society," at the time of their consideration by this Court. If we had asked, therefore, in *Eisenstadt, Griswold, Ingraham, Vitek,* or *Stanley* itself whether the specific interest under consideration had been traditionally protected, the answer would have been a resounding "no." That we did not ask this question in those cases highlights the novelty of the interpretive method that the plurality opinion employs today.

The plurality's interpretive method is more than novel; it is misguided. It ignores the good reasons for limiting the role of "tradition" in interpreting the Constitution's deliberately capacious language. In the plurality's constitutional universe, we may not take notice of the fact that the original reasons for the conclusive presumption of paternity are out of place in a world in which blood tests can prove virtually beyond a shadow of a doubt who sired a particular child and in which the fact of illegitimacy no longer plays the burdensome and stigmatizing role it once did. Nor, in the plurality's world, may we deny "tradition" its full scope by pointing out that the rationale for the conventional rule has changed over the years, as has the rationale for [the California law at issue here];[1] instead, our task is simply to identify a rule denying the asserted interest and not to ask whether the basis for that rule—which is the true reflection of the values undergirding it—has changed too often or too recently to call the rule embodying that rationale a "tradition." Moreover, by describing the decisive question as whether Michael's and Victoria's interest is one that has been "traditionally *protected by* our society," (emphasis added), rather than one that society traditionally has thought important (with or without protecting it), and by suggesting that our sole function is to "*discern* the society's views," (emphasis added), the plurality acts as if the only purpose of the Due Process Clause is to confirm the importance of interests already protected by a majority of the States. Transforming the protection afforded by the Due Process Clause into a redundancy mocks those who, with care and purpose, wrote the Fourteenth Amendment.

In construing the Fourteenth Amendment to offer shelter only to those interests specifically protected by historical practice, moreover, the plurality ignores the kind of society in which our Constitution exists. We are not an assimilative, homogeneous society, but a facilitative, pluralistic one, in which we must be willing to abide someone else's unfamiliar or even repellant practice because the same tolerant impulse protects our own idiosyncracies. Even if we can agree, therefore, that "family" and "parenthood" are part of the good life, it is absurd to assume that we can agree on the content of those terms and destructive to pretend that we do. In a community such as ours, "liberty" must include the freedom not to conform. The plurality today squashes this freedom by requiring specific approval from history before protecting anything in the name of liberty.

The document that the plurality construes today is unfamiliar to me. It is not the living charter that I have taken to be our Constitution; it is instead a stagnant, archaic, hidebound document steeped in the prejudices and superstitions of a time long past. *This* Constitution does not recognize that times change, does not see that sometimes a practice or rule outlives its foundations. I cannot accept an interpretive method

---

1. California courts initially justified [the] conclusive presumption of paternity on the ground that biological paternity was impossible to prove, but ••• the preservation of family integrity became the rule's paramount justification when paternity tests became reliable.

that does such violence to the charter that I am bound by oath to uphold.

II

The plurality's reworking of our interpretive approach is all the more troubling because it is unnecessary. This is not a case in which we face a "new" kind of interest, one that requires us to consider for the first time whether the Constitution protects it. On the contrary, we confront an interest—that of a parent and child in their relationship with each other—that was among the first that this Court acknowledged in its cases defining the "liberty" protected by the Constitution, and I think I am safe in saying that no one doubts the wisdom or validity of those decisions. Where the interest under consideration is a parent-child relationship, we need not ask, over and over again, whether that interest is one that society traditionally protects.

Thus, to describe the issue in this case as whether the relationship existing between Michael and Victoria "has been treated as a protected family unit under the historic practices of our society, or whether on any other basis it has been accorded special protection," is to reinvent the wheel. The better approach—indeed, the one commanded by our prior cases and by common sense—is to ask whether the specific parent-child relationship under consideration is close enough to the interests that we already have protected to be deemed an aspect of "liberty" as well. On the facts before us, therefore, the question is not what "level of generality" should be used to describe the relationship between Michael and Victoria, but whether the relationship under consideration is sufficiently substantial to qualify as a liberty interest under our prior cases.

* * *

The evidence is undisputed that Michael, Victoria, and Carole did live together as a family; that is, they shared the same household, Victoria called Michael "Daddy," Michael contributed to Victoria's support, and he is eager to continue his relationship with her. Yet they are not, in the plurality's view, a "unitary family," whereas Gerald, Carole, and Victoria do compose such a family. The only difference between these two sets of relationships, however, is the fact of marriage. The plurality, indeed, expressly recognizes that marriage is the critical fact in denying Michael a constitutionally protected stake in his relationship with Victoria: no fewer than six times, the plurality refers to Michael as the "*adulterous* natural father" (emphasis added) or the like. However, the very premise of [our prior decisions] it is that marriage is not decisive in answering the question whether the Constitution protects the parental relationship under consideration. These cases are, after all, important precisely because they involve the rights of *unwed* fathers. * * *

III

Because the plurality decides that Michael and Victoria have no liberty interest in their relationship with each other, it need consider neither the effect of [the California law] on their relationship nor the State's interest in bringing about that effect. It is obvious, however, that the effect of [the California law] is to terminate the relationship between Michael and Victoria before affording any hearing whatsoever on the issue whether Michael is Victoria's father. This refusal to hold a hearing is properly analyzed under our [prior] cases, which instruct us to consider the State's interest in curtailing the procedures accompanying the termination of a constitutionally protected interest. California's interest, minute in comparison with a father's interest in his relationship with his child, cannot justify its refusal to hear Michael out on his claim that he is Victoria's father.

* * *

IV

The atmosphere surrounding today's decision is one of make-believe. Beginning with the suggestion that the situation confronting us here does not repeat itself every day in every corner of the country, moving on to the claim that it is tradition alone that supplies the details of the liberty that the Constitution protects, and passing finally to the notion that the Court always has recognized a cramped vision of "the family," today's decision lets stand California's pronouncement that Michael— whom blood tests show to a 98 percent probability to be Victoria's father—is not Victoria's father. When and if the Court awakes to reality, it will find a world very different from the one it expects.

SELECTED BIBLIOGRAPHY

❂ ❂ ❂

INDEX OF CASES CITED

❂ ❂ ❂

GENERAL INDEX

❂ ❂ ❂

Selected Bibliography

Speeches and Articles by Justice Brennan

Forward: Neither Victims Nor Executioners, 8 Notre Dame J.L. Ethics & Pub. Pol'y 1 (1994).

The Worldwide Influence of the United States Constitution as a Charter of Human Rights, 15 Nova L. Rev. 1 (1991).

The Criminal Prosecution: Sporting Event or Quest for Truth? A Progress Report, 68 Wash. U.L.Q. 1 (1990).

Why Have a Bill of Rights? 9 Oxford L.J. Legal Stud. 425 (1989).

Are Citizens Justified in Being Suspicious of the Law and the Legal System?, 43 U. Miami L. Rev. 981 (1989).

Reason, Passion, and the "Progress of the Law," 10 Cardozo L. Rev. 3 (1988).

The Equality Principle in American Constitutional Jurisprudence, 48 Ohio St. L.J. 921 (1987) (the identical text—but for one word—also appeared as *The Equality Principle: A Foundation of American Law*, 20 U.C.D. L. Rev. 673 (1987)).

Color-blind, Creed-blind, Status-blind, Sex-blind, 14 Hum. Rts. 30 (Winter 1987).

Constitutional Adjudication and the Death Penalty; A View from the Court, 100 Harv. L. Rev. 313 (1986).

The Bill of Rights and the States: The Revival of State Constitutions as Guardians of Individual Rights, 61 N.Y.U. L. Rev. 535 (1986).

In Defense of Dissents, 37 Hastings L.J. 427 (1986).

The Constitution of the United States: Contemporary Ratification, 19 U.C.D. L. Rev. 2 (1985), *reprinted in*, 27 S. Tex. L.J. 433 (1986), *reprinted in*, Interpreting the Constitution (J. Rakove, ed. 1990).

State Constitutions and the Protection of Individual Rights, 90 Harv. L. Rev. 489 (1977).

State Supreme Court Judge v. United States Supreme Court Justice: A Change in Function and Perspective, 19 U. Fla. L. Rev. 225 (1966).

Supreme Court and the Meiklejohn Interpretation of the First Amendment, 79 Harv. L. Rev. 1 (1965).
Constitutional Adjudication, 40 Notre Dame Law. 559 (1965).
United States Supreme Courts: Reflections Past and Present, 48 Marq. L. Rev. 437 (1965).
Educators and the Bill of Rights, 113 U. Pa. L. Rev. 219 (1964).
Some Aspects of Federalism, 39 N.Y.U. L. Rev. 945 (1964).
International Due Process and the Law, 48 Va. L. Rev. 1258 (1962).
The Bill of Rights and the States, 36 N.Y.U. L. Rev. 761 (1961).

BOOKS ABOUT JUSTICE BRENNAN

E. Joshua Rosenkranz & Bernard Schwartz, eds., *Reason & Passion, Justice Brennan's Enduring Influence* (W. W. Norton & Co., 1997).
Hunter R. Clarke, *Justice Brennan, the Great Conciliator* (Carol Publishing, 1995).
Roger Goldman & David Gallen, *Justice William J. Brennan, Jr., Freedom First* (Carroll & Graf Pub., 1994).
Peter Irons, *Brennan vs. Rehnquist, The Battle for the Constitution* (Alfred A. Knopf, 1994).
Robert D. Richards, *Justice Brennan's Legacy to the First Amendment* (Parkway Pub., 1994).
Kim Isaac Eisler, *A Justice for All, William J. Brennan, Jr. and the Decisions that Transformed America* (Simon & Schuster, 1993).

ARTICLES ABOUT JUSTICE BRENNAN

In Memoriam: William J. Brennan, Jr., 111 Harv. L. Rev. (1997) (symposium).
Sandra L. Wood & Gary M. Gansle, *Seeking a Strategy: William J. Brennan's Dissent Assigments*, 81 Judicature 73 (1997).
Hunter R. Clark, *The Pulse of Life in Justice Brennan's Jurisprudence*, 46 Drake L. Rev. 1 (1997).
Donna F. Coltharp, *Writing in the Margins: Brennan, Marshall, and the Inherent Weakness of Liberal Judicial Decision-Making*, 59 St. Mary's L.J. 1 (1997).
Michael Mello, *Adhering to Our Views: Justices Brennan and Marshall and the Relentless Dissent to Death as a Punishment*, 22 Fla. St. U.L. Rev. 591 (1995).
Stephen J. Wermiel, *The Nomination of Justice Brennan: Eisenhower's Mistake? A Look at the Historical Record*, 11 Const. Comment. 515 (1994).
Alan I. Bigel, *Justices William J. Brennan, Jr. and Thurgood Marshall on Capital Punishment: Its Constitutionality, Morality, Deterrent Effect and Interpretation by the Court*, 8 Notre Dame J.L. Ethics & Pub. Pol'y 1 (1994).
B. Glenn George, *Visions of a Labor Lawyer: The Legacy of Justice Brennan*, 33 Wm. & Mary L. Rev. 1123 (1992).

Joel E. Friedlander, Comment, *Constitution and Kulturkampf: A Reading of the Shadow Theology of Justice Brennan*, 140 U. Pa. L. Rev. 1049 (1992).

Jamie D. Batterman, Comment, *The First Amendment Protection of the Freedoms of Speech and the Press and Its Effect on the Law of Defamation as Seen Through the Eyes of Justice Brennan: His Impact and its Future*, 13 Whittier L. Rev. 233 (1992).

Rodney A. Grunes, *Justice Brennan and the Problem of Obscenity*, 22 Seton Hall L. Rev. 789 (1992).

Guido Calabresi, *Antidiscrimination and Constitutional Accountability (What the Bork-Brennan Debate Ignores)*, 105 Harv. L. Rev. 80 (1991).

Frank I. Michelman, *Super Liberal Romance, Community, and Tradition in William J. Brennan, Jr.'s Constitutional Thought*, 77 Va. L. Rev. 1261 (1991).

Edward de Grazia, *Freeing Literary and Artistic Expression During the Sixties: The Role of Justice William J. Brennan, Jr.*, 13 Cardozo L. Rev. 103 (1991).

Dean H. Hashimoto, *Justice Brennan's Use of Scientific and Empirical Evidence in Constitutional and Administrative Law*, 32 B.C.L. Rev. 739 (1991).

Essay: The Jurisprudence of William J. Brennan, Jr., 139 U. Pa. L. Rev. 1319 (1991) (symposium).

Glenn A. Phelps & John B. Gates, *The Myth of Jurisprudence: Interpretive Theory in the Constitutional Opinions of Justices Rehnquist and Brennan*, 31 Santa Clara L. Rev. 567 (1991).

A Focus on Justice Brennan, 27 Cal. W.L. Rev. 233 (1991) (symposium).

Owen Fiss, *A Life Lived Twice*, 100 Yale L.J. 1117 (1991).

Harry F. Tepker, Jr., *Justice Brennan, Judge Bork, and a Jurisprudence of Original Values*, 43 Okla. L. Rev. 665 (1990).

A Tribute to Justice William J. Brennan, Jr., 104 Harv. L. Rev. 1 (1990) (symposium).

Nat Hentoff, *The Constitutionalist*, New Yorker, March 12, 1990, at 45.

Kenneth Casebeer, *Running on Empty: Justice Brennan's Plea, the Empty State, the City of Richmond, and the Profession*, 43 U. Miami L. Rev. 989 (1989).

Stanley H. Friedelbaum, *Justice Brennan and the Burger Court: Policy Making in the Judicial Thicket*, 19 Seton Hall L. Rev. 188 (1989).

Earl M. Maltz, *False Prophet—Justice Brennan and the Theory of State Constitutional Law*, 15 Hastings Const. L.Q. 429 (1988).

Laura Krugman Ray, *Justice Brennan and the Jurisprudence of Dissent*, 61 Temp. L.Q. 307 (1988).

Raoul Berger, *Justice Brennan vs. the Constitution*, 29 B.C.L. Rev. 787 (1988).

Reason, Passion, and Justice Brennan: A Symposium, 10 Cardoza L. Rev. 25 (1988).

Jonathan Van Patten, *The Partisan Battle Over the Constitution: Meese's Jurisprudence of Original Intention and Brennan's Theory of Contemporary Ratification*, 70 Marq. L. Rev. 389 (1987).

Glenn A. Phelps & Timothy A. Martinez, *Brennan v. Rehnquist: The Politics of Constitutional Jurisprudence*, 22 Gonz. L. Rev. 307 (1987).

Edward V. Heck, *Justice Brennan and Freedom of Expression Doctrine in the Burger Court*, 24 San Diego L. Rev. 1153 (1987).

Justice William J. Brennan, 20 John Mar. L. Rev. 1 (1986) (symposium).

John Denvir, *Justice Brennan, Justice Rehnquist, and Free Speech*, 80 Nw. U.L. Rev. 285 (1985).

The Mind of Justice Brennan: A Twenty-five Year Tribute, Nat'l Rev., May 18, 1984, at 30.

Tribute to Mr. Justice Brennan, 1981 Ann. Surv. Am. L. 11 (April 1982) (symposium).

Edward V. Heck, *Justice Brennan and the Development of Obscenity Policy by the Supreme Court*, 18 Cal. W.L. Rev. 410 (1982).

Edward V. Heck, *Justice Brennan and the Heyday of Warren Court Liberalism*, 20 Santa Clara L. Rev. 841 (1980).

A Tribute to Justice William Brennan, 15 Harvard C.R.-C.L. L. Rev. 279 (1980) (symposium).

Edward V. Heck, *The Socialization of a Freshman Justice: The Early Years of Justice Brennan*, 10 Pacific L.J. 707 (1979).

Mr. Justice Brennan, 4 Rut.-Cam. L. Rev. 5 (1972) (symposium).

Mr. Justice Brennan, 11 Cath. U.L. Rev. 1 (1962) (symposium).

Nomination of William Joseph Brennan Jr.: Hearings Before the Senate Committee on the Judiciary, 85th Congress, 1st Sess. 28., *reprinted in* 103 Cong. Rec. 3945 (1957).

Index of Cases Cited

Key to symbols:

*   Justice Brennan wrote the opinion for the Court or otherwise announced the Court's judgment

†   Justice Brennan wrote a dissenting opinion in the case

‡   Justice Brennan wrote a concurring opinion in the case

Abdul Wali v. Coughlin, 754 F.2d 1015 (2d Cir. 1985): 121–22

Ambach v. Norwick, 441 U.S. 68 (1979): 46, 231

Armstrong v. Manzo, 380 U.S. 545 (1965): 137, 166

**Baker v. Carr*, 369 U.S. 186 (1962): 3

**Bantam Books, Inc. v. Sullivan*, 372 U.S. 58 (1963): 8, 18

†*Barr v. Matteo*, 360 U.S. 564 (1959): 9

‡*Bethel School District No. 403 v. Fraser*, 478 U.S. 675 (1986): 47

**Board of Education v. Pico*, 457 U.S. 853 (1982): 50, 52, 97

†*Board of Regents of State Colleges v. Roth*, 408 U.S. 564 (1972): 239

‡*Boos v. Barry*, 485 U.S. 312 (1988): 61

Bradwell v. Illinois, 83 U.S. 130 (1873): 210

Brandenburg v. Ohio, 395 U.S. 444 (1969): x, 59–60

†*Braunfeld v. Brown*, 366 U.S. 599 (1961): 106, 108–09

Brinegar v. United States, 338 U.S. 160 (1949): 179

Brown v. Board of Education, 347 U.S. 483 (1954) [*Brown I*]: 217, 223

Brown v. Board of Education, 349 U.S. 294 (1955) [*Brown II*]: 217

†*Brown v. Glines*, 444 U.S. 348 (1980): 110, 112, 113, 117

‡*Brown v. Louisiana*, 383 U.S. 131 (1966): 56

Califano v. Webster, 430 U.S. 313 (1977): 219

Callins v. Collins, 510 U.S. 1141 (1994): 140

Cantwell v. Connecticut, 310 U.S. 296 (1940): 48

Chaplinsky v. New Hampshire, 315 U.S. 568 (1942): 38

Chappell v. Wallace, 462 U.S. 296 (1983): 112

Cohen v. California, 403 U.S. 15 (1971): 39–40, 42

Committee for Public Education & Religious Liberty v. Nyquist, 413 U.S. 756 (1973): 88

Community for Creative Non-Violence v. Watt, 703 F.2d 586 (D.C. Cir. 1983): 58

Counselman v. Hitchcock, 142 U.S. 547 (1892): 131

*Craig v. Boren, 429 U.S. 190 (1976): 207, 219, 229

Craig v. Harney, 331 U.S. 367 (1947): 6

CSC v. Letter Carriers, 413 U.S. 548 (1973): 30

*Edwards v. Aguillard, 482 U.S. 578 (1987): 95–102

*Eisenstadt v. Baird, 405 U.S. 438 (1972): 197–204, 239

*Elrod v. Burns, 427 U.S. 347 (1976): 27–36

Engel v. Vitale, 370 U.S. 421 (1962): 68, 69, 72, 78, 80–81, 88, 94, 97, 98

Epperson v. Arkansas, 393 U.S. 97 (1968): 95, 97, 100, 101

Erznoznik v. Jacksonville, 422 U.S. 205 (1975): 40–41

Everson v. Board of Education, 330 U.S. 1 (1947): 109

*FCC v. Metro Broadcasting, 497 U.S. 547 (1990): 216

†FCC v. Pacifica Foundation, 438 U.S. 726 (1978): 37–43, 59

†Flemming v. Nestor, 363 U.S. 603 (1960): 107

Food Employees v. Logan Valley Plaza, Inc., 391 U.S. 308 (1968): 56

*Frontiero v. Richardson, 411 U.S. 677 (1973): 205–13

F.S. Royster Guano Co. v. Virginia, 253 U.S. 412 (1920): 228

‡Furman v. Georgia, 408 U.S. 238 (1972): 139–50

Gideon v. Wainwright, 372 U.S. 335 (1963): 151

*Gilbert v. California, 388 U.S. 263 (1967): 152–54

*Ginsberg v. New York, 390 U.S. 629 (1968): 23

*Ginzburg v. United States, 383 U.S. 463 (1966): 18

*Goldberg v. Kelly, 397 U.S. 254 (1970): 133–38, 140

†Goldman v. Weinberger, 475 U.S. 503 (1986): 110–17, 118

*Grand Rapids School District v. Ball, 473 U.S. 373 (1985): 97

Grannis v. Ordean, 234 U.S. 385 (1914): 137

†Gregg v. Georgia, 428 U.S. 153 (1976): 140

Griswold v. Connecticut, 381 U.S. 479 (1965): 197, 199–203, 239

Hamilton v. Alabama, 368 U.S. 52 (1961): 158

†Hazelwood School District v. Kuhlmeier, 484 U.S. 260 (1988): 44–52

Hirabayashi v. United States, 320 U.S. 81 (1943): 219

Holt v. United States, 218 U.S. 245 (1910): 130–31

Humphrey v. Cady, 405 U.S. 504 (1972): 162

Illinois ex rel. McCollum v. Board of Education, 333 U.S. 203 (1948): 97

Illinois State Employees Union v. Lewis, 473 F.2d 561 (7th Cir. 1972): 32, 34

Ingraham v. Wright, 430 U.S. 651 (1977): 239

Interstate Circuit, Inc. v. Dallas, 390 U.S. 676 (1968): 19, 25–26

*Jacobellis v. Ohio, 378 U.S. 184 (1964): 18

Jones v. North Carolina Prisoners' Union, 433 U.S. 119 (1977): 123

†Kahn v. Shevin, 416 U.S. 351 (1974): 219

*Keyishian v. Board of Regents, 385 U.S. 589 (1967): 50, 51

†Kime v. United States, 459 U.S. 949 (1982):54

†Kirby v. Illinois, 406 U.S. 682 (1972): 151

Korematsu v. United States, 323 U.S. 214 (1944): 121

Kusper v. Pontikes, 414 U.S. 51 (1973): 32

*Lamont v. Postmaster General, 381 U.S. 301 (1965): 11–14

Larkin v. Grendel's Den, Inc., 459 U.S. 116 (1982): 81

†Lehman v. City of Shaker Heights, 418 U.S. 298 (1974): 40

‡Lemon v. Kurtzman, 403 U.S. 602 (1971): 78–81, 86–89, 95–98

†Lynch v. Donnelly, 465 U.S. 668 (1984): 85–94, 98

*Malloy v. Hogan, 378 U.S. 1 (1964): 127–28

Mapp v. Ohio, 367 U.S. 643 (1961): 168, 172

†Marsh v. Chambers, 463 U.S. 783 (1983): 78–84, 86, 87, 93

Martin v. City of Struthers, 319 U.S. 141 (1943): 13

†*Mathews v. Eldridge*, 424 U.S. 319 (1976): 166

M'Culloch v. Maryland, 17 U.S. (4 Wheat.) 316 (1819): 173

*Memoirs v. Massachusetts, 383 U.S. 413 (1966): 20

Meyer v. Nebraska, 262 U.S. 390 (1923): 231

†*Michael H. v. Gerald D.*, 491 U.S. 110 (1989): 235–42

†*Miller v. California*, 413 U.S. 15 (1973): 16

Miranda v. Arizona, 384 U.S. 436 (1966): 127, 128, 130

‡*Moore v. City of East Cleveland*, 431 U.S. 494 (1977): 238

*NAACP v. Button, 371 U.S. 415 (1963): 6, 13, 106

National Insurance Co. v. Tidewater Co., 337 U.S. 582 (1949): 238

*New York Times Co. v. Sullivan, 376 U.S. 254 (1964): xiii, 3–10, 32

O'Connor v. Donaldson, 422 U.S. 563 (1975): 163

Olmstead v. United States, 277 U.S. 438 (1928): 184

†*O'Lone v. Estate of Shabazz*, 482 U.S. 342 (1987): 118–24, 161

O'Neil v. Vermont, 144 U.S. 323 (1892): 143

†*Parham v. J.R.*, 442 U.S. 584 (1979): 125, 160–67

†*Paris Adult Theatre I v. Slaton*, 413 U.S. 49 (1973): 15–26, 79

People v. Defore, 150 N.E. 585 (N.Y. 1926): 175

Planned Parenthood of Central Missouri v. Danforth, 428 U.S. 52 (1976): 163

*Plyler v. Doe, 457 U.S. 202 (1982): 226–34

Prince v. Massachusetts, 321 U.S. 158 (1944): 164

Railway Express Agency v. New York, 336 U.S. 106 (1949): 203–04

Reed v. Reed, 404 U.S. 71 (1971): 199–200, 206, 210, 212, 213

‡*Regents of the University of California v. Bakke*, 438 U.S. 265 (1978): 214–25

Reid v. Covert, 354 U.S. 1 (1957): 182

Roe v. Wade, 410 U.S. 113 (1973): 198

*Roth v. United States, 354 U.S. 476 (1957): 6, 15–18, 20–23, 38

*Rutan v. Republican Party of Illinois, 497 U.S. 62 (1990): 28

†*San Antonio Independent School District v. Rodriguez*, 411 U.S. 1 (1973): 218–19, 226, 229

Schacht v. United States, 398 U.S. 58 (1970): 56, 63

Schenk v. United States, 249 U.S. 47 (1919): 2

*Schmerber v. California, 384 U.S. 757 (1966): 127–32, 151

†*Schneckloth v. Bustamonte*, 412 U.S. 218 (1973): 158

‡*School District of Abington Township v. Schempp*, 374 U.S. 203 (1963): 68–79, 83, 89, 97, 99, 100, 103, 231

Shanley v. Northeast Independent School District, 462 F.2d 960 (5th Cir. 1972): 52

*Shapiro v. Thompson, 394 U.S. 618 (1969): 135, 191–96, 226, 233

Shelton v. Tucker, 364 U.S. 479 (1960): 51

*Sherbert v. Verner, 374 U.S. 398 (1963): 103–09, 135, 193

Simmons v. United States, 390 U.S. 377 (1968): 156–57

*Smith v. California, 361 U.S. 147 (1959): 18

Smith v. Goguen, 415 U.S. 566 (1974): 57

Specht v. Patterson, 386 U.S. 605 (1967): 163

*Speiser v. Randall, 357 U.S. 513 (1958): 9, 52, 107, 135

Spence v. Washington, 418 U.S. 405 (1974): x, 53, 56–58, 60, 62

Stanley v. Georgia, 394 U.S. 557 (1969): 24

Stanley v. Illinois, 405 U.S. 645 (1972): 213, 239

Stone v. Graham, 449 U.S. 39 (1980): 97–101

†*Stone v. Powell*, 428 U.S. 465 (1976): 177

*Stovall v. Denno, 388 U.S. 293 (1967): 152–54

Street v. New York, 394 U.S. 576 (1969): 53, 61

Stromberg v. California, 283 U.S. 359 (1931): 6, 53, 57

Terminiello v. Chicago, 337 U.S. 1 (1949): 59

*Texas v. Johnson, 491 U.S. 397 (1989): 53–65

Thomas v. Collins, 323 U.S. 516 (1945): 50, 108

Tigner v. Texas, 310 U.S. 141 (1940): 228

Tinker v. Des Moines Independent Community School District, 393 U.S. 503 (1969): 44–45, 47–52, 56

Torcaso v. Watkins, 367 U.S. 488 (1961): 76

Towne v. Eisner, 245 U.S. 418 (1918): 42

Trimble v. Gordon, 430 U.S. 762 (1977): 230

‡ *Trop v. Dulles*, 356 U.S. 86, 99 (1958): 141, 142, 148

Turner v. Safley, 482 U.S. 78 (1987): 123

† *United States v. Ash*, 413 U.S. 300 (1973): 125, 151–59

† *United States v. Calandra*, 414 U.S. 338 (1974): 170, 172, 175

* *United States v. Eichman*, 496 U.S. 310 (1990): 54

United States v. Grace, 461 U.S. 171 (1983): 56

† *United States v. Guest*, 383 U.S. 745 (1966): 194

United States v. Jackson, 390 U.S. 570 (1968): 194

† *United States v. Leon*, 468 U.S. 897 (1984): 168–79

United States v. O'Brien, 391 U.S. 367 (1968): 53–54, 56, 58, 60

† *United States v. Verdugo-Urquidez*, 494 U.S. 259 (1990): 180–87

* *United States v. Wade*, 388 U.S. 218 (1967): 152–59

Vitek v. Jones, 445 U.S. 480 (1980): 239

Wallace v. Jaffree, 472 U.S. 38 (1985): 97, 98

‡ *Walz v. Tax Commission*, 397 U.S. 664 (1970): 82, 93

Weber v. Aetna Casualty & Surety Co., 406 U.S. 164 (1972): 220

Weeks v. United States, 232 U.S. 383 (1914): 168, 174–75

Weems v. United States, 217 U.S. 349 (1910): 142

* *Weinberger v. Wiesenfeld*, 420 U.S. 636 (1975): 219

West Virginia Board of Education v. Barnette, 319 U.S. 624 (1943): 47, 52, 53, 57, 61–62, 70, 76, 83

Whitney v. California, 274 U.S. 357 (1927): 24

Wilkerson v. Utah, 99 U.S. 130 (1879): 141

Williams v. Rhodes, 393 U.S. 23 (1968): 32

Williamson v. Lee Optical Co., 348 U.S. 483 (1955): 200

Wisconsin v. Yoder, 406 U.S. 205 (1972): 103, 104, 231

Wolf v. Colorado, 338 U.S. 25 (1949): 172

General Index

Adams, John, 185 n.8
affirmative action, 214–25

Black, Hugo L., 16, 22, 128
Blackmun, Harry A., 28, 52, 140, 207
blood tests, 127–32
Brandeis, Louis D., 24, 184
Brennan, William J., Jr.: changes in viewpoint, 16–26, 79; Court's refusal to review cases, reaction to, 54, 140; deference to other authorities, 98–99, 110–11, 117, 118–24, 160–61, 164–65, 167; history and tradition, use of, 7, 30, 35 n.22, 82–83, 92–93, 150, 185, 210–11, 237–42; on original intent, 68–72, 77, 82–83, 92–93, 139, 141–42, 183, 185–86, 235–37
Bryan, William Jennings, 95
Burger, Warren E., 160, 163, 199–200, 206–07, 226–27
Bush, George, 54

Calhoun, John C., 7
Cardozo, Benjamin, 175
Carlin, George, 37–38, 41, 43
children: Bible reading in schools, 68–77; commitment of, 160–67; compulsory education of, 103–04; free speech rights of, 37–38, 40–41, 44–52; illegal immigrants, education of, 226–34; school prayer, 68; teaching evolution in public schools, 95–102
churches: financial support to, 78; separation from state. *See* Establishment Clause
civil servants, 27–36

Clark, Tom C., 68
Cleland, John: *Memoirs,* 16
communism, 11–14
counsel, right to, 151–59
cruel and unusual punishment, 139–50

Daley, Richard J., 27, 29
Darrow, Clarence, 95
death penalty, 139–50
defamation, 3–10
Douglas, William O., 16, 22, 128, 139
due process, procedural: commitment of minors, 160–67; hearing, requirement of a, 133–38; witness identification, 151–59
due process, substantive: death penalty, 139–50; parental rights, 235–42; right to privacy, 197–204; right to travel, 191–96

Eighth Amendment, 139–50
equal protection, 188–90; affirmative action, 214–25; gender discrimination, 205–13; illegal immigrants, discrimination against, 226–34; illegitimacy, discrimination on basis of, 235–42; level of scrutiny, 188–89, 196, 200n. 7, 205–07, 210–11, 215–16, 218–20, 226–27, 228–32; marital status, discrimination on basis of, 197–204; race discrimination, 214–25; residency, discrimination on basis of, 191–96
Equal Rights Amendment, 206–07
Establishment Clause, 66–67; Bible reading in public schools, 68–77; holiday displays on

253

Establishment Clause (*continued*)
public property, 85–94; legislative prayer, 78–84; *Lemon* test, 78–79, 95; prayer in public schools, 68
evolution, teaching of, in public schools, 95–102

Federal Communications Commission (FCC), 37–38
federalism, 1
Field, Stephen J., 143
Fifth Amendment, 127–32
First Amendment. *See* Establishment Clause; freedom of association; free exercise of religion; free speech and press
Fortas, Abe, 44
Fourteenth Amendment, 1; incorporation of Bill of Rights, 1. *See also* due process, procedural; due process, substantive; equal protection
Fourth Amendment. *See* search and seizure
Frankfurter, Felix, 97, 238
freedom of association, 27
free exercise of religion, 66–67, 78, 103–04; in the military, 110–17; in prison, 118–24; working on the sabbath, 103–09
free speech and press: advertisements, 3; audience, 12–14, 39–41, 43, 49–50; children, 37–38, 40–41, 44–52; defamation, 3–10; flags, desecration of, 53–65; indecency, 37–43; not absolute, 2, 15; obscenity, 15–26; school newspapers, 44–52

Ginsburg, Ruth Bader, 206–07
Goldberg, Arthur J., 201

Harlan, John Marshall, II, 16, 19, 25, 39, 42, 192
holidays, 85
Holmes, Oliver Wendell, Jr., 2, 64, 130–31

illegal substances, 67, 104

Jackson, Andrew, 30, 35
Jackson, Robert H., 62, 121, 179, 203–04
Jefferson, Thomas, 7, 30, 70, 210 n.13

Kennedy, Anthony, 237
King, Rev. Martin Luther, Jr., 3

legislative districts, 3
libel, 3–10

Madison, James, 6–7, 9, 70, 183
Marshall, John, 173
Marshall, Thurgood, 16, 139–40, 147, 148, 227
McCarthy, Joseph, 11

NAACP, 27
natural law/natural rights, 2, 185–86
Nineteenth Amendment, 205

obscenity, 15–26
O'Connor, Sandra Day, 85–86, 98, 237

parental rights, 235–42
peyote, religious use of, 67, 104
political patronage, 27–36
political protest, 44, 47–48, 54–65
Powell, William, 28, 41, 42, 207, 215
privacy, right to, 197–204

Reagan, Ronald W., 57
Red Scare, 11
Rehnquist, William H., 53, 57, 63 n.11, 180, 237
religion. *See* Establishment Clause; free exercise of religion
Religious Freedom Restoration Act, 104

Scalia, Antonin, 58, 236–37
schools, public: affirmative action in, 214–25; Bible reading in, 68–77; illegal immigrants, education of, 226–34; newspapers, censorship of, 44–52; religion in, 68, 78; teaching evolution in, 95–102
schools, sectarian, 78
Scopes "Monkey Trial," 95
search and seizure: blood testing, 127; exclusionary rule, 168–79; outside the U.S., 180–87
Sedition Act of 1798, 7
self-incrimination, 127–32
separation of church and state. *See* Establishment Clause
Sixth Amendment, 151–59
slander, 3–10
Stevens, John Paul, 41–42, 59
Stewart, Potter, 16, 23, 28, 38, 139, 147, 194

travel, right to, 191–96

Un-American Activities Committee (U.S. House), 11–12
U.S. Post Office, 12–14

vagueness, 17–19

welfare, 133–38, 191–96
White, Byron, 139, 169, 238
Williams, Roger, 66

STEPHEN L. SEPINUCK, J.D., LL.M., is a professor and associate dean at Gonzaga University School of Law in Spokane, Washington. He has taught seminars on American Constitutional History and Judicial Decision Making, as well as a variety of courses on commercial law subjects. He has authored several articles; this is his first book.

✿ ✿ ✿

MARY PAT TREUTHART, J.D., LL.M., is a professor at Gonzaga University School of Law, where she teaches Constitutional Law, Criminal Procedure, Family Law, and Woman and the Law. She is a former legal services program director who has written and lectured about constitutional issues.